PROFIT BRAND

To Ming
Always and forever

PROFIT BRAND

HOW TO INCREASE THE PROFITABILITY, ACCOUNTABILITY & SUSTAINABILITY OF BRANDS

NICK WREDEN

KOGAN PAGE

London and Sterling, VA

Publisher's note

Every possible effort has been made to ensure that the information contained in this book is accurate at the time of going to press, and the publishers and author cannot accept responsibility for any errors or omissions, however caused. No responsibility for loss or damage occasioned to any person acting, or refraining from action, as a result of the material in this publication can be accepted by the editor, the publisher or the author.

First published in Great Britain and the United States in 2005 by Kogan Page Limited

120 Pentonville Road
London N1 9JN
United Kingdom
www.kogan-page.co.uk

22883 Quicksilver Drive
Sterling VA 20166–2012
USA

ISBN 978-0-7494-5018-2

British Library Cataloguing-in-Publication Data

A CIP record for this book is available from the British Library.

Library of Congress Cataloging-in-Publication Data

Wreden, Nick.
    ProfitBrand : how to increase the profitability, accountability, and sustainability of your brand / Nick Wreden.
        p. cm.
    Includes bibliographical references and index.
    ISBN 0-7494-4465-7
    1. Brand name products—Management. 2. Brand name products—Marketing. 3. Marketing. 4. Relationship marketing. 5. Customer relations. I. Title. II. Title: Profit brand.
HD69.B7W73 2005
658.8'27—dc22
                                        2005001872

Typeset by Saxon Graphics Ltd, Derby, United Kingdom

Contents

List of figures

List of tables

Acknowledgements

An author may get the glory, but it is others who deserve the credit. In this case, the credit goes to my wife, Ming, and daughter, Crystal. The hundreds if not thousands of hours of work steal precious time from conversation, trips and the daily tasks that families willingly do for one another. No book ever gets written without the support and love of family. It also requires their patience, and the patience of mine has been legendary.

Others deserve credit, too. Phyllis Harholdt provided her editing skills, but more importantly provided an inspiration. She has always listened hard to conventional wisdom and then gone ahead and done what she thought was needed. I cannot forget my beloved sister, Jeanne, who is also willing to write a book that challenges conventional stasis. Pauline Goodwin of Kogan Page deserves great thanks for understanding that books are not always about echoing the past but also about illuminating the future. Marcus Osborne gave me faith that ProfitBranding concepts had international appeal. The many penetrating questions from those who have attended my seminars have helped clarify many issues concerning quantification. And once again, a hearty thank-you to Mick and the boys.

understanding that, as with other strategic investments, pay-offs may be years in the future. It also means embedding branding executives, who are capable of much more than selling an offering after it has been developed, into corporate strategy development and execution. Branding executives must be involved in product development, human resources, capital expenditures, research and development (R&D) and every other vital corporate decision.

Branding executives have lessons to learn, too. For branding to be justified as a strategic investment, marketing and other activities must be managed and measured by the criteria that guide other strategic investments. No longer can branding make its own rules, justifying investments with the soft and fuzzy intangibles that wrap every brand. Hard-nosed scrutiny by CEOs and CFOs who want quantification must not be feared, but welcomed. Meeting such scrutiny means that branding will ultimately get the respect – and the investment – it deserves.

As a result, branding must raise its eyes from the details and deadlines of advertising, public relations and trade shows to the strategic imperatives of business: profitability, accountability and sustainability.

Profitability is fundamental. That seems obvious, yet far too often branding is discussed without mention of profitability. Why make the substantial operational and marketing investments required to build and sustain a brand unless they result in greater profitability? Without profitability, ultimately there is no brand, no matter how great the buzz or creative the image.

Marrying branding to profitability offers more than brand survival. Profitability represents a metric that is relevant and understandable to everyone from the post-room worker to an international investor. Unlike many branding benchmarks, such as 'brand equity' or impression, profitability can be calculated with standardized, commonly accepted formulas, making it a universal benchmark for determining success or failure.

If brands are going to be judged by profitability, then CEOs and CFOs must raise the importance of profitability in strategy. Often profitability plays second fiddle to market share or sales growth. This is a mistake. While increased market share can lead to economies of scope and/or scale, no strong connection exists between market share and profitability. Richard Miniter, author of *The Myth of Market Share* (2002), cites a study of more than 3,000 companies. The study found that, more than 70 per cent of the time, companies with the largest market share did not have the highest rate of return. Not long ago, Chase Manhattan Mortgage originated the most home mortgages in the United States. Washington

Introduction

'I skate to where the puck is going to be, not where it has been.'
Wayne Gretzky, Ice Hockey Hall of Fame

Listen to the language of CEOs and CFOs. Return on investment. Internal rate of return. Efficiency. Productivity. Cost-justification. Cash flow. Contribution margin. And most important of all: profit.

Now listen to the language of branding. Creativity. Imagination. Impact. 'Position'. Buzz. Impressions. Image.

No wonder the worlds of branding, finance and management collide. But too much is at stake – brand power, profitability and customer relationships – for the conflict to continue.

It is time for CEOs, CFOs and branding managers to speak a common language. CEOs and CFOs must learn the language of the customer. Sometimes that means concepts that do not fit on a balance sheet, including trust, loyalty, service, experience, emotion and reputation. At the same time, branding executives must learn the language of business. Even though branding has a softer side than, say, manufacturing, branding executives can no longer sidestep the need for rigour and quantifiable benchmarks that drive the rest of the organization.

The common language must be based on the fundamental recognition that branding is a strategic investment. It is as vital to an organization's future as investment in innovation, personnel and machinery. For CEOs and CFOs, that means giving branding the investment it requires. It means not cutting branding funds at the first hint of a slowdown. It means

Mutual was fifth largest. Yet Washington Mutual reported US $452 million in net earnings, while Chase lagged with less than US $123 million. Look at GM and Sears. Both have dominant market share without equivalent profitability.

Companies focused on market share see business in terms of competition. As a result, they spend more time trying to out-manoeuvre and out-promote their competition, robbing time and energy from trying to understand customers. Of course, companies must be aware of competitors. But more effort must be spent in learning how competitors are creating and maintaining customer relationships than in trying to 'beat' them.

Companies seeking sales growth often use expensive promotions or price cuts to juice sales. Sales may increase temporarily, but at the high cost of lower profitability and loyalty. Customers attracted by price often defect quickly for lower prices elsewhere.

Instead of chasing sales or market share, the prime directive must be profitability growth. What good is it to increase sales or market share if profitability declines? Driving for sales growth often causes poor pricing or investment decisions. Market share cannot be taken to the bank. As one perceptive Australian executive pointed out, 'Volume is vanity, and profit is sanity.'

Profitability also provides a valuable tool for segmentation. While customers are usually discussed in reverent tones, it must be remembered that there are 'good' customers and 'bad' customers. The good customers are the 20 per cent, on average, who generate 80 per cent of the profits. 'Bad' customers are the estimated 15 per cent who are unprofitable.

Because maximizing profitability requires an emphasis on good customers, brand management must include customer equity, or the lifetime profitability of customers. Using customer profitability as a primary branding metric focuses the organization on retention, especially retention of profitable customers. Knowing customer profitability also improves corporate profitability and enables more cost-effective alignment of services and offerings. Just as important, the measurement helps address – or even avoid – unprofitable customers.

Branding objectives must follow strategic objectives. For customer profitability to succeed as a branding metric, it is imperative that CEOs and CFOs place greater importance on profitability than on sales or market share.

The next strategic imperative is accountability. Without accountability, resources are wasted and responsibility diffused. Without accountability, branding does not get the CEO and CFO attention it requires. In a survey among companies from *The Times* 1000, fewer than 57 per cent of finance directors believed investment in marketing was necessary for long-term corporate growth; 27 per cent thought marketing investment to be only a short-term tactical measure; and 32 per cent said marketing was the first budget they would cut in hard times.

Accountability requires measurement. Measurement ensures that branding goals set will be branding goals achieved. Branding executives understand that they are handicapped by a current lack of measurement. In a survey by the CMO (Chief Marketing Officer) Council, almost 80 per cent of senior marketing executives said they were dissatisfied with their ability to demonstrate the business impact and value of their activities.

From the perspective of CEOs and CFOs, branding accountability requires measurement tied to profitability. While branding intangibles may be hard to measure, the results are not. How many customers bought how much? How much did it cost to acquire them, and how often did they buy? How much profit did the last campaign generate? It is long past time for branding executives to embrace the balance-sheet language of the financial community as enthusiastically as they have embraced the ethereal language of creatives. No company can afford to invest for long in branding without a measurable return that enables both profitability and accountability.

While CEOs and CFOs must demand accountability, they must not use measurement as a stick for punishment. Rather, measurement must be a tool to improve future efforts. Branding requires art as well as science, and branding success cannot be guaranteed even if all variables are known and tracked. Measurement works best when it is used to unify resources, track progress and improve future efforts.

Profitability and accountability drive the third branding imperative: sustainability. Sustainability is critical, since by some estimates 80–95 per cent of products fail to become brands. Even long-established brands like Oldsmobile can lose their way and get ploughed under. Sustainability is also important because more than two-thirds of purchases are just one-off buys. Only a brand focused on sustainability will take the steps that lead to second, third or even a lifetime of purchases.

Because of the imperatives of profitability, accountability and sustainability, companies must focus more on retention branding than acquisition branding. Advertising, public relations and other aspects of acquisition branding get the lion's share of attention. By contrast, retention branding – or the effort to keep customers – is treated like an unwanted stepchild. Most firms do not even track retention rates.

A brand is not built by acquiring customers; it is built by keeping them. Most competitive product advantages can be duplicated. The one advantage that cannot be duplicated is a customer relationship. Retention branding focuses a company on those customers and relationships, not products and transactions. Retention branding also drives profitability and sustainability. As loyalty expert Frederick Reichheld pointed out, 'It is not how satisfied you keep your customers; it is how many satisfied customers you keep!'

The final theme of this book is operational excellence. The best, most award-winning advertising or other effort cannot build a brand unless promises are backed up with service and other organizational performance. As a result, companies must pay close attention to the systems, processes and people that deliver the emotional, experiential and economic value that make up a brand. Brands die without the ability to execute accurately, consistently and responsively. What good does it do to generate thousands of leads if phones are not answered properly or orders shipped on time?

Ensuring profitability, accountability and sustainability requires ProfitBranding, not such trends *du jour* as e-brands or so-called 'immutable laws'.

ProfitBranding reflects a fundamental branding shift recognized by many but understood by few. Companies no longer sell. Customers buy. That means companies must stop defining themselves in terms of their offerings (eg a 'car manufacturer') and start defining themselves in terms of customer value (a 'mobile, interactive and entertainment environment').

ProfitBranding represents an innovative, comprehensive approach to brand building. It reflects the integration – or fusion – of traditional marketing with technology, measurement and operations. It fuses customer requirements and organizational capabilities to deliver value. Acquisition and retention branding complement one another. Online and offline branding are interlinked. And employees and managers focus on the same customer goals. As a result, ProfitBranding sets strategies for today's customer economy and the emerging demand economy, builds profitable customer relationships and enables brand management and growth based on data, not opinion.

Get out your calculators. The time to start ProfitBranding is now.

1

Branding: yesterday, today and tomorrow

'Markets are conversations. Their members communicate in language that is natural, open, honest, direct, funny and often shocking. Most corporations, on the other hand, only know how to talk in the soothing, humorless monotone of the mission statement, marketing brochure and your-call-is-important-to-us busy signal. Same old tone, same old lies. No wonder networked markets have no respect for companies unable or unwilling to speak as they do.'

Christopher Locke *et al*, *Cluetrain Manifesto* (2001)

Why do brands fail?

Every company wants a brand like Coca-Cola, Cadbury, Sony or Haier. These brands represent a consumer, business or regional shorthand for what a company does and how well it does it. Brands are a valuable corporate asset that can increase profitability, sales and even share value. Brands shrink sales cycles. They bolster competitive prowess and help launch new offerings. They enable higher pricing. In consumer electronics, for example, the price difference between branded and unbranded products is as high as 50–60 per cent. No wonder branding has moved to the top of corporate strategic goals.

As a result, companies make substantial branding investments. About US $1.4 trillion was spent on marketing in 2002 alone. In 2003 companies spent an estimated US $750 billion on marketing research. The US Department of Labor estimates that advertising, marketing, promotions, public relations (PR) and sales managers held about 700,000 jobs in 2002. The concept of branding supports a large industry encompassing books, seminars and agencies.

Yet despite such investment, concentration and exposure, branding remains inconsistent. Depending on the source, 80–95 per cent of all products fail to become brands. Indeed, branding failures are the stuff of legend. In 1979, Clairol introduced 'Touch of Yoghurt'. Few bought the yoghurt-based shampoo. Some who did ate it, making them ill. In the mid-1990s, Mattel introduced 'Earring Magic Ken' as a Barbie companion. Not many parents saw the appeal of a male doll with an earring in his left ear, mesh T-shirt and a large gold neck chain. Other well-known examples include the Ford Edsel, New Coke, Sony Betamax and McDonald's Arch Deluxe.

Branding has not suffered for its failures. Don Schultz and Jeffrey Walters cite studies in their book *Measuring Brand Communication ROI* (1997) that indicate marketing now represents 50 per cent or more of corporate costs, up from about 20 per cent after the Second World War. By contrast, manufacturing and operations have reduced their demands from 50 per cent of total corporate outlays in the 1950s to about 30 per cent today.

With so much effort and expertise devoted to branding, why are there so many branding failures? The usual suspects are poor timing, lack of understanding, product shortcomings or inadequate funding. These can kneecap any brand. But efforts have failed with generous budgets and the best brains money can buy. Even Microsoft with its billions could not salvage desktop software 'Bob' and bCentral. So what causes one offering to be transformed into a brand and another to slink off product shelves with its tail between its legs?

Brands fail primarily because they do not address current branding imperatives. Branding imperatives represent the ocean in which all brands must swim. Based on market characteristics, customer requirements and competitive realities, brand imperatives establish the ground rules for acquiring, identifying, retaining – and profiting from – customers. These imperatives include buyer–seller relationships, branding goals, organizational processes, technology and, most importantly, measurement.

While eternal truths about human behaviour remain constant, brand imperatives change over time. Shaped by technological, economic or social forces, brand imperatives reflect new customer demands, competitive realities and even new media. In other words, they represent social, economic and technological 'brandscapes' – the forces that shape awareness, selection, relationships and reputation.

Just as generals lose when they fight current battles with past tactics, companies lose when they fail to adapt to current branding imperatives. The most generous budget, synergistic strategy or innovative 'positioning' will not establish or salvage a brand if the efforts are based on the wrong brand imperatives. Not only will the effort be like pushing a rock uphill, but it will be the wrong hill as well.

Many look to Cadbury, Nivea, Sony and other brands as models to emulate. However, it is critical to remember that these brands established their dominance during an era when branding imperatives were different. Using the same tactics that propelled them to the top of the heap then does not guarantee success today. In fact, it may even be counter-productive. It's more than 'the branding rules have changed'. What has changed is the game.

It is important to recognize that brand imperatives have changed from yesterday. It is more important to recognize that imperatives will inevitably shift again. To surf the tides of change instead of being swamped by them, executives must keep an eye on emerging imperatives. Such a beyond-the-headlights view enables companies to steal a march on competitors and forge customer relationships just when loyalties are emerging.

As a result, companies seeking to brand must abandon the comfortable homage to old imperatives, adapt to current realities and build the foundation for emerging ones. Essentially, these brand imperatives can be divided into three eras – mass economy, customer economy and the evolving demand economy.

MASS-ECONOMY BRANDING: MINDLESS PURSUIT OF 'SHARE-OF-MIND'

On 2 April 1993, a branding era rode off into the sunset. On a day immortalized as Black Friday, Philip Morris dropped the price of its best-selling Marlboro cigarettes by 40 cents a pack.

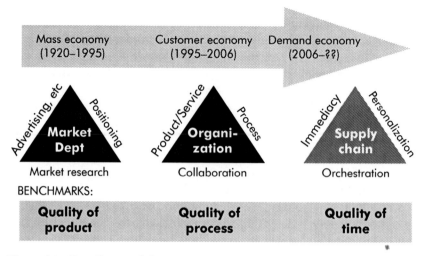

Figure 1.1 Branding models

Marlboro remains a classic branding story. The cigarette quintessentially identified with the jut-jawed Marlboro Man was once marketed to women. In 1927, a Marlboro ad read, 'Women quickly develop a discerning taste. That is why Marlboros now ride in so many limousines, attend so many bridge parties and repose in so many handbags.' But by 1954, increased competition and other factors caused Marlboro's market share to decline to less than 1 per cent. Marlboro then committed itself to a smart and prescient brand programme. By using powerful mass marketing tools to purvey a masculine image, Marlboro eventually became the world's best-selling packaged product. Its pricing premium produced more US revenues than such well-known companies as Campbell Soup, Kellogg's and Gillette.

The price cut not only dethroned the Marlboro Man from his horse but also symbolized the end of the golden age of mass-economy branding, when mass media promoted mass-produced products to mass markets. Manufacturers held the upper hand over customers. They controlled information flow, and customers had no easy way to check promises. They controlled where products could be bought, and for how much.

Mass market branding rewards were great. Consumers paid for the reduced risk of a brand: 'No one ever got fired for buying IBM.' Since size and market share conferred significant production advantages, sales growth became a strategic goal. This drove branding efforts to focus on acquisition. If customers left, markets were growing fast enough and mass-media tools were so effective that replacement customers could be acquired elsewhere.

The emphasis on sales and market share growth led companies to 'sell what we make'. Marketing departments and agencies served as broadcast towers for one-way messages – 'buy new, buy now' – to markets. Armed with market research, they used increasingly sophisticated advertising and PR. Strategies were based on tried-and-true formulas like the '4 Ps' (product, price, place and promotion), which emerged during the 1930s, and AIDA (awareness, interest, desire and acquisition), which 19th-century door-to-door salespeople developed. The effect was to reduce purchasers to receptacles for products and messages: 'targets' to be 'profiled' before they were 'captured'.

Mass-economy branding tools were so powerful that many forgot that just because it could be sold did not mean it was worth selling. A decline in quality offered an opening to Japanese firms, who married mass market efficiencies with a quality advantage to develop world-class brands.

Mass-economy brand imperatives included:

- *Mass media:* Until 1955, the BBC operated Britain's only television service, followed by ITV. In the United States, viewers had only three channels until the advent of cable. The limited number of television and magazine options gave mass-media advertising and PR tremendous power.
- *Sales and market growth:* Companies followed the pied piper of sales and market share growth for everything from compensation to budgeting. The universal assumption was that sales or market growth translated into profitability – sooner or later.
- *Awareness:* 'Awareness' represented the primary branding currency in the mass economy. If an offering, reinforced by adequate distribution, pierced a level of awareness, then it had a better-than-even chance of crossing the chasm to become a brand. Mass media and sufficient budgets made awareness fairly easy to achieve. But in the customer economy, awareness is not enough. Awareness is required, just as putting the key in the ignition is required to drive a car. But just as the ability to start a car does not mean the driver will arrive on time, neither does the creation of awareness mean a brand will be established.

  Awareness as a strategic, and not minor, branding goal has problems. Awareness represents a low bar that is only minimally connected to profitability. What good is awareness if few sales result? Additionally, the single-minded pursuit of awareness with so little return wastes resources. Compounding the problem, consumers have grown adept at blocking the interrupt-based marketing that seeks to increase awareness. What they can't block with technology or other tools, they don't remember. How many commercials are talked about when the name of the advertiser is forgotten? Finally, the goal of branding is not awareness. It is not even an initial sale. It is repeat sales to customers based on a profitable relationship.

- *Positioning:* Rightly believing that branding was becoming more difficult because audiences were confused by too many communications, the 1970s marketing classic, *Positioning: The battle for your mind* (1986) by Al Ries and Jack Trout – and its numerous reiterations over the past three decades – promoted positioning as a tool to 'break through the clutter'. Perception is the essence of positioning. As outlined in the book, positioning consists of creating a 'position', or psychic identity, in prospects' minds. Ideally, this position is based on being 'first' in a particular competitive category. If someone else is already first in a category, then companies should redefine themselves in a new category to be 'first'. Powerful mass media made the task of creating 'a leadership position' comparatively easy. The mental niche was so important that Ries and Trout emphasized that 'it's better to be first in the mind than to be first in the marketplace'.

Ries and Trout's books are entertaining but, in essence, make a case for manipulation. The preface lays it out: 'Positioning has nothing to do with the product... [it] is what you do to the mind of the prospect.' In other words, 'positioning' is based on the premise that prospects can be made to believe, through advertising, PR and other vehicles, what offerings mean to them.

In the mass economy, when companies could generally control how offerings were portrayed, positioning could work. In fact, positioning was the horse that the Marlboro Man rode to the peak of his branding power. Positioning was ideal for the hierarchical, command-and-control paradigm of the mass economy. It was also ideal for agencies and marketing departments. It justified the bulk of advertising and PR while removing the onus of accountability. Achieving the goal of 'first in the mind' was sufficiently fuzzy to allow marketing departments routinely to pat themselves on the back, at least until a 'repositioning' was required by a new vice-president or even agency.

But positioning produced several ramifications that make it a losing tactic in the customer economy. First, it led companies towards manipulating information to control their position: at a minimum, 'same old tone, same old lies', as the *Cluetrain Manifesto* points out. As a result, markets have become disillusioned and cynical. In 1964, 41 per cent of consumers had a favourable view of advertising and only 14 per cent unfavourable, according to a survey by the American Association of Advertising Agencies (AAAA). By 2004, a Yankelovich survey found that only 28 per cent had a wholly positive view of marketing, while 36 per cent were wholly negative. No wonder branding has got harder.

Positioning ignores a basic principle of communications theory. Communication does not occur just because a speaker (or company) speaks. It occurs only when the message is accepted. Companies think an offering is positioned when they advertise a particular message, but unless consumers accept it their efforts are for nought. A company can 'position' service as part of its brand ('your business is important to us'), but such positioning does more harm than good if customers only hear that message while on hold.

In the highly competitive world of the customer economy, the goal of 'being first in a segment' essentially results in companies letting themselves be defined by what their competitors have already done, or segmenting themselves into customer irrelevance. As legendary management consultant Peter Drucker said, 'Customers do not buy what we think we sell them.' In other words, they buy products on their terms, not our 'positions'.

The perception-based foundation of positioning has two risks. What if performance does not match the perception? That hurts the brand and future sales. Perception is also fragile. Unexpected events – competitive product introductions, product mishaps or even bad reviews – can cause the value of 'positioned' brands to plunge overnight.

Positioning – declaring yourself a leader in one category or another – is easy, especially compared to the task of discovering and meeting specific customer requirements. When offerings are failing, operational issues, service capabilities or pricing are usually at fault – not the position. Unless these are addressed, positioning – or repositioning – will amount to no more than grandiose generals deploying war resources that don't exist. As one insightful direct mail expert said, 'It is not about share of mind. It's a show of hands.'

The problems with positioning do not mean that offerings should not be differentiated, or markets targeted and segmented. Differentiation, segmentation and targeting are tangible, based on the current or desired requirements of a specific group. By contrast, positioning is intangible, based on the impossible-to-measure 'share of mind'.

Despite its power, mass-economy branding had an Achilles heel: lack of effective measurement. Measurement was based on audiences (readers, viewers, etc), financial metrics (cost-per-thousand, distribution costs, etc), response (leads, calls, etc), production (sales, units shipped, etc) or perceptions (awareness, satisfaction, etc). Such measurements were expensive to gather, were often long after the fact and, most importantly, could not easily link branding cause and sales effect.

CUSTOMER ECONOMY: CUSTOMERS DEFINE BRANDS

This golden age of mass-economy branding began to tarnish in the 1980s. Leveraging their distribution and 'shelf display' chokepoints, Tesco, Wal-Mart and other large retailers began dictating pricing, packaging, delivery and other areas that were once the exclusive domain of manufacturers. Once-homogeneous markets segmented.

The monolithic force of mass media fragmented, making brand building harder and more expensive. From 1960 to 2004, the number of US magazines grew fourfold to 18,000 titles – and that is not counting such alternative media as blogs and online newsletters. The magazine *Advertising Age* estimates the average consumer was subjected to 3,000 messages daily in 1990, up from 1,500 in 1960. US broadcast networks, which attracted 71 per cent of the prime-time audience during the 1991–92 season, only captured 52 per cent in the 2003–04 season, according to Nielsen Media Research.

Mass-media advertising is losing power. In one study, McKinsey & Company looked at the market share and advertising expenditures of worldwide car manufacturers from 1995 to 1998. In some cases, more advertising led to greater market share; in other cases, less. But the study concluded: 'What's troubling about the distribution, however, is the relatively large number of companies that lose share whether they spend more or spend less on measured advertising.' According to a Nielsen Media Research study in 2000, only 12–13 per cent of viewers who see an ad can recall it on the same night.

Additionally, the Internal Revenue Service, the US tax agency, looked at the relative ad spending by profitable and unprofitable companies. Profitable companies with more than US $100 million in sales spent 1.18 per cent of sales on advertising. Unprofitable companies spent 1.27 per cent. The same ratios held true for smaller companies. No wonder

McDonald's now devotes a third of its US marketing budget to television, down from two-thirds five years ago.

Manufacturers also helped dig the grave of mass marketing. Brand extensions introduced more products in more categories. McKinsey & Company estimates that the number of products on supermarket shelves tripled from 1991 to 2001. In 2003 alone, 26,893 new food and household products were introduced, including 115 deodorants, 187 breakfast cereals and 303 women's fragrances, according to Mintel International Group. TNS Media Intelligence, which has 2 million products in its database, is adding an average of 700 per day. No wonder customers are confused and companies find it hard to stand out.

Product parity has become the norm. Everyone has access to the same manufacturing technology and branding tools. This makes it difficult to differentiate. For example, T-Mobile International, the world's second-largest international mobile operator with US $16 billion in sales, tried differentiating itself through innovation. The company grew skilled at bringing out products two or three months before competitors but found that 'no one cared', says Andras Kondor, vice-president of CRM. The lesson for T-Mobile: 'We have to get our revenue growth from our current customers,' says Kondor.

And then came the internet. Because of the way it has transformed processes, supply chains and information access, the internet has sparked the biggest revolution in branding since the first television commercial was transmitted in 1930. The internet allows customers to get information without relying on the manufacturer or retailer. Products and delivery can be customized. Pricing dynamics have been altered. Every aspect of business – especially marketing – is still struggling to understand the imperatives of this new medium.

As a result, the mass economy is fading into history. Today, it is the customer economy. According to US research firm Forrester Research, the customer economy is shaped by customers who 'demand better products at lower prices, higher levels of service in routine business interactions, satisfying experiences, and access to all of these things at any moment via the web, e-mail, phone, store or kiosk'.

The splintering of the mass media, increased retailer power and new purchasing options have taken branding power away from companies and put it into the hands of customers. No longer can companies position brands; now it is customers who define brands, based on economic, emotional or experiential attributes. Marketing axioms like the '4 Ps' become much less relevant, partly because they don't acknowledge the role of the customer or the importance of processes and profitability.

Brand imperatives of the customer economy include:

- *Access:* Access takes various forms. The internet opens a new sales channel. It gives companies greater access to customers through e-mail, websites and even internet telephony. It also gives purchasers greater access to companies. Support, for example, can be round the clock instead of 9-to-5. More importantly, it gives consumers access to pricing, performance and other information that was once hard to find. The information can be found not only via Google but, much more powerfully, from other customers.

  In the mass economy, customers were isolated. But, thanks to the internet, customers can now band together for increased corporate attention or better pricing. Dissatisfied customers can damage brands at the speed of e-mail. Upset with Toshiba customer service, a Japanese consumer put up a website. The site included a recording of a customer service representative saying 'I'm not going to apologize for being impolite. Why should I?' The site generated more than 7 million visits. Eventually, Toshiba had to apologize publicly. Additionally, opinion-gathering sites like Epinions.com or customer reviews on Amazon can shape a brand more than any positioning effort. In the mass economy, companies had to satisfy the bulk of their customers. Now, they cannot afford to dissatisfy even one.

- *Relationships:* The mass-economy emphasis on sales or market share growth led to a focus on customer acquisition. Product and sales development took precedence over customer development. Accounting and other systems did not distinguish between revenue from a new customer and revenue from an old one. Companies eagerly stood at the front door to greet new customers and collect commissions, blissfully unaware of the customers walking out the back door.

  One brand imperative of the customer economy is optimized relationships, not maximized transactions. That is because increased competition, customer-to-customer communication and the declining power of mass-economy tools have made it more difficult to replace customers who walk. To create and maintain the relationships that are at the heart of every brand, companies are turning to CRM (customer relationship management) and such tactics as 'one-to-one marketing'. Ironically, companies are waking up to the importance of relationships at the same time that customer willingness to enter into relationships is diminished. Customers, recognizing their value, have become more demanding – and more fickle.

- *Processes:* Product quality, a brand differentiator in the mass economy, is now a given. Today, it is the quality of processes – service, delivery, billing, support – that makes a brand stand out. While once marketing departments built brands, now 'the organization is the brand', shaping brands by everything from how phones are answered to delivery timeliness. As a result, brand imperatives have shifted away from product attributes. Now, they are 'essentially a seller's promise to deliver a specific set of features, benefits and services to the buyers', says Philip Kotler, distinguished professor of international marketing at Northwestern University.

- *Measurement:* In the mass economy, information about behaviour, operations and supply chains was a black hole. Data were suspect because they were self-reported (television viewing books) or lacked trackability (who redeemed coupons?). Often, measurement was not even a goal. A study in the *Journal of Advertising Research* analysed 135 'successful' advertising campaigns. Fewer than 1 per cent had any quantifiable objectives. Without quantifiable objectives, how can progress and accountability be tracked?

  Measurement has substantially evolved in the customer economy, aided by increased processing power, sophisticated software and the internet's ability to capture actions. Despite the new flood of information, however, companies still have trouble establishing causal links between marketing activity and customer activity. Knowing the number of website 'hits' is as interesting – but ultimately as useless – as knowing levels of awareness in the mass economy.

  Marketing has tried to meet the demand for measurement with various artificial metrics – creativity, awareness, impressions and others. Unfortunately, such measurements have little proven link to profitability or even brand success. Indeed, awareness could even be a negative. Just look at the fallout linked with the scandals associated with the Italian firm Parmalat or the Japanese dairy company Snow Brand. Such artificial metrics also could not fit within the cells of a spreadsheet or find a home on a balance sheet, making them hard to integrate with organizational metrics used elsewhere.

  Increasing measurement prowess has had an unintended side effect – increased calls for branding accountability within executive suites. Understandably, top executives want to know how well the brand is meeting organizational goals and how well the organization is meeting customer goals. Since the dawn of the mass economy, the difficulty of effective measurement has made marketing the least accountable part of the organization. 'I know that 50 per cent of my advertising is wasted. The only trouble is, I don't know which half' is a well-known industry phrase commonly attributed to department store magnate John Wanamaker. Could any other part of the organization get away with saying 'I know that 50 per cent of my production is rejected. But I do not know why' or 'I know that 50 per cent of my deliveries are late. Oh, well'?

Calls for accountability make branding professionals uncomfortable, especially since they sense, as the *Cluetrain Manifesto* underscores, that branding power has shifted away from them. Advertising, PR and other marketing generated by a department or agency can no longer establish a brand. The activities that create a brand today, such as quality, service, fulfilment and innovation, consistently delivered over time, are in the hands of process owners in logistics, manufacturing and information systems. Look at the latest buzzword to sweep through the world of branding – 'experiential branding'. Regardless of the merits of that strategy, the responsibility for delivering an enhanced experience is in the hands of almost every department – except for marketing.

DEMAND ECONOMY: LOOK AHEAD TO AVOID BEING LEFT BEHIND

If the customer economy made the mass economy fade, what will replace the customer economy? It is vital to think about that now. Many brands faltered as the world moved from the mass economy to the customer economy. The ground rules changed, but companies persisted in using mass-economy tactics like positioning in a world that required attention to relationships, access and accountability. Keeping an eye on the future allows companies to start building and strengthening brands based on emerging imperatives. And they can avoid the waste that results when the branding techniques of a fading era are used in a new one.

The next branding era is the 'demand economy'. Signs of the demand economy are emerging now, but it will become dominant in the next two or three years. Drivers of the demand economy include globalization, wireless technologies, customization capabilities and, of course, the internet.

Think customers today are demanding? According to Forrester, the customers of tomorrow will 'make today's customers look like saints'! That's because the demand economy will give customers the tools and choices needed to demand immediate, personalized fulfilment. Customers won't want just offerings; they will want service, support and offerings just for them – now. If the symbolic buzzword for the customer economy was 24/7, standing for availability 24 hours a day, seven days a week, the standard for the demand economy will be 60/24 – ready every minute of every hour of every day.

Brand imperatives of the demand economy include:

- *Integrated supply chains:* In the customer economy, competition is based on organizational competencies. Competition in the demand economy will be based on the organization, orchestration and integration of supply chains, or an ecosystem of suppliers, manufacturers, partners and customers. It will take a coordinated, interactive supply chain to deliver tailored solutions to customers whenever and wherever they want. Companies will have to be able to communicate customer requirements quickly down to the deepest supplier tier, and be able to communicate with customers based on current, accurate information from suppliers. Companies will change from enterprises to syndicates, or interlocking networks of strategic alliances and joint operations.

  No company will be able to brand, no matter how much is spent on marketing, without an integrated end-to-end supply chain. Every branding decision will incorporate a supply chain component. For example, promotions could immediately incorporate a 15 per cent discount to boost demand if orders drop below forecasts.

- *Increased accessibility:* Now, it's anywhere, any time. Soon it will be everywhere, every time, thanks to wearable wireless devices that interconnect us all. The number of mobile subscribers tops 1 billion. Wireless users outnumber PC users. Consumers and businesses will be able to establish their own private 'internets' with the specific information and resources they need. Companies and consumers will be able to reach each other around the clock according to customer-driven rules. Customer-, location- and even activity-specific information can be sent to customers no matter where they are or what they are doing. Even now, consumer products giant Unilever suggests mobile recipes while customers shop.

  Currently, most marketing drives towards dead ends. Ads and PR deliver messages and stop. It is up to purchasers to take the next step. That will change in the demand economy, which will be marked by multiple channels (web, e-mail, instant messaging (IM), information appliances) to interact with customers. Interactive TV (iTV), now in its earliest stages of adoption, will allow consumers to order products seen on favourite programmes. Scanning technology will allow instant ordering from ads, coupons, even street posters. These technologies will force companies to learn how to guide customers interactively from initial interest through deeper levels of involvement. The ultimate brand goal will not be awareness, but incorporation into the 'personal networks' that individuals use to link to their families and friends as well as interests.

- *Immediacy:* Availability was a door opener to the customer economy, enabling customers to obtain offerings through a variety of channels. The bar gets higher in the demand economy with immediacy – the ability to satisfy demands immediately at the onset of desire.

  The spread of wireless and other technologies will accelerate immediacy. New brands will be formed and industries reshaped by 'pervasive computing' – an environment enabled by mobile computers, embedded systems (computer operating systems that are built into cars and industrial equipment) and other devices that can all communicate with each other. By 2010, researchers predict that computing will have become so integrated into our lives that people will not even realize that they are using computers.

  The requirement for immediacy will force companies to shrink delivery windows from days to hours, telephone hold times from minutes to seconds and e-mail responses from hours to minutes. Distribution will become more critical, since consumers will want goods and services as soon as possible. 'Time' will become a bigger driver of value than 'price'.

- *Personalization:* In his book *The Global Village* (1992), Marshall McLuhan observed that new technology has an interesting side effect. It brings back an activity that had faded from the scene. In the age of the craftsman and guild, every product was made to personal specification. Tomorrow, new technologies will move us away from mass production to products as personalized as tastes in music. Personalization is an important differentiator now. But current personalization is primitive, limited by cost, time and technological capabilities. Customers 'personalize' items by choosing colour and options for standardized items.

  Customers want more. They want actively to shape information and offerings. Look at the successes of the Apache web server, Linux operating system and other open-source innovations. Sumerset Houseboats allows customers to design boats, negotiate pricing and monitor construction. Each boat is 'as individual as its owner'.

Advanced build-to-order capabilities that include nanotechnology (the ability to rearrange atoms to create offerings) will enable even complex products to be produced specifically for one customer. Web services will enable businesses and consumers to 'assemble' service, production and other capabilities from a variety of sources. Companies will use wireless and embedded technologies to tailor services and products based on customer location, context and preferences. Already, for example, Mattel allows customers to personalize Barbies based on 6,000 options. Orange enables phone customers to personalize services and handsets. The Malaysian shoe company Lewre delivers customized shoes.

- *Measurement:* Marketing departments and agencies are now often judged on 'creativity' that fuels campaigns to build awareness. While creativity is always important, benchmarks will change substantially, based on how well prospects are guided from interest to profitability. A primary metric will be the depth, length and profitability of customer relationships. The fact that 20 million people saw an ad will not be as important as knowing that 100,000 interactively engaged with the marketing effort, resulting in 12,345 customers with an average lifetime value of US $12,342.

The most interesting characteristic of the demand economy will be integration. Companies will not sell products but produce solutions that will involve complex supply chains, joint ventures, strategic partners and even competitors. Already, a new GM business helps customers find the car they want based on preferences and budget – whether the car is made by GM or not. IBM and other technology firms have long sold offerings from competitors as part of a solution, even if they have similar offerings. In effect, this changes branding strategies from focusing on 'selling' to customers to 'buying' for them. Obviously, companies will have to become much more knowledgeable about customers to fulfil this new role.

Marketing departments will have to play a new role in the demand economy. Already, marketing departments risk irrelevance. Few marketing executives become CEOs. The role of the marketing department has already diminished in the customer economy as CEOs have adopted marketing as one of their strategic responsibilities. Marketing executives will have to become more skilled in business process management, supply chain management, multiple technologies and financial analysis.

CONCLUSION

Branding as a discipline has been around since the late 1800s, when Campbell's, Heinz and other companies created brands as a way to deal with consumer concerns about mass-produced products. Branding skills grew more sophisticated throughout the 20th century, fuelled by the huge growth in demand after the Second World War. Companies approached branding with a sense of 'stewardship'. Executives saw their job as protecting market share and reputation.

But the mass-economy environment that grew so many great brands has lost its fertility. Customers are no longer helpless supplicants prostrate before the power of brands. Now they are gods, demanding homage. No wonder so many marketing professionals long for the days when mass media and positioning were so powerful. It is difficult going from sovereign to serf.

As Philip Morris recognized when it made its best-selling product compete on price rather than brand, the world has changed. Marketers must adapt strategies and tactics to the branding imperatives of the customer economy. Attempting to brand using antiquated tactics wastes resources, especially when marketing expenses can account for more than 30 per cent of a brand's cost, according to Forrester.

Customers are no longer interested in keeping 'SuperBrands' or other corporate trophies shiny. They are looking for offerings that innovate, add value or convenience, or simplify lives or operations. It won't make any difference what companies say a brand does; the only thing that counts is the value actually delivered. As a result, mass-economy approaches to branding must fade away. Branding must incorporate customer-economy imperatives, including relationships, access and accountability. Companies must start understanding that customers define brands, based on their experience and the words of their peers, not on how companies position them.

Ultimately, branding in the customer economy means viewing prospects as candidates for relationships, not markets for products. Admittedly, it's not as easy as before, when boosting marketing budgets could boost brands. But, remember, part of the power of brands derives from the difficulty in their creation.

Table 1.1 Branding model comparisons

	Mass Economy (1945–1995)	Customer Economy (1995–2006)	Demand Economy (2006–??)
Characteristics	Mass-produced products and services	Customer-oriented products and services	Personalized products and services
Target	Mass markets	Market segments	Profitable customers
Customer insight	Market research	Databases, analysis	Customer collaboration
Goals	Sales/market growth	Profitability growth	Customer equity growth
Customer contact	Single channel	Multichannel	Unified multichannel
View of customer	Revenue source	Asset to be nurtured	Co-creator of value
Branding responsibility	Marketing department	Organization	Supply chain
Dominant branding strategy	Positioning	1:1 marketing	ProfitBranding
Metrics	Sales growth, market share	Loyalty, cost-to-serve, profitability	Customer, account, product penetration
Primary communications vehicles	Broadcast media	Targeted (direct mail, telemarketing, segmented publications)	Targeted, interactive (internet, iTV, wireless)
Barriers to entry	Capital, distribution, media gatekeepers	Intellectual capital, technological integration	Alliances, global supply chain capabilities
Role of technology	Minimal	Important, but with integration and other difficulties	Seamless and vital to branding
Product development drivers	Internal	Markets	Customers
Fulfilment capabilities	Slow, using internal capabilities	Fast, using outsourced facilities	Immediate, using digital capabilities

Takeaways

- Have your branding initiatives been losing effectiveness? Do you still have the same branding goals as a decade ago? Are you still using the same tactics?
- How do you characterize your relationship with customers? How do customers characterize their relationship with you? Are the answers the same? If not, why?
- Are executives demanding accountability for branding money spent? Are current measurements providing the insights sought? What metrics are they looking for? Can marketing executives deliver?
- Why do you want to brand? Sales growth? Market share growth? Increased profitability?
- Do you have a vision of the relationship between your brand and your customers? Is that vision shared throughout the organization?

2

Forging a ProfitBrand in the customer economy

'The purpose of business is not to make a sale, but to make and keep
a customer.'

Peter Drucker, legendary management consultant

Attracted by its rapid growth, American Express acquired IDS Financial
Services and its 5,000-member sales force. American Express then
discovered that IDS was losing a client almost every time another signed
up. The reason: IDS was spending US $16 on acquisition for every US $1
it spent on retention.

That story illustrates why so many brands fail and so much branding
money is wasted. When strategic goals focus on sales or market growth,
branding strategies stress acquisition. Acquisition activities – ads, PR,
trade shows, direct mail – then consume 80–90 per cent of the branding
budget. According to one survey, 72 per cent of senior marketing executives said their primary role was to drive leads for sales. 'Sales and
marketing' gets its own department and star billing. Even compensation
is based on immediate sales. Retention is an afterthought, with no single
organizational voice to represent existing customers.

Acquisition branding is important. Yet what should brands do about
the fact that more than two-thirds of buyers fail to make a repeat
purchase, according to McKinsey & Company? Or that US businesses
lose half of their customers every five years, as researcher Find/SVP
reported? Or that such customer loss reduces profits by 17 per cent?

Customers who buy once and never again mean the initial acquisition investment is wasted. Additional investments are required to find 'replacement' customers. *Harvard Business Review* estimates that attracting a new customer costs 5–10 times more than retaining one; Bain & Co estimates it costs 10 times more. A study by the US Office of Consumer Affairs Studies reported that acquisition cost is five times greater than retention. For example, it costs retail financial services firms US $280 to find a new customer and only US $57 to keep one, according to the research firm Gartner.

In the mass economy, markets grew so fast and mass media was so effective that retention was an afterthought. Lost customers could be easily replaced. But the imperatives are different in the customer economy, when customer acquisition costs and complexity rise every year. In 2001, a *Sales & Marketing* survey indicated an average cost of US $113.25 for a sales call. Research from publisher McGraw-Hill pegged the average sales call cost at US $336.

The satellite television provider DirecTV understands the importance of retention. In 2001, attrition at DirecTV declined from 1.7 per cent to 1.5 per cent, far below the industry average of 2.5 per cent. That is significant, since every tenth of a percentage point represents about 120,000 customers. Since DirecTV estimates that it costs about US $550 to acquire a customer and only US $50 to retain one, the decline in attrition saved the company about US $12 million in acquisition costs.

Retention branding generates profitability. Existing customers represent recurring revenue through licensing, support, training, customization and other services. Older customers require less service and fewer costs than new ones. A rule of thumb is that businesses should not invest more than 20 per cent of what was spent to acquire a customer to retain that customer. Motivated by trust and loyalty, existing customers are less price sensitive than prospects. Satisfied customers refer new ones. This helps sustain the brand and represents a low-cost source of leads. In retail, loyal customers spend an average of 3 times more – and as much as 20 times more – than customers who are not loyal, according to Newgistics, a returns-management vendor.

Bain & Co has estimated that increasing retention rates by only 5 per cent can increase profits by 25 per cent. Massachusetts-based Bernie & Phyl's Furniture 'absolutely' credits growth from US $15 million in 1998 to US $100 million in 2004 to a focus on retention instead of acquisition.

Retention is also key to sales recovery. When sales dip, some firms frantically try to attract new customers to reverse the slide. A wiser move is to leverage the customer base. In most industries, companies have only a 5 per cent chance of selling to a new prospect. Those chances increase to 50 per cent when selling to an existing customer. To generate rapid results, the California Milk Processor Board (CMPB) initially targeted its famed 'got milk' campaign at those who drank milk several times a week, especially since those milk lovers constituted 70 per cent of the California market.

Customers who walk represent a threat. While satisfied customers tell 4–5 others about pleasant experiences, unhappy customers tell 8–13 others. That number rises exponentially if they air their dissatisfactions on the internet. Those they tell are twice as likely to believe 'negative' information as they are positive news. Most worrying of all: they will continue to discuss their dissatisfaction for up to 23 years!

All these factors are important. But the most important reason to focus on retention branding is this: 80 per cent of profits come from 20 per cent of customers.

Despite its substantial impact on profitability, it is estimated that fewer than 20 per cent of companies track retention. Statistics are depressing for the ones that do. The Yankee Group estimates that annual 'churn', or customer loss, in the mobile phone industry ranges from 21 per cent to about 80 per cent. If AT&T Wireless reduced churn by only 10 per cent, lifetime customer value would increase by US $360 million over two years. Still fewer companies track customer life cycles or reasons for customer defection.

Furthermore, companies treat existing customers worse than prospects. A major cause of dissatisfaction among mobile and magazine subscribers is that better deals are offered to new customers than to existing ones. As one subscriber vented in an online forum: 'I have paid [wireless provider] Cingular thousands of on-time dollars over the past several years. Yet, they give a better phone plan to new customers who have never paid them a dime. When my current contract ends, they won't be able to "hear me now"… or at all.'

This lack of retention branding is short-sighted. A 5 per cent increase in retention can result in a bottom-line profit increase of up to 75 per cent, depending on industry. Michigan State University estimated that US $1 spent on acquisition generates US $5 in revenue, while every dollar spent on retention creates US $60 in revenue. British Airways calculated that retention efforts return US $2 for every dollar invested.

The customer economy is changing executive attitudes, however. The single biggest concern for CEOs globally today is customer retention, according to a Conference Board survey. A Gartner survey revealed that more than 75 per cent of 600 enterprises rated customer loyalty and increased sales from current customers more important than sales to new customers. In a memo, Microsoft CEO Stephen Ballmer wrote, 'Our biggest growth opportunity is with our existing base of Office users.' Feargal Quinn, the founder of Ireland's Superquinn chain, proselytizes the 'boomerang principle'. The goal is not to maximize individual transactions, but to ensure that shopping experiences make customers want to return to Superquinn.

Ironically, retention has grown harder just as its importance has emerged. Consumers are more cynical. Rewards for disloyalty are greater. Look at how credit card companies simplify balance transfers, or how software firms offer specialized help for users of competitive products.

After its IDS acquisition, American Express shifted the focus from acquisition to retention. When a study indicated that IDS typically handled only 15 per cent of a client's financial assets, the sales force concentrated on developing relationships by selling lifetime personal financial plans instead of single investments or insurance policies. IDS soon became American Express's most profitable division.

RETENTION BRANDING: DOING BUSINESS ON CUSTOMER TERMS

All companies, especially start-ups, must continue acquisition efforts to replace customers who move, defect or even die. Expansion and growth generate profits. However, the bulk of branding efforts – and budgets – must move from acquisition branding to retention branding. Acquisition branding generates sales and market growth, but retention branding is critical for the most important growth of all – profitability. Retention branding also builds the foundation for brand sustainability.

Acquisition branding focuses on capturing customers. Retention branding seeks to capture – and keep – customer relationships. Without a relationship, the potential for ongoing purchases declines. Companies may even lose contact with former customers. In a single year, about 10 per cent of postal addresses and 30 per cent of e-mail addresses change. Unfortunately, however, the term 'relationship' is frequently misunderstood.

Companies speak of relationships in economic terms. In their eyes, relationships mean selling customers more, more often, at less cost. This one-sided approach may be good for making quarterly numbers, but it is bad for relationships. It's estimated that 80 per cent of customer problems are caused by management policies that are cost driven, rather than customer driven. A RoperASW 'Corporate Reputation Scorecard', based on interviews with 6,500 adults, found that 63 per cent felt that most large US corporations were 'greedy'; 52 per cent felt they were 'arrogant'.

While sales are vital, gains will come from increasing the value of the brand to the customer, not necessarily the value of the customer to the company. This is a difficult shift for those with mass-economy branding imprinted on their genes. After classifying customers as 'targets', it's hard to accept customer control over relationships.

In the customer economy, relationships must be on customer terms. This is defined as matching sales, service, communications and support to specific desires, requirements and value that are defined by customers. Interactions must erase points of pain, increase customer profitability/satisfaction or eliminate uncertainty, from the customer's point of view. Branding strategies that overlook the requirement to be profitable by focusing instead on being 'number one in our market' or 'the industry's best-known offering' are doomed to failure. In the customer economy, brand sustainability means relationships on customer terms.

Doing business on customer terms has allowed Intuit to remain the leader in tax preparation software, despite concerted efforts by larger competitors to dethrone it. In 1995, the company found a bug in its flagship tax program. Although the bug affected fewer than 1 per cent of customers, management immediately offered a new copy of TurboTax to any who requested it. No proof of purchase was required, even though this opened the firm up to sending copies to those using pirated software. Intuit also offered to pay the tax and penalties caused by the bug, if necessary. Compare Intuit's actions on behalf of its customers with how Intel acted with flaws in the Pentium chip and how Firestone acted with its tyres. Firestone even blamed customers for 'underinflation'.

Doing business on customer terms requires approaching issues and processes from the customer's perspective. It's 'How does the customer want it done?', not 'What can we sell to the customer?'. For example, ABB Automation routinely services assemblies containing competitors' products. 'Doing things the customer doesn't expect is what gives us our competitive edge,' said John Barnes, vice-president and general manager. Doing business on customer terms even requires willingness to refer prospects to competitors if immediate requirements cannot be met. PC distributor MicroAge offers data on rivals' inventory when it is out of stock. When storage vendor EMC had quality problems, it offered to replace its systems with new ones from its primary competitor, IBM.

Both customers and companies benefit from doing business on customer terms. Customers, obviously, get offerings based on what they need, not what companies need to sell, and better service. Customers become more loyal when they gain relevant, timely interactions and information. Companies increase retention, gain valuable insights and build a competitive edge. Doing business on customer terms also promotes operational excellence. According to Accenture, large-scale initiatives typically fail at companies when managers know little about what customers want.

Doing business on customer terms is the essence of ProfitBranding. Mass-economy brands could be built by using mass-economy acquisition branding tools to increase sales volume. But sustainable brands in the customer economy require relationships. As a result, a ProfitBrand is defined as 'a long-term *profitable* bond between an offering and customers. This relationship is based on trust and loyalty, backed by everyday operational excellence and measured by customer equity'.

A ProfitBrand has six characteristics:

- *Attention:* 'Awareness' was the Holy Grail of mass-economy branding. In the customer economy, when consumers are exposed to thousands of messages daily, awareness is no longer enough. Now, it's attention. Attention results when messages are relevant, based on timing and interests. Without such relevancy, efforts to achieve awareness are no more than background static to markets skilled at blocking messages.
- *Transactional excellence:* Brands start with a single transaction. If that transaction goes poorly from the customer's perspective, no ProfitBrand can be built. A Pew Charitable Trusts survey found that poor service had driven 46 per cent of consumers out of a store during the preceding year. Undoubtedly, many will not go back. Brands fail because companies do not have the people, processes and systems to fulfil expectations raised by marketing. Brands succeed when they get operational basics right. According to a study from the US consultancy Frank About Women, 83 per cent of women buy more when in a store with good customer service, and 89 per cent will choose one store over another based on better customer service.
- *Trust:* Trust = ProfitBrand. Trust is a powerful, yet fragile, competitive advantage. It cannot be bought; it is only earned over time through transactions judged successful from the customers'

perspective. Trust begins with reputation and third-party endorsements/testimonials, extends through the elimination of financial and other risks, and is confirmed with reliability and consistency over multiple transactions. To create trust, promises made must be promises kept – again and again. Trust building not only encompasses customers, but extends to employees, suppliers, media and other constituencies. Trust is especially important on the web, where products can't be handled. Says *Harvard Business Review*: 'Price does not rule the Web; trust does.'

The Vanguard Group, the fastest-growing US mutual fund company over the past decade, uses trust to brand. Unlike competitors, Vanguard educates customers, rather than pitches to them. On its website, warnings against investing in certain funds are displayed for customers with a low tolerance for risk. Another warning suggests deferring investment until after dividend distribution dates. Vanguard understands that a relationship based on trust is worth more than a quick sale. 'Trust is our number-one asset at Vanguard. We recognize you can't buy trust with advertising; you have to earn it by always acting in the best interests of customers,' CEO Jack Brennan said.

- *Loyalty:* Out of 550 CEOs surveyed in a Conference Board study, 45 per cent said customer loyalty was a top strategic issue. It's clear why. Loyalty leads to retention, a primary driver of profitability. Based on loyalty surveys conducted for 10 years, the bank First Tennessee estimates that every one-point increase in customer loyalty adds US $8 million to its bottom line.

- *Advocacy:* Trust and loyalty create advocacy, or the willingness of customers to recommend offerings. Such advocates pass along e-mails, provide testimonials and/or references and are willing to try a firm's new offerings. A study based on the surveys and purchasing histories of 4,000 customers in six industries published in *Harvard Business Review* found that the best predictor of growth was the answer to the question, 'How likely is it that you would recommend X to a friend or colleague?' The signature of a ProfitBrand is a network of advocates working on its behalf.

- *Profitability:* This is the most critical element of branding, yet so rarely discussed. Without profitability, no brand will survive. Without profitability, there's no point to branding. Without profitability, awareness, position and creativity mean nothing. Every brand activity, relationship and metric must be focused on profitability.

IBM provides a premier example of a mass-economy brand that has made the transition to a ProfitBrand based on these characteristics. In 1993, IBM was in deep trouble. The unthinkable was being asked: 'Can IBM survive?'

The board of directors selected Louis Gerstner Jr as CEO. Although he had no technology experience, Gerstner quickly diagnosed IBM's problem – insularity that had left it unable to do business on customer terms. Employees spent more time working on slide presentations than dealing with customers. Compliance with internal regulations took precedence over customer requirements.

So Gerstner did two things, based on his experience with IBM as a customer. First, he banned complex slide presentations. Second, instead of following the conventional wisdom of dividing the company into 13 loosely linked 'Baby Blues', he focused the company on offering integrated solutions that represented doing business on customer terms. No longer would IBM offer only home-grown technology.

In his words, 'We were going to build this company from the customer back, not from the company out.' He started with IBM Global Services, a small division, and drove it to 'look at technology through the eyes of the customer' by working with Oracle, Sun and 'God forbid, Microsoft'. Since then, IBM's revenue has grown from US $64.5 billion to US $89.1 billion. IBM Global Services employs 180,000, up from 7,600 in 1992.

Gerstner turned IBM around because of a key insight. In the customer economy, companies are no longer sellers of internal offerings. Instead, they are buyers for customers. In other words, a ProfitBrand is based on adding value and solving problems on behalf of customers, whether or not an immediate product sale is involved. A relationship is then established, based not on what companies sell but on how well they 'buy' for customers, even – as IBM had to swallow hard to accept – offerings from competitors.

THREE ES OF PROFITBRANDING: EMOTIONAL, EXPERIENTIAL AND ECONOMIC VALUE

Customers give a ProfitBrand their attention, loyalty, advocacy and money based on the emotional, experiential and economic value they receive. Each ProfitBrand must incorporate one or more of these elements into its product, service and marketing efforts.

Emotional requirements

The heart drives purchases more than the head, even for the most jaded purchasing manager. Customers must feel an emotional connection to their purchases. This emotional connection results from two sources. The first is relationship depth, quality and length. ProfitBrands answer key questions for customers. Am I more important than just a transactional sale? Does the company respect my value? Is it willing and able to take care of future requirements? Can it do business on my terms? Finally, and most importantly, is this company worth having a relationship with?

The answers are often found in operational excellence. Customers develop an emotional connection to a ProfitBrand when phones are answered quickly, service is timely and products are reliable.

The other source of the emotional connection is psychic rewards. Does the ProfitBrand portray the image the customer wants? Does it fit in with relevant values and experiences? Any car provides transport, but one reason buyers purchase Lexus vehicles is to make a statement to the neighbours. Advertising and other marketing play vital roles in developing and supporting such emotional attachments, even after purchasers become customers. It is also important to remember that constituencies such as retailers and distributors, media, investors and employees also have emotional attachments to a ProfitBrand. These constituencies must believe that the company understands and cares about their interests.

Experiential requirements

Emotional appeals can persuade prospects to try an offering, but it is experiential factors that make them stay. Every ProfitBrand has to provide a satisfactory experience. Sometimes this experience is based on sensory experiences, such as when characters pose with children at Disney parks. At other times it makes customers feel better about themselves or their place in the world. The experience can simplify life's complexities with on-time deliveries, expert service and fast resolution of disputes.

Good experiences are based on offerings working as promised. They must be easy to use and maintain, and perform according to the expectations of both novice and expert. Resources must be easily available, ranging from clear manuals to hotlines. Remember that these experiences are from the customer perspective. A complex error message from the infamous 'blue screen of death' may help Microsoft engineers, but it does nothing for the firm's customers.

Providing positive experiences can range from lifetime guarantees to reducing daily frictions. British Airways, for example, identified US residents who used the airline to fly within Europe but did not use it for transatlantic flights. A team dedicated to retention developed several experience enhancements, including faster processing of customs and immigration documents, private suites and even valet services. Business from the target segment increased substantially.

ProfitBrands also unify customer experiences. Online experiences are as satisfactory as offline. Customer knowledge is universally accessible by employees so most transactions can be handled in a single contact. Each transaction includes knowledge about earlier transactions. Customers receive service value, whether they deal direct or through retailers. A quality experience also results from personalization.

Remember, however, that meeting experiential criteria requires effective operational capabilities, backed by policies and procedures created from the customers' perspective.

Economic requirements

ProfitBrands must provide economic value to the customer. They must provide a greater return to the customer than the customer paid. They must perform as promised and meet expectations for quality and longevity.

Economic value requires operational excellence. Systems and processes must ensure that quality offerings are accurately delivered on time. Economic value encompasses integrated implementations of key technologies, including logistics, order processing and other systems. Information must be accessible to employees, suppliers and even customers who need to know. In a world where customers can be anywhere, operational excellence must also extend internationally where necessary.

Doing business on customer terms delivers economic value. Customers must have alternatives to meet their requirements, which can range from the internet to retail showcases. Customer interactions must be built on relevancy and timing. Offerings, information and communication must be based not on what the company wants to sell, but what customers may need to buy. This is not new. Solutions-based sales anchored in the customer perspective have always generated the greatest returns.

Economic value also derives from effective internet usage. The internet is much more than a new marketing and sales channel. Ultimately, the internet enables more effective supply chains as well as the ability to work collaboratively with partners, customers and suppliers. Without an effective, coordinated supply chain, the ability to deliver customer value is limited. In terms of branding, the supply chain will be the same defining characteristic of the demand economy as the mass media was to the mass economy.

PROFITBRANDING PROCESS: FIND, KEEP, GROW AND PROFIT

The imperatives for branding in the customer economy include trust, loyalty and profitability. Branding also means meeting experiential, emotional and economic requirements. How can that knowledge be leveraged into developing ProfitBrands?

Like anything else of value, it requires a consistent process. That process can be defined simply. Find. Keep. Grow. Profit.

- *Find:* ProfitBrands start with finding the 'right' customers – those who represent the most current and long-term value. Identifying the right customers requires understanding the characteristics and requirements of existing profitable customers, and targeting similar prospects.
- *Keep:* During the mass economy, companies focused on acquisition. Acquisition is the most difficult and laborious part of branding. For a variety of reasons, acquisition branding cannot continue to fuel growth. In the customer economy, companies must focus on retention. Higher retention rates, based on loyalty, trust and transactional excellence, inevitably lead to lower costs, greater profits and better word of mouth. Retention depends on delivering customer value based on emotional, experiential or economic requirements. It also requires customer-driven benchmarks and measurement as well as an organization capable of doing business on customer terms.
- *Grow:* Successful brands work to increase the profitability of existing customers. This profitability results from increasing retention and customer life cycles. It also results from increasing customer (share-of-wallet), account or product penetration through cross-selling, up-selling or other strategies. Other growth results from customer advocacy, when happy customers refer other customers.

- *Profit:* The branding goal in the customer economy is not sales or market growth, but profitability growth. Without profitability growth, brands cannot be sustained. Profit is also the metric that is understood – much better than 'passion' or 'creativity' – throughout an organization and such key constituencies as the financial community. Profit drives accountability. And, ultimately, profit benefits customers.

CONCLUSION

Companies say they understand that a customer in hand is much more valuable than a prospect to be acquired. While many talk the talk, however, few walk the walk. Acquisition branding gets the bulk of corporate resources; retention efforts are an afterthought. Organizations have sales and marketing executives, but responsibilities for retention are scattered among customer service, marketing, support and other departments. Sales are tracked daily; retention, rarely.

That must change. Companies waste resources when they focus single-mindedly on acquiring that first sale, believing that is enough to brand. The first sale is easy. An initial purchase can be triggered with promotions, special pricing or advertising/PR based on trying 'new' or 'improved'. But it is the second, third, fourth and continuing purchases that are hard. Breaking that difficult barrier between the first and subsequent sales is what separates products from brands.

The key to profitable, repeat purchases is retention branding. Retention branding benefits companies as well as customers. Operational goals seek to build trust and loyalty. Retention branding moves a company away from focusing on increasing transactional efficiencies and towards increasing effectiveness by doing business on customer terms. It stresses the everyday operational excellence that builds the emotional, experiential and economic connections with customers. And retention branding introduces relevant measurement, adding the accountability required in the customer economy.

Doing business on customer terms does not mean giving away the company store. On the contrary, it means closer attention than ever before to true costs and profitability. Doing business on customer terms forces companies to understand which customers are profitable and which are not. It requires reducing costs by delivering only targeted, relevant communications to customers and prospects, not mass market broadsides. It requires retention branding efforts to keep customers loyal, reducing the costs of finding 'replacement' customers.

In fact, companies that do business on customer terms emphasize cost control and profitability. In his book *Loyalty Rules!* (2001), Frederick Reichheld highlights the companies that focus on retention: Harley-Davidson, Enterprise Rent-A-Car, Vanguard Group and others. These industry leaders are renowned for both low-cost structures and service. They produce profitable dividends, not just to shareholders but to employees and managers as well.

Brands in the customer economy must shift focus to reflect the importance of retention to profitability. Every company must have a retention plan as well as an acquisition plan, since each requires different research, activities and measurements. Because of its ability to generate higher returns, the amount of resources devoted to retention branding must increase substantially.

Even organizational structures must change. Sales and marketing departments are universally dedicated to selling products or, for the most advanced companies, acquiring customers. What department is focused on ensuring the customer stays with the company? Often, it is not customer service, which is generally structured around dealing with customer complaints.

New skills are also required. Branding professionals must become knowledgeable about financial and supply chain issues. They must demonstrate a new willingness to be measured on results, just as other parts of the organization are. And they must learn new skills in measurement and segmentation, all centred around profitability and sustainability.

The shift from acquisition to retention branding is not easy. But it pays off in increased profitability, lower costs and increased loyalty.

Takeaways

- Why did customers choose your company over the competition? Why are customers staying with you instead of defecting?
- Are your branding efforts more focused on gaining awareness than attention? What are you doing to ensure the relevancy of communications to prospects and customers?
- Are you spending more on acquisition or retention? What are current retention branding efforts? Who is responsible for retention? What

metrics measure acquisition and retention efforts? Are they trending up or down? How long do customers stay with your firm (customer life cycle)?

- Describe the emotional, experiential and economic value you provide to customers. Would your customers give the same answer?
- Are branding efforts limited to your advertising, PR and other marketing efforts? Are operational, supply chain and merchandising capabilities integrated with your branding?

3

Customer equity: the key to accountability

'Customer equity effectively explains success and failure in business… The companies with the highest retention rates also earn the best profits. Relative retention explains profits better than market share, scale, cost, position or any other variable associated with competitive advantage.'
  Frederick F Reichheld and Thomas Teal, *The Loyalty Effect* (1996)

Branding has a dirty little secret. It doesn't know how to count. Look at common branding goals. 'Awareness'. 'Visibility'. 'Impact'. 'Image'. These cannot be measured well, and no two measurements of the same goal will generate the same number. Without accurate measurement, there is no accountability. Without accountability, profitability is not assured. Without accountability, brand sustainability is threatened. Marketers are painfully aware of this fact, especially when they are asked to justify budgets. As a result, they grasp at anything that can communicate solid 'measurement'. Unfortunately, these measurements have little relevance to CEOs and CFOs.

One of the most popular pseudo-measurements is 'brand equity'. After the recognition that brands have value emerged during the 1980s, brand equity emerged to answer the obvious question: how valuable? The concept was outlined in the landmark book, *Managing Brand Equity: Capitalizing on the value of a brand name* (1991) by David Aaker.

The concept of brand equity, which sought to overcome the inability of traditional accounting to measure intangible strategic assets like perceived quality, brand and channel resources, rose to PowerPoint fame in marketing for several reasons. It appeared to quantify intuitive recognition about the value of brands. It incorporated two brand strengths – its standing with purchasers and perception among prospects and customers. And it provided a means to rank winners and losers in branding wars. But what exactly is brand equity?

Brand equity definitions are as scattered as branding definitions. *Strategic Brand Management: Building, measuring and managing brand equity* (2003) by KL Keller lists nine definitions, some contradictory. *Brandweek* magazine says brand equity is 'determined by a calculation of Familiarity, Quality and Purchase Intent'. According to *BusinessWeek*, the consultancy Interbrand 'looks at how much of a boost each brand delivers, how stable that boost is likely to be in the future, and how much those future earnings are worth today'. Delve into any methodology from major consultancies regarding brand equity calculation, and it is apparent that the effort has all the intellectual rigour of a voodoo spell – a dash of corporate history, a gaggle of retail numbers, an extra helping of distribution, a sampling of questionnaires.

Because of the lack of a common methodology, brand equity calculations result in pie-in-the-sky numbers. Look at this one definition, again different from those above: 'Essentially, a brand's value is derived by multiplying its annual net after-tax profits, adjusted to exclude the earnings expected for an equivalent generic product, by a discount rate that reflects the brand strength as defined as the brand's ability to influence the market, the stability of its consumer franchise, the ability to sustain demand in the face of technological change, and the strength of supporting communications.'

Using this definition, two people could not come up with the same number based on all the impossible-to-define variables. This imprecision – at a time when CEOs and CFOs are demanding accountability – means 'brand equity' lacks validity as a decision-making benchmark. How can strategies be executed when metrics lack consistency?

This imprecision causes other problems as well. Brand equity does not provide any insights about operational cause and effect. If brand equity increases by 10 per cent, what caused it? The latest campaign? A new product? Better service? Brand equity does not deliver answers.

Brand equity has no direct linkage to profitability. Thanks to its famous sock puppet, Pets.com had great brand equity, according to some calculations. Unfortunately, the firm was unprofitable, and ultimately kamikazed out. Rumour has it that Pets.com sold more of its oh-so-cute mascots than it did pet supplies. Undoubtedly, Eastern Airlines, Ipana toothpaste, Heathkit (Daystrom), Marathon chocolate bars, Cellnet, Oldsmobile and many, many more also had great brand equity, but it makes little difference now. They are all defunct.

Brand equity has other flaws as well. It excludes the most important component of any brand: the customer. If it is agreed that the value of a brand is derived – either partly or completely – from relationships with customers, then any branding measurement that excludes customers is suspect. Additionally, since brand equity derives from product value, using it as a guiding star leads companies to focus on products at a time when a customer focus is critical.

Finally, and most importantly, brand equity is irrelevant to customers. In the history of the world, only two things have never happened. No one has washed a rental car. And no one has bought anything based on brand equity. Customers buy on value, service, price or other issues, but never purchase based on the relative brand equity of two offerings. Why should companies pay attention to an issue that customers ignore? As a result, brand equity has as much value to those interested in profitability and accountability as leeches and bleeding have to those focused on medical efficacy. But there is one brand value calculation that the CEO and CFO can embrace – customer equity.

CUSTOMER EQUITY: IMPORTANCE OF LIFETIME CUSTOMER VALUE

Do brands have value? Absolutely. But attempting to measure this value through brand equity provides little benefit and distracts a company away from the task of retaining profitable customers. Ultimately, it is loyal customers – not a fallible calculation – who are responsible for brand value and sustainability.

The pay-offs from loyalty have long been recognized. A half-century ago, W Edwards Deming, the father of quality-based management, wrote that quality improvement produces loyal customers. In turn, loyal customers create greater market share, higher profits, higher share price and a more effective work force.

Customer equity, which *Harvard Business Review* first wrote about in the early 1990s, has one universally recognized definition – the lifetime value (LTV) of customers, discounted by time. This value results from the current and future customer profitability as well as such intangible benefits as testimonials and word of mouth. Customer equity incorporates the loyalty to buy again and again, the faith to recommend and the willingness to forgive inevitable mistakes. Like intellectual property or reputation, customer equity cannot be found on the balance sheet, but it is just as valuable.

Customers have financial value, but traditional accounting systems cannot calculate that value for three reasons (customer equity differs from present-value or discounted-cash-flow accounting by focusing on individual customers and accounting for customer retention and defection). First, these systems cannot distinguish the relative value of customers. Revenue from new customers is lumped together with revenue from older, more valuable customers. Or the high costs associated with low-profit customers are pooled with the minimal expenses from high-profit customers. CEOs and CFOs can extract totals and averages, but a lot of information about specific customer profitability and expenses is buried by those averages. See Tables 3.1 and 3.2.

Another failing is an inability to track process costs. Some companies do track gross profit from each customer. More difficult to track are subsequent 'below-the-line' costs, such as those involved in selling, administering and servicing customers. Companies also have difficulty tracking the capital costs associated with each customer resulting from either late payments or special inventories, or the costs associated with failures (defects, late deliveries, etc). Two customers can share the same gross profit, but one is unprofitable if it buys rarely, demands frequent service and pays late.

Finally, accounting systems deliver rearview-mirror insights. They sum up past transactions. By contrast, customer equity can look forward, incorporating the profitability from past, current and future purchases.

Customer equity is the pay-off for retention branding. Essentially, customer equity consists of adding up total revenue related to a customer, and subtracting all associated product, service and other costs. If companies can separate revenue, expenses and cash flow for quarter-to-quarter comparisons, doesn't it make more sense to separate revenue, expenses and cash flow by customer? Isn't it more valuable to see an analysis of profit and loss from customer to customer than it is from quarter to quarter? Wouldn't such an analysis help pinpoint cost-cutting or profit-enhancing initiatives? Chapter 4 explores customer equity calculations in greater detail.

Customer equity starts with the profit from an initial sale. Over time, more profits come from additional sales, and from the lower costs of

Table 3.1 Traditional view of profitability

	Q1	Q2	Q3	Q4
Total revenue	9,074	10,571	32,641	7,294
Cost of sales	8,004	9,269	20,220	7,288
SG&A	4,226	4,993	6,642	3,491
Total expenses	12,230	14,262	26,862	10,779
Income before taxes	(3,156)	(3,691)	5,779	(3,485)
Taxes	(1,309)	(1,551)	(2,241)	(1,437)
Net income	(4,465)	(5,242)	3,538	(4,922)

Table 3.2 Why not view profitability by customer?

	Bill	Aisha	Bob	Emily
Total revenue	9,074	10,571	32,641	7,294
Cost of sales	8,004	9,269	20,220	7,288
SG&A	4,226	4,993	6,642	3,491
Total expenses	12,230	14,262	26,862	10,779
Income before taxes	(3,156)	(3,691)	5,779	(3,485)
Taxes	(1,309)	(1,551)	(2,241)	(1,437)
Net income	(4,465)	(5,242)	3,538	(4,922)

serving existing customers. Additional profits result from referral or word-of-mouth sales. While referral sales are likely to be small initially, they can be significant during later years of a relationship.

These profits are cumulative. Of course, profits decrease with customer attrition, but according to *Harvard Business Review* the decline in profits is not as great as the decline in customers because of the increasing profitability of remaining customers.

Customer equity has numerous advantages over brand equity. While brand equity is product oriented, customer equity incorporates the realization that, ultimately, it is customers, not products, who are the source of profits. Unlike brand equity, customer equity focuses on long-term value building, not short-term transactional sales. While complicated brand equity sums are in the eye of the beholder, customer equity can be calculated by anyone, on the back of an envelope. See Figure 3.1.

Figure 3.1   Brand versus customer equity

All that is required is numbers that every company already is – or should be – calculating. These include revenue, customer acquisition (or marketing) costs, costs of goods/services and retention rates. Ideally, companies should also track leads, referrals and customer life cycles. They should also be able to determine the profitability of specific products or services.

By adding up revenue, subtracting relevant costs and incorporating retention rates, companies can determine the long-term profitability of every customer and determine the appropriate levels of service. Because of its ease of calculation, customer equity can be understood from the boardroom to the post-room. It is easier to understand the impact and importance of, say, responsiveness, if employees know that every customer who goes represents a long-term loss in profitability of US $687. By contrast, how much does the loading dock worker care that brand equity equals US $468 million?

Smart companies realize the importance of customer equity. About five years ago, Skelton Tomkinson, a heavy machinery shipper in Australia, realized that some customers were costing more than they were worth. The firm raised fees on non-machinery accounts to drive off unprofitable customers; other unprofitable accounts were sold. Revenues dropped to US $8.2 million.

Concentrating on customer equity energized the firm. Revenues have climbed back to US $20 million, and net profits have increased by 98 per cent since 1999. Now, managing director Brad Skelton says, 'I run my company with this saying: volume is vanity, and profit is sanity.'

Customer equity represents a virtuous circle. Customer equity focuses a firm on retention, which leads to customers buying more, more often. Since it costs less to sell to existing customers, costs are lower and profitability rises. Once US retailer Sears began analysing its business by asking 'Who are our most profitable customers?' instead of 'What are our most valuable brands?' it began turning the corner back to profitability.

Customer equity is the defining metric of the customer economy. By quantifying the impact of loyalty and retention, customer equity adds accountability to branding. It delivers a customer-focused perspective to financial decision making. It provides investment justification for the vital intangibles – service, innovation, loyalty – that are hard to fit within the cells of a spreadsheet. Additionally, customer equity pinpoints the value of relationships, helps segment customers and focuses the company on customers, not products or market share.

Price Automotive Group, a US chain of car dealers, credits retention with a 'cost-per-vehicle-sold' that is 30 per cent below the industry average. Instead of the acquisition-based promotions typical of most car dealers, Price primarily uses retention branding that relies on direct marketing, strong community presence and benefits for loyalty.

'Our marketing programme is designed to maintain an active customer relationship for all service needs and future auto purchases. We track relationships, and contact customers by mail and phone to win them back if there is any change in their maintenance services with us. This effort earns back a significant number of customers for ongoing service, which strengthens the relationship and positions us as the leading choice for their next purchase,' says a Price executive.

Customer equity advantages include:

- *Improved profitability:* Loyal customers are disproportionately more valuable than new ones. McKinsey & Company estimated that an existing customer generates twice as much quarterly revenue as a new one, and that a 10 per cent increase in repeat customers translates into a 9.5 per cent revenue increase. This profitability results from additional purchases with decreasing cost of sales. It takes four times as much effort to sell to a new customer as to an existing one. Another source of profits is cross-selling – purchases of related offerings – or up-selling – purchases of higher-value items. Existing customers cost less to serve. Industry studies show that the cost of keeping a customer is as little as 20–25 per cent of the cost associated with customer acquisition. Highly profitable credit card giant Capital One has consistently focused on customer equity. Its average customer acquisition cost is estimated at US $55, while customer equity is more than US $500. At the other end of the spectrum, the average customer loss rate of 10–30 per cent annually reduces annual profits by approximately 17 per cent.

- *Increased accountability:* Are campaigns generating short-term sales without creating long-term customer value? Customer equity provides objective data that determine which branding efforts worked and which activities produced the best ROI. This helps gain greater support and funding for branding. Because retention and profitability are tracked, marketing, service and other programmes can be linked to increases (or declines) in customer equity. Brand equity may stroke CEO egos, but the figure provides no help for those responsible for attracting and keeping profitable customers.
- *Segmentation insights:* All customers are not created equal. High-profit customers generate 6–10 times as much profit as low-profit customers. The value of customers is not always determined by size. Often, the largest customers are the most expensive to serve, have longer sales cycles and lower profit margins. US financial services firm Fidelity Investments found that 10 per cent of its 'Private Access' customers – those with more than US $2 million in assets – were unprofitable. Knowing which customer segments are unprofitable can dramatically improve the ROI of acquisition campaigns. By identifying highly profitable, profitable and unprofitable customers, customer equity not only helps promote retention of the best customers but also improves prospect targeting. Why spend to acquire new customers that are likely to be unprofitable or disloyal?
- *Investment insights:* Customer equity can illustrate how much to pay to acquire a customer. That is important. More than one company has failed by focusing on sales or market growth and paying too much for customers. CDnow Online, for example, spent about US $40 to acquire a customer even though customer equity was no more than US $25. It is also why many mergers and acquisitions fail; companies pay too much for the customers they are acquiring. AT&T spent US $110 billion to acquire TCI and MediaOne. That represented a staggering US $4,200 for each customer. Simple analysis would have shown that, even in the most optimistic scenario, customer equity would never match the acquisition cost. Customer equity also indicates how much to invest in retaining a customer or how much prices must be raised to maintain profitability.

- *Organizational focus:* By numerically indicating how well trust, loyalty and profitability are being nurtured, customer equity moves an organization away from a focus on one-time transactions and towards retention and repeat sales.
- *Increased advocacy:* Loyal customers refer other customers. This not only lowers sales costs but generally results in better prospects. Consulting firm Bain & Company said customers referred by loyal customers have a 37 per cent higher retention rate. Recommendations from family and friends drive consideration of more than 50 per cent of car brands.
- *Other benefits:* eBay and Cisco have found that the support costs of referred customers are lower than those acquired through other means. Referred customers tend to use those who referred them for guidance instead of calling support desks. Additionally, loyal customers are less receptive to competitive lures and are more forgiving of mistakes.

LOYALTY: FOUNDATION OF CUSTOMER EQUITY

The birth and death of brands are based on disloyalty. Every customer who is lured away bleeds the sustainability of your brand and builds the brand of a competitor. That is why the essence of so many branding campaigns is based on encouraging disloyalty: 'We honour competitor coupons', 'Turn in a satellite dish and get three months' cable free', etc.

That is one reason loyalty, which represents an enthusiastic commitment to a relationship based on a ProfitBrand's long-term ability to do business on customer terms, is so important. Loyalty keeps customers from defecting when competitors come knocking. Loyal customers also buy more, more often. They can trigger a chain reaction of additional sales from other prospects.

But companies make several mistakes about loyalty. The first is confusing 'customer satisfaction' for loyalty. Just because customers are 'satisfied' does not always mean they will buy again. Neither do repeat sales indicate loyalty. 'Loyalty' can result from high switching costs or proprietary technology. About 70 per cent of repeat purchases are made out of indifference or inertia, not loyalty. One theory for this phenomenon is that customers have a fairly wide satisfaction 'range'. It is fairly easy to satisfy customers within this broadly self-defined range.

But force of habit is not a force that builds a ProfitBrand. ProfitBranding involves not only keeping customers satisfied but, more importantly, keeping satisfied customers. Companies seeking to ProfitBrand must also move customers beyond basic 'satisfaction' to loyalty and even advocacy.

At the same time, some 'loyal' customers are not worth retaining. When customers don't generate sufficient profits to justify support and other expenses, even the most 'loyal' customer must be dropped or moved to less expensive support or sales.

Another common mistake concerns loyalty marketing, typified by loyalty cards. If these programmes do not have the right vision, they can be ineffective branding tools and decline into expensive administrative burdens. Companies start loyalty programmes and invest in CRM to earn more future customer money. While understandable, such motivation risks potential failure. Loyalty programmes are most successful when they reward customers for previous purchases. That is instantly understandable to anyone who has a wallet full of unused cards just needing a stamp or two to qualify for a 'free' meal or cup of coffee. Loyalty programmes must be on customer terms – no making customers jump through hoops to claim a reward – and be relevant.

Another common motivation is the belief that 'the more we know about customers, the more they will want to do business with us'. That is fine when it is used to improve service or products, but typically it is used to bombard customers with multiple sales promotions and communications As one customer put it, 'Are loyalty programmes the reward or punishment for being a customer?' Loyalty programmes are discussed in greater detail in Chapter 12.

CUSTOMER EQUITY: GETTING STARTED WITH DATA AND TRACKING

The first step for customer equity is relevant data collection. This includes customer information, purchase history and basic financial information such as costs and revenue. Although such data are critical to sustainability and accountability, few companies gather even basic information. 'It is amazing to me how many large corporations track their sales but don't do a very good job of tracking sales to whom,' said David Reibstein, marketing professor at Wharton School of the University of Pennsylvania. 'Shipping departments handle some of that information, but knowing who bought what has not always been tracked closely by marketing.'

Next, all the data must be consolidated, whether in a spreadsheet or a data warehouse. Database and system design are complex topics, but worthy of study. The most important principles: place customer data in a single location (at most companies data are scattered among multiple departments or even divisions); also ensure that they are accurate and current. According to *Data Management Review*, '12 per cent of all customer data are inaccurate'. Consulting firm PricewaterhouseCoopers said 75 per cent of companies studied reported problems from poor data quality. The problem has grown even greater with web-based self-service. How many 'Mickey Mouses' from Bulgaria reside in corporate databases?

The importance of data accuracy cannot be overstated. Achieving this goal must be a strategic priority, and will require about 75 per cent of the effort required to determine customer equity. But unless companies are using 'clean' data, they risk both making poor strategic decisions and angering customers. What other asset is as valuable as accurate, complete data about customers? How can any brand hope to establish a relationship based on trust and loyalty if it cannot even correctly identify anyone as 'Mr' or 'Ms'?

Make the data accessible throughout the organization. This helps ensure consistent customer interactions and helps eliminate the 'transfer-and-repeat-the-problem' response that irritates so many customers. Although this capability may require investments in technology, training and enhanced organizational capabilities, it pays off in lower costs, increased sales and stronger brands.

Collect data concerning acquisition branding. Unless these costs are known, customer equity cannot be accurately calculated. Key data include number of customers acquired; acquisition ratio of customers to prospects, broken down by segment, campaign or channel; marketing costs; total sales and profits; and typical purchase behaviour of new customers.

Then, track retention over a particular period (month, quarter, year). According to Frederick Reichheld in *Loyalty Rules!* (2001), fewer than 20 per cent of firms track retention, the primary indicator of loyalty. The period must be long enough to accommodate occasional purchasers. Calculate retention by dividing the number of customers at the start of a period by the number of the same customers who are still with you at the end of that period. Do not count new customers – those who make a first purchase – that joined during that period. Track the retention rate over time. Downward trends signal trouble. Also track retention rates by division and product for comparative analysis. Retention rates below 80 per cent require corrective action.

Establish a customer life cycle. A life cycle starts with an initial purchase and extends through a period after the last purchase (to account for the potential for customer recovery). Understand purchasing, service and other characteristics of the life cycle. Calculate the average length of time customers stay before defecting. To start, look at the customers who defected during a particular period, including those who make just a one-off purchase. How long, on average, had they been with you before they defected? What were the type and amount of their purchases?

These basic measurements can help drive retention strategies. If, for example, customers typically leave after 12 months, seek to extend their life cycles by making special offers at 9 months. They are also useful for capturing 'defection signals'. Do purchase amounts or frequency decline before defection? Do payment cycles lengthen? Does service frequency change? Common characteristics may serve as 'triggers' for corrective actions before customers actually defect.

Build an environment focused on retention. Bells are often rung when new customers are signed. What happens when customers leave? Do executives even know? Are the reasons for defection understood? Are there attempts at customer recovery? Establish a system that signals when customers defect, or fail to make a purchase after a set period. Companies also send out press releases to announce new customers. Why not also send out releases to announce the anniversary of a long-term customer?

Compensation strategies must also reflect the importance of retention. Compensation schemes are typically based on total new revenue. Although this helps stimulate sales growth, it also encourages sales forces to sell on price. Customers who buy solely on price are least likely to be loyal. At least a portion of compensation must be based on retention and customer equity. This encourages sales forces to focus on prospects likely to generate the greatest returns over time.

Ensure that everyone in the organization understands the importance of retention, especially the retention of profitable customers. According to the management consulting firm The Gallup Organization, 'Retention programs often fail to involve front-line employees who are key to creating emotional attachment and customer engagement.' In a study of fast-food chains, Gallup found that diners who had quality interactions with the order-takers were five times more likely to return. Current or former customers of AT&T and MCI who felt that customer service representatives were not helpful were, respectively, 6.6 and 5.7 times more likely not to consider using that carrier in the future. To drive home its importance, award bonuses to everyone in the corporation based on retention gains.

Set goals. In a survey of 950 executives in 35 countries, Deloitte Consulting found that manufacturers are 60 per cent more profitable and more likely to exceed goals for growth when they set explicit customer retention targets.

Finally, and most importantly, segment customers by customer equity or relative profitability. Services must also be segmented by customer equity. Segmentation is covered in detail in Chapter 5.

CONCLUSION

VideoPlus grew to US $25 million by 1998 by leasing dishes, selling satellite time and creating content for CDs and tapes. But that year VideoPlus lost money and was forced to lay off half of its employees. The loss was a wake-up call. Afterwards, instead of going after sales in multiple categories, VideoPlus concentrated on serving the requirements of its most profitable customers. Profits have increased 67 per cent annually.

This illustrates the gains possible from concentrating on profitability growth instead of short-term transactions. While concentrating on immediate sales and market growth may win temporary applause from the financial community, the strategy will backfire if profits also do not grow.

The key to profitability growth, of course, is customer equity. Customer equity, combined with knowledge about retention rates and customer life cycles, illustrates exactly what customers are worth. Knowing the value of customers provides a measurable rationale for retention branding, outlines what can be spent on acquisition, retention and service, and focuses the organization on building relationships instead of increasing transactions. Customer equity is vital for brand sustainability. If a firm is not growing customer equity, it will fail, inevitably. Customer equity also provides a better benchmark than brand equity for ensuring the accountability of marketing.

Since brand equity is usually linked to product value, it leads to a strategic focus on sales growth, which always leads to the risk of attracting 'wrong', or unprofitable, customers. Unprofitable customers ultimately lead to higher costs, which hurts profitability. Brand equity must be retired like a commercial from the 1970s. Companies that focus on brand equity place brands on a higher pedestal than customers. Brands are only magnets to attract new customers, and anchors to hold existing ones. It must never be forgotten that it is customers, not brands, that deliver profits.

Unfortunately, marketing and finance have long had an adversarial relationship. Marketing talked in terms of emotions and relationships; finance's language was shaped by formulas and spreadsheets. Customer equity represents a common language both can speak.

Takeaways

- Does everyone in the organization understand the importance of acquiring and keeping profitable customers? Is retention stressed at orientation and through ongoing training?
- How loyal are your customers? How do you define loyalty? What programmes are in place to develop and maintain loyalty? How well are they working?
- What is your retention rate? How long does the average customer stay with you? Why do customers leave? What activities signal potential defection?
- How complete, accurate and integrated are customer data? How are data collected on customers being used? Are customer data 'owned' departmentally or shared organizationally?
- Are you compensating sales forces and the rest of the organization for improvements in retention?

4

How to calculate customer equity

'Those friends thou hast, and their adoption tried.
Grapple them to thy soul with hoops of steel.
But do not dull thy palm with entertainment of
each new-hatched, unfledged comrade.'

Shakespeare, *Hamlet*

Companies want to focus on customer value. But they rarely know how valuable customers are. So it is time to get out the calculators.

Customer equity represents LCV (lifetime customer value) (also known as lifetime value – LTV). This value includes not only the profit from purchases, including services, but also such auxiliary income as referrals or advertising based on exposure to customers. It can also include the intangible value resulting from testimonials, word of mouth, input into product development and even the cachet a large customer can bring. The total is discounted by the time value of money, which is based on the concept that a unit of money today is worth more than one tomorrow. Generally, customer equity starts negative at the beginning of a relationship, reflecting acquisition costs, and grows positive over time.

Customer equity calculation starts by totalling the revenue from past, current and future expected purchases and, optionally, adding a conservative sum for intangible values. Subtract the cost of goods. Also subtract the cost-to-serve. This includes the costs of support, warranties, returns, etc. Finally, subtract acquisition branding costs. The total sum is then discounted by NPV (net present value).

Various methods can calculate customer equity. As with most branding activities, elements of imprecision colour them all. Someone who signs up in response to direct mail may have been influenced by an earlier ad in a trade publication, a connection that is hard to track and value. But the precise value of customers is less important than their relative value. Such knowledge allows more precise and cost-effective marketing and service segmentation.

The primary customer equity calculations are described below, but others exist. Each approach has advantages and disadvantages, generally based on the trade-offs between complexity and simplicity. More advanced calculations of customer equity use modelling and other statistical techniques to differentiate between the future value of two customers whose value may be equivalent today. Such modelling incorporates the difference in customer equity for a financial service, for example, between a customer who just got married and one who has just retired.

The first step in customer equity calculation is collecting relevant data. Some come from financial statements or CFOs; other data come from customer databases. Finding the data can be difficult, since companies have set up systems built around products, not customers. In many cases the data are aggregated, complicating the task of finding data on specific customers.

Accounting data consist of:

- *Acquisition costs:* These are the marketing expenses that attract prospects and turn them into customers. Acquisition costs vary widely. Credit card vendors spend from US $50 to US $75 per customer while mortgage lenders spend about US $250. Obviously, brand sustainability depends on acquisition costs not exceeding customer value.

  Even though acquisition cost calculation can get quite sophisticated, most simply divide marketing expenses by the number of customers captured during a period. That number is applied equally to all customers. Obviously, such a simplistic approach has problems. Ideally, acquisition costs can be broken out by channel, campaign or even customer.

  Critics have pointed out that most acquisition cost calculation fails to account for previous attempts to attract customers and other methods to convert prospects, including product discounts and free delivery. That is true, but it is better to be approximately correct than exactly wrong.

- *Cost-of-goods-sold (COGS):* For manufacturing firms, COGS represents materials, labour and factory overhead. For service businesses, COGS is generally known as 'cost of sales', which can include salaries, research, etc. Costs of sales or COGS are subtracted from sales to determine gross margin. Gross profit is gross margin less operating expenses.

- *Cost-to-serve:* This is the cost required to provide the offering and related service, and to maintain the relationship (eg loyalty discounts). It must also capture volume and other discounts, which few companies track well and which can considerably distort a relationship's profitability. Cost-to-serve generally declines over time as customers become more familiar with offerings.

- *Net present value (NPV):* A common accounting calculation, NPV reflects the fact that the value of money generally declines over time. The value of tomorrow's money depends on interest rates and risk factors.

- *Profit:* As one wit explained, profit is 'what's left over after everyone has been paid' (technically, gross sales minus COGS minus operating expenses).

Customer data come from databases with customer demographics (address, phone, e-mail, number of employees, etc), organizational issues (departments, superiors, purchasing processes, etc), financial (products, amounts, dates, etc), field sales and/or telephone representatives and other sources that record customer interactions. Ideally, the data also contain total revenue, gross margin and all costs directly attributable to each customer.

Databases should also incorporate data about communications relevancy, including frequency and type of communication. After customers overwhelmingly indicated that they wanted to 'direct dialogue based on their own needs', IBM's 'Focusing on You' programme reduced the amount of information given to customers. As always, the relevancy of communications to customer issues is more important than communications volume. Customer data consist of the following:

- *Retention rates:* Retention, the opposite of attrition, is calculated by dividing the number of customers at the beginning of a period by the number of customers at the end of a period. Retention rates are closely linked to customer life cycles, or the period a customer stays with a firm. Generally, the longer a customer stays with a firm, the greater the customer equity. Additionally, the longer the relationship, the greater the likelihood of continued loyalty as well as increased referrals.

Retention rates have the greatest value when tracked over time. Each month firms should examine three numbers (see Table 4.1). The first is the number of customers who have done business with the firm during a relevant period (week, quarter, year) preceding the current period. The second is the number of customers recovered. These are the lapsed customers who had previously purchased, but who had not done business with the firm in the period preceding the current one and resumed doing business with the firm during the current period. And the third number must be the number of customers who did not do business with the firm during the current period.

This chart presents valuable insights concerning retention, showing over time whether the number of active customers is growing or declining, how many customers are defecting (or on the verge of defection), and whether efforts to recover customers are working.

- *Customer life cycles:* Customer life cycles are determined by the start and end of relationships. This is subject to interpretation. Does a relationship start when a customer signs a contract, when payment is received or when the product is installed? It is also tough to determine the end of a relationship. If customers have not purchased anything in six months, are they 'inactive' customers or have they defected? Companies miss potential sales – and loss of relationships – by failing to contact 'inactives'. If a customer still has not bought after being contacted as an 'inactive', then the relationship is over. Customer life-cycle tracking provides a good picture of relationship strength and brand sustainability. Executives must take action if average customer life cycles start to shrink.

Table 4.1 Retention analysis

	Period 1	Period 2	% change
Existing customers	5,000	5,200	4
Recovered	125	119	(5)
Inactive	480	580	21

- *Referrals:* These are new customers that result from customer recommendations. Not only is positive customer word of mouth an inexpensive source of new business, but it is a strong indicator of loyalty. Additionally, customers obtained by referral tend to be more loyal than those acquired by other means.
- *Intangibles:* These include testimonials, the benefits of tapping customer competencies and even the allure of the 'right' customers. Such customers can be industry advocates who provide credibility or vocal advocates who help generate leads. They can also be customers with tremendous opportunity for growth, such as the first customer in a large account that could lead to substantial account penetration. Some customer equity calculations add as much as 3–5 per cent to revenues to account for intangibles. A more plausible amount is 1–3 per cent.

CUSTOMER EQUITY: RUNNING THE NUMBERS

Customer equity calculations, in order of complexity, are recency, frequency and monetary value (RFM), average customer equity, customer equity dashboard, retention-based, 'fill-in-the-blank', standard and customer P&L. All approaches have advantages and disadvantages.

RFM

The principles behind RFM (sometimes called RFV for recency, frequency, value), which have been a staple of the direct mail industry since the 1930s, are intuitively clear. Customers who purchased recently are more likely to buy again. This makes them more valuable than those who have not purchased for a period. First-time customers have a 30 per cent chance of becoming long-term profitable customers. If they buy three times relatively quickly, their chance of becoming long-term customers more than doubles. Customers who purchased frequently are more likely to buy again compared to customers who have rarely made purchases. Finally, customers who spent the most money are more likely to buy again. It is RFM principles that lead direct mail cataloguers to send first-time buyers a discount coupon after the initial order. Other cataloguers offer free shipping or gifts with a second purchase.

Essentially, RFM consists of scoring and ranking each customer. Recency, frequency and monetary value each receive a score of 1 to 5. This score depends on how optimum purchase behaviour is defined. For example, customers who have bought within the past month may be scored a '5' while those who bought a year ago get a '1'. This varies according to industry and purchase patterns. Customers who bought during the past year may get a '5' while those who bought five years ago may get a '1'.

The same philosophy applies to frequency and monetary value. Purchases last week may be worth a '5'; last year, '1'. For some, for example, purchases totalling US $1,000 could rate a '5'; for others, it might take US $100,000.

Each customer then winds up with a three-digit score ranging from '555' (the highest rating in recency, frequency and monetary value) to '111' (lowest). Generally, the digits are rearranged so the highest number comes first. In other words, a customer scoring a '1' on recency, '3' on frequency and '4' on monetary value would be represented by '431' for analysis. Customers are then grouped from highest score to lowest. See Table 4.2.

Table 4.2 Calculating RFM, part 1

Scoring

Buy interval	Frequency	Total buy
<1 mth = 5	>40 = 5	>$50K = 5
1–3 mths = 4	30–40 = 4	$20K – $50K = 4
3–6 mths = 3	20–29 = 3	$10K – $20K = 3
6–9 mths = 2	10–19 = 2	$5K – $10K = 2
>9 mths = 1	<10 = 1	<$5K = 1

Customer	Last buy*	Frequency	Total $	RFM score =	
A	05/04	12	6K	422	422
B	01/04	18	9K	322	322
C	11/03	35	40K	244	442
D	07/04	1	1K	511	511
E	01/03	6	5K	112	211
F	03/04	40	90K	355	553
G	05/03	5	2K	111	111
H	07/04	20	9K	532	532

*Reference date for last buy is 07/04

Obviously, the customers with the highest RFM scores represent the most valuable customers. They are presumed more likely to buy more, more often. Customer scores must also be trended over time. As Jim Novo points out in his excellent book about RFM, *Drilling Down* (2001), 'rising scores indicate the potential value of the customer is rising; falling scores indicate decreasing potential value – and signal the customer is becoming less likely to continue on as a customer'. Novo suggests establishing 'trip wires' if RFM numbers (or some other indicator, such as help desk calls) reach a predetermined point that signals potential defection. A trip wire is a signal for a sales call, communications or other activity designed to refurbish a customer relationship. See Table 4.3.

The US casino Harrah's Entertainment uses RFM with spectacular results. It identifies customers who have spent a threshold amount during previous visits, but who haven't visited recently. The casino sends them a coupon redeemable during the next visit. The programme resulted in 6.5 per cent sales growth in two quarters.

Cal Farley's Boys Ranch and Affiliates, which serves at-risk children, used RFM to generate an 11.7 per cent greater response than the response from a control group. Additionally, a dollar spent soliciting the RFM-selected group generated 192 per cent more donations than a dollar spent with the control group. SilverMinds Direct, a UK retailer that sells classic CDs, improved revenues by more than 5 per cent by segmenting its 250,000 customers using RFM. ROI was estimated at 2,000 per cent.

Advantage: RFM easily identifies good customers. Trending results also quickly indicate which customers are strengthening or weakening their relationship with you. *Disadvantage:* It fails to quantify actual customer

Table 4.3 Calculating RFM, part 2

Customer	RFM score	
F	553	Most valuable/loyal
H	532	
D	511	
C	442	
A	422	
B	322	Recovery campaign
E	211	
G	111	

value. Even customers crowned as 'best' by RFM may not be the most profitable owing to high service requirements or purchases or low-margin products.

Average customer equity

The simplest way of calculating customer equity is to multiply the average sale per customer by the average number of times customers buy per year (or other period) by the average number of years (or other period) that customers buy from you (customer life cycle).

To calculate average sale per customer, divide total sales by the total number of customers. A variety of methods, varying in precision, can calculate the average number of times customers buy per year. These range from dividing the number of purchase orders or other transactions by the number or customers, or totalling all customer transactions and dividing by the number of customers. Average customer life cycles to determine the typical customer retention period.

For example, if 5,000 customers bought US $10 million of goods, the average sale per customer is US $2,000 (US $10,000,000 / 5,000). Each customer buys, on average, twice monthly, or 24 times a year. Customers are retained for an average of five years. The average customer equity is US $240,000 (US $2,000 × 24 × 5).

Advantage: This is a simple, back-of-the-envelope method for demonstrating the value of a customer. Everyone from the boardroom to the post-room can understand how much is lost with a defecting customer. *Disadvantage:* The biggest disadvantage, of course, is this method does not incorporate costs, and thus does not reflect profitability. Averaging all customers, both profitable and unprofitable, cloaks the contributions and costs associated with individual customers.

Customer equity dashboard

A common objection to customer equity calculations is 'the finance department will not give me the information' or 'we don't record when (or how often) customers make purchases'. Such objections are baffling. Information concerning overall costs and revenues can be found in every financial statement, and invoicing data can show the recency, frequency and value of transactions. Other information, such as retention rates, can also be collected and calculated.

But, sometimes, management is no more than the art of the possible. To deal with such roadblocks, a customer equity dashboard, modelled on balanced scorecards and other executive dashboards, can provide a barometer of the strength of customer relationships. Instead of specific financial data, a customer equity dashboard uses data from marketing, shipping, competitive research, customer analyses and other sources.

A customer equity dashboard is based on a 4 × 4 matrix. On the *x* axis are 'strength of relationship', 'performance', 'transactions' and, optionally, 'environment'. On the *y* axis are four customer categories: 'numbers', 'retention', 'experience' and 'spending'.

A customer equity dashboard attempts to quantify an intangible such as 'strength of relationship'. Such quantification can include number of customers, number of referrals and number of products purchased. Spending associated with 'strength of relationship' includes total sales and share-of-wallet. The numbers associated with each category must be tracked over time to show trends.

Table 4.4 provides examples of the type of information that can be collected. The metrics behind each intangible can vary by industry and by company.

Advantage: No calculator is required, and such numbers as the 'number of leads' or conversion rate should be easily obtainable. The trends in each area also indicate specific, actionable areas for improvement. A declining number of transactions should trigger a response. *Disadvantage:* Again, these numbers represent cumulative totals and provide no indication of which customers or activities are profitable or unprofitable. It also requires collecting – and updating – a lot of information from multiple departments, which makes it applicable only to the largest customers.

Retention-based customer equity

Some argue that, if retention is at the heart of customer equity, then retention must be at the heart of customer equity calculations. Retention-based customer equity illustrates the impact that retention has on lifetime customer value for each time period.

Calculations require a base of customers, a retention rate and an average sale per customer. First, determine the average first-year customer sale by dividing annual sales by the number of 'original' customers. If 1,000 customers generate US $1,000,000 in sales, the average sale is US $1,000. For the second year, multiply the number of

Table 4.4 Customer equity dashboard

	Strength of relationship	**Performance**	**Transactions**	**Environment**
Customer numbers	No. of customers No. of referrals No. of products per customer No. of customers within account	No. of active customers Change in referrals Change in no. of products Change in purchase frequency, volume or amount	No. of leads No. of customers by segment No. of customers by channel Conversion rate	Competitive rankings
Customer retention	Retention rate Customer life cycle	By product, segment and campaign	Percentage using new products No. of service calls	Industry averages
Customer experience	Accountability to customer benchmark No. of complaints/ compliments	By channel By product By process	Time on hold On-time deliveries Process effectiveness	Industry averages
Customer spending	Sales/market share Customer equity by segment	By product, segment and campaign	Up-sell/ cross-sell Referrals RFM	Competitor profitability

first-year customers by the retention rate. If, for example, the base number of customers from the first year is 1,000, and the retention rate is 60 per cent, then the number of second-year customers who have been retained is 600 (1,000 × 0.60 = 600).

Second- and subsequent-year sales are determined by multiplying the number of retained customers by the average sale (based on that year's gross sales and total customers). First-, second- and subsequent-year sales are added to determine gross cumulative sales. Then acquisition costs for the original group of customers (which can be represented by the total

Table 4.5 Retention-based equity

	First year	Second year	Third year	Total
Total number of customers	1,000	1,100	1,200	
Retention rate	60%	70%	75%	
Number of retained customers		600 (1,000×0.6)	420 (600×0.7)	
Annual sales	$1,000,000	$1,100,000	$1,300,000	$3,400,000
Average sale per customer	$1,000	$1,000 ($1,100,000/1,100)	$1,083 ($1,300,000/1,200)	
Average annual sale to retained customers	$1,000,000	$600,000 (600×$1,000)	$454,860 (420×$1,083)	$2,054,860

Acquisition costs	$150,000
Three-year gross customer equity	$1,904,860 ($2,054,860–$150,000)
Customer equity	$1,904.86 ($1,904,860/1,000)

marketing budget for the first year) are subtracted. The result is divided by the total number of original customers to determine customer equity. It is important to divide by the number of original customers, rather than existing customers, so that the effect of retention can be demonstrated.

Advantage: This demonstrates the positive effect from retention on customer equity. A small increase in retention can dramatically impact customer equity over several years. It also accounts for acquisition branding costs. *Disadvantage:* Specific profitable and unprofitable customers remain hidden because costs are not accounted for. The decreasing value of money over time is not accounted for.

Fill-in-the-blank

This represents a four-step, fill-in-the-blank methodology for calculating customer equity. The first step determines the average number of customers during a period, including those gained from referrals. Steps two and three examine revenues and costs. Step four uses those inputs to calculate average sale, profit margin, number of lifetime sales and other data to determine customer equity.

Advantage: For the arithmetically challenged, this represents an easy way to calculate customer equity. It also incorporates referrals, which can play a major role in customer equity and which few companies emphasize enough. Finally, costs are accounted for. *Disadvantage:* It fails to reflect how NPV affects cumulative lifetime value. It shows only average sales and fails to account for the profitability of individual customers.

Table 4.6 Fill-in-the-blank customer equity calculation

		Formula	Result
Step 1: Customers			
A	Number of months in period*		
B	Number of customers at beginning of period		
C	New customers from all sources except referrals		
D	New customers from referrals		
E	Customers lost during period		
F	Customers net at end of period	(B+C+D–E)	
G	Average number of customers during period	(B+F)/2	
H	Average customer life cycle	(years)	
Step 2: Revenues			
I	Total revenues**	$	
J	Number of sales in period		
Step 3: Costs			
K	Cost of goods, fulfilment, etc	$	
L	Acquisition costs	$	
M	Total costs	K+L	$
Step 4: Customer equity calculations			
N	Average life/relationship with customer (same as H)		(years)
O	Number of referrals in lifetime	(D/G)×(12/A)×N	
P	Average sale	I/J	$
Q	Profit margin	I–M/I	%
R	Number of sales in lifetime	[(J×12/A)×N]/G	
S	Customer equity	(1+O)×P×Q×R	$

*Number of months evenly divisible by 12
**Includes product, service, other revenues

Standard

The standard calculation examines sales, all costs and retention rates for groups of customers. It also discounts the results by NPV. It provides a framework for investigating what-if scenarios. For example, what happens to customer equity if advertising costs are decreased or retention rates increase?

Table 4.7 Standard customer equity – formula

Multiply	Retained customers × sales per customer
Add (optional)	Other benefits (referrals, etc)
Total	
Subtract	Cost of goods, etc
Subtract (optional)	Cost-to-serve
Subtract (optional)	Overhead costs allocated to customers
Discount	Net present value (NPV)
Subtract	Acquisition cost
Total	Total customer equity ($)
Divide by	Original number of customers

Table 4.8 Standard customer equity, part 1

Sales	Year 1	Year 2	Year 3
Customers	1,000	500	300
Retention rate	50%	60%	70%
Sales per customer	$500	$500	$500
Total retention sales	$500,000	$250,000	$150,000

Costs	Year 1	Year 2	Year 3
Cost of goods %	50%	50%	50%
Actual cost of goods	$250,000	$125,000	$75,000
Fulfilment cost %	12%	12%	12%
Fulfilment costs	$60,000	$30,000	$18,000
Cost-to-serve %	25%	25%	25%
Cost-to-serve costs	$125,000	$62,500	$37,500
Total costs	$435,000	$217,500	$130,500

Table 4.9 Standard customer equity, part 2

	Year 1	Year 2	Year 3
Total sales	$500,000	$250,000	$150,000
Total costs	$435,000	$217,500	$130,500
Gross profit	$65,000	$32,500	$19,500
NPV@10%	1	1.2	1.33
NPV calculation	$65,000/1	$32,500/1.2	$19,500/1.33
NPV profit	$65,000	$27,083	$14,661
Acquisition costs	$50,000		
CE calculation	$15,000/1,000	$27,083/1,000	$14,661/1,000
Annual CE	$15	$27.08	$14.66
Cumulative CE	$15	$42.08	$56.74

The standard customer equity calculation starts by selecting a group of customers for a specific period. Retention rates are calculated to determine how many of those original customers remain in subsequent years. The number of retained customers is multiplied by the sale per customer to get gross sales. Next, the costs for that group of customers are subtracted from gross sales to calculate gross profit. (More sophisticated calculations can also subtract allocated overhead.) The NPV of gross profit is then calculated based on a predetermined interest rate (and, optionally, estimated risk). Acquisition costs are subtracted from the first year's profits. The annual and cumulative customer equity can then be calculated using the original number of customers.

An extended explanation regarding this type of calculation is 'Building Successful Retail Strategies Using Customer Lifetime Value' by Arthur Middleton Hughes. The website is www.dbmarketing.com/articles/Art181.htm.

Advantage: This method provides a complete picture of customer equity for a selected group of customers over the customer life cycle. It accounts for the time value of money and illustrates how small changes in retention rates can dramatically affect customer equity. *Disadvantage:* It requires the greatest investment of time, and again, averages out all customers.

Customer P&L

The ultimate customer equity goal is to calculate the specific profitability of each customer. But creating a 'customer P&L' is difficult. The main issue is allocating process costs, which form the bulk of relationship costs. For customer P&Ls to work with larger firms, a more advanced financial system, ABC (activity-based costing), is required. While traditional accounting, invented by a 15th-century Italian monk, identifies 'hard' costs like land, labour and materials, ABC is used to track 'soft' costs such as inputs and processes. ABC breaks down every process into its component activities. For example, the specific cost of loading a delivery truck can require knowing the time and other resources required to palletize cartons, operate a forklift, number cartons and even finish paperwork. ABC can even allocate the cost of capital to specific customers.

A customer P&L starts by looking at activities in six categories: sales, ordering, production, shipping, collections and returns and post-sales support. Issues include the number of sales calls required to close, ordering preference (web, phone, etc), frequency of order changes, type and frequency of post-sales support, etc.

Companies like Chrysler that have implemented ABC have saved millions by identifying excess costs and improving pricing. However, implementation is difficult. Still, customer P&Ls must be the long-term goal for companies seeking data that determine appropriate service levels as well as pricing. Customer P&Ls can also align sales force compensation with true customer value.

Roadway Express, a US trucking firm, operates in an unforgiving industry whose margins average a paltry 2.5 per cent. Because it creates customer P&Ls using ABC, Roadway can calculate the actual costs of specific activities for each customer. Thanks to ABC, Roadway turned away more than 350,000 tons of business one year because it was able to calculate that the cost of service exceeded the new revenue. Sales went down, but Roadway's revenue per ton increased by 4 per cent.

'We see [ABC] as a competitive advantage,' says Roadway CIO Robert Obee. 'We know the difference in profitability between different services, so we know how to grow our profitability. That can lead us to move away from, or not emphasize, certain types of business.'

Be willing to show customers their P&Ls. It helps them understand the impact of demands, and thus provides a roadmap for improved relationships. For example, customers may agree to higher prices for smaller orders and bigger discounts for larger orders once they understand the impact of those orders on costs.

CUSTOMER EQUITY OBSTACLES: DIFFICULTIES OF DATA CAPTURE

Companies without a direct relationship with customers have the greatest difficulty calculating customer equity. Because they usually work through retailers, distributors or other intermediaries, many manufacturers often do not even know the names of their customers, much less details on their purchases. Distributors, who fear losing control of the relationship, are notorious for refusing to share information about ultimate customers.

Mass market retailers also have problems collecting relevant data. How can they distinguish the profitability of individual customers among the millions who visit daily, especially when a customer may visit one outlet or branch one day and another the next? Everyone who seeks closer customer relationships, from proponents of one-to-one marketing to advocates of experiential marketing, has stumbled over this conundrum.

There are no easy answers. Ultimately, technology will provide a solution, through RFID and other tracking sensors, 'always-on' wireless connectivity and even a digital, cashless economy. Burger King is experimenting with terminals that enable payment and can help capture customer information for promotions and loyalty campaigns. Until similar technologies are widely deployed, the best solutions consist of strengthening relationships with intermediaries and encouraging customers to open their own direct dialogue. For example, manufacturers can encourage web visits by including detailed instructions on websites.

For manufacturers who deal through intermediaries, the best solution is to enable resellers and distributors to do business on customer terms more easily. Companies have reported successes in setting up formal programmes that start by passing *well-qualified* leads to retailers, resellers and distributors. These programmes include lead generation and management, financing programmes, information-sharing support and other communities, help desk and cooperative advertising programmes. They also reward retailers and distributors for sharing information.

For example, US distributor Avnet Hall-Mark's programme gives resellers an opportunity to view, evaluate and track pre-qualified leads through a web-based portal. The system allows both Avnet and its resellers to measure the efficiency of branding investments as well as see what vertical markets and technologies offer the best returns. Avnet also offers enhanced training, education and go-to-market services for resellers as well as classes in helping customers meet requirements for regulatory compliance. For smaller resellers, Avnet will develop specific branding programmes. The efforts helped its resellers close US $165 million in business over a 15-month period. Avnet also benefited, with a 17 per cent jump in revenue and a phenomenal 1,700 per cent improvement in earnings.

For mass market retailers, one solution lies in such technology as 'contactless cards' that only need to be waved near a reader to pay for items or transmit information. For example, more than 5 million US consumers can use RFID tokens to pay for petrol as well as McDonald's hamburgers. Similar contactless cards can be used in mass transit and vending machines in Hong Kong. Mobile phones are being introduced that will not only make and receive phone calls and receive e-mail but also do everything from pay for groceries and unlock doors to operate appliances and buy cinema tickets. The devices are part of a move toward 'pervasive computing', in which everything is networked to everything else. Along with financial information, such devices will capture personal and other transactional information for manufacturers, much like 'loyalty cards' capture information from customers today.

Another customer equity obstacle is that few companies have consolidated systems in place to determine product and account penetration, referrals or even customer life cycles. Most accounting systems, which specialize in identifying corporate or product profitability, lack the detail that provides a true picture of all customer costs, including manufacturing, distribution, sales, marketing, order management and support/warranties. While an average cost can be determined, actual costs per customer can be skewed by volume, levels of support and product mix.

Also required are systems that capture retention levels, loyalty rates, add-on sales and acquisition costs. The first, and most important, place to start is with source codes. Every prospect and customer must be tagged with a source code indicating the ad, referral or other source of the business. Source codes are invaluable not only for determining marketing effectiveness but for grouping customers by campaign to determine ROI and customer equity.

Without customer-focused data, brands can suffer. When profitability is seen solely in terms of products, managers view service, support, quality and the other investments in retention as costs, easily cut. As one McKinsey consultant put it, 'Any time we did a cost-reduction study, we went straight after the quality department. It never could justify its programmes on economic terms.' The economic impact may be debatable, but quality, service and innovation represent required and necessary branding investments. Cutting costs at the expense of customers decreases loyalty, increases churn and creates pressures for greater acquisition spending to attract 'replacement' customers.

Finally, all customer equity calculations have elements of uncertainty. A small customer may be unprofitable today, but represents tremendous potential for tomorrow. New management at long-term customers can end a brand relationship. Changes in markets, products and even economic trends can alter assumptions. As a result, every customer equity calculation must be analysed in the light of customer and market realities.

One answer is that business success results from adapting to such inevitable changes better than competitors. But a better argument is that unpredictability makes a stronger argument for retention branding. If we can, as William Shakespeare counsels, 'grapple them to thy soul with hoops of steel', then the chances of defection are reduced, and constancy as well as profitability can be the hallmark of customer relationships.

ACQUISITION EQUITY:
WHAT ARE PROSPECTS WORTH?

Customer equity calculates the value of retained customers. Strategies to boost customer equity include increasing marketing effectiveness, defined as attracting the most qualified prospects at the lowest cost, or increasing the value of new customers. As a result, branding professionals must also become adept at calculating acquisition equity, which incorporates acquisition costs, marketing efficiency and ROI.

Marketing efficiency is calculated by dividing by the number of prospects who became customers in a period by the total number of prospects. Calculations can be broken down by channel or campaign. Obviously, that percentage does not reflect the quality of those prospects. Therefore, if a campaign generated 25,000 prospects, and 225 became customers, the marketing efficiency is just under 1 per cent (225 / 25,000 = 0.009).

Acquisition equity requires calculating the total gross margin for the first purchases by customers captured in a period, campaign or channel, then subtracting the marketing costs associated with that period, campaign or channel. This number may be negative because initial purchases may not cover acquisition outlays. As the direct mail industry has understood for years, retention branding is vital because customers may not be profitable until the second, third or later purchases. Divide the result by the number of customers to generate the acquisition equity. This number provides a picture of how effective the marketing campaigns were in terms of profitability. If, for example, a campaign generated US $500,000 from 750 customers as a result of a campaign costing US $550,000, the acquisition equity is (US $66.67) (([US $500,000 – $550,000)] / 750 = (US $66.67). Of course, with such a negative acquisition equity, retention becomes even more important so later purchases make the customers profitable and justify the initial marketing investment.

ROI represents return divided by total investment. To calculate marketing ROI, subtract the marketing investment from the gross margin, and divide by the marketing investment. For example, suppose that marketing for a new product is expected to generate US $500,000 in sales. The cost of goods is US $250,000 and sales/fulfilment expenses are US $100,000. The marketing campaign costs US $100,000.

[(US $500,000 – US $250,000 – US $100,000) – US $100,000)] / US $100,000
= US $50,000 / US $100,000
= 50 per cent ROI

ROI provides a great tool for comparing marketing investment alternatives. If a standard direct mailing of 500,000 pieces costs US $290,000 with a 0.9 per cent response rate and a cost per sale of US $64 and a net profit per cost of US $75, the ROI is about 16 per cent. If sweetening the direct mail offer with a US $25 coupon increased the response rate to 1.6 per cent, then the ROI would increase to more than 22 per cent. Using ROI, it is more cost effective to include the US $25 coupon, despite spending US $200,000 more on the campaign.

In the 1990s, knowing little about the effectiveness of its promotions, Kellogg's began examining the ROI of the nearly US $500 million it was spending annually on promotions. The ROI analysis determined that 59 per cent of its trade promotions lost money, almost overshadowing the 41 per cent that made money. Kellogg estimated that it could save US $64 million annually by basing its promotions on ROI.

How do you get the numbers required for ROI calculation? One source is historical data from previous campaigns. A more important source is often overlooked by many – testing. The insights from a small test can substantially improve results and avoid wasting resources.

James Lenskold provides an extensive exploration of ROI in his excellent book, Marketing ROI: The path to campaign, customer and corporate profitability (2003). Lenskold also examines the concept of hurdle rates, where marketing investments are not made unless they exceed a minimum threshold.

Two main arguments are made against ROI. First, it provides little insight into the quality or long-term profitability of new customers. Additionally, using ROI can provide a weapon for those who argue against branding expenditures, since the easiest way to increase ROI is to decrease the spending on branding.

CONCLUSION

ProfitBrands are built on customer equity, which is roughly the total lifetime value received from a customer minus acquisition and other costs. The pay-offs from customer equity include greater profitability, increased loyalty and more referrals. As a benchmark, it establishes branding accountability. As a measure, it provides justification to CEOs and CFOs for acquisition and retention branding. And as a mission, it focuses the organization on retention.

Companies relentlessly track product profitability, often out to several decimal places. It is surprising – and unfortunate – that so few track customer equity, especially since it is customers – not products – that ultimately determine profitability. Companies must begin to devote resources to track accurately the forces that drive customer profitability, including customer life cycles, retention or referrals.

A variety of methods, ranging from simple to complex, can calculate customer equity. It is important to generate specific numbers to drive branding accountability and identify both profitable and unprofitable customers. With these numbers, managers can measure progress towards specific goals, cost-justify branding for spreadsheet-driven CEOs and CFOs and provide empirical – not just emotional – proof for the power of branding. More important, customer equity forces organizations to measure success and profitability in terms of their customer relationships.

Customer equity calculation can be difficult, especially for companies with deeply ingrained systems for calculating product profitability. But it is absolutely essential to make the effort. Even partial data will yield tremendous insights. And if the outcome is no more than a new emphasis on retention and a greater appreciation for the fact that customers vary tremendously in terms of costs and profitability, the effort will be worth it.

Customer equity is based on the only immutable law: without customers there are no profits, and without profits there is no brand.

Takeaways

- Is long-term strategy focused on increasing customer profitability or product/service profitability? Why?
- What steps can you take to collect the information required to determine customer equity? Have you looked at moving toward ABC?
- Have you estimated current customer equity, either as group or individually? Has this number been distributed throughout the organization so employees understand the value of retention?
- Do your marketing support firms understand the concepts of acquisition and customer equity?
- What programmes drive increases in customer equity? Name the specific individuals who are directly responsible for ensuring that profitable customers stay and increase their equity. What are the metrics for their performance?

5

Divide and conquer: take care of customers worth taking care of

'It is not possible to be all things to all people, so marketsegmentation is the way to avoid this temptation.'
Robert S Kaplan and David P Norton, *The Balanced Scorecard* (1996)

How did Capital One become one of the world's largest and most profitable credit card issuers? Analysing the market in the late 1980s, Capital One noticed that competitive banks were charging all customers the same, despite differences in profitability. So it used a proprietary customer equity analysis and identified two primary segments. Profitable customers were nicknamed 'love 'ems' while unprofitable customers were called 'kill yous'. So Capital One came up with a sophisticated poaching strategy: it would go after the 'love 'ems', but charge them less than their current provider while still making a profit. And it would leave the 'kill yous' for their competitors.

Capital One determined that strategic execution rested on encouraging balance transfers to a credit card with a lower APR (annual percentage rate) than competitors. The strategy was smart because unprofitable customers – those who do not carry balances – had no incentive to transfer. But those who carried balances eagerly jumped. They saved money on their monthly interest payments, while Capital One got all their interest payments – and future business.

Companies have long recognized the importance of segmentation, whether based on RFM, behaviour, demographics or attitudes. While individual actions cannot be predicted, it is easy to be confident that, for example, 30 per cent of a group will buy two products a year. Segmentation enables targeting, differentiation and personalization. It minimizes waste by enabling a better match between offers, sales and support levels. Finally, segmentation powers differentiation of offerings, service, pricing and value.

Segmentation strategies are shifting from attitudinal (demographics) to behavioural (purchase activity, usage). One emerging area of behavioural segmentation is influence. CRM vendor Avaya reported that its customers are developing greater interest in segmenting customers based on influence. Customers can also segment themselves. Sears, Roebuck sells tyres that are 'good, better, best'; FedEx offers morning and two-day delivery at different rates. However, the most effective behavioural segmentation is based on relative profitability, even one as simple as 'love 'ems' and 'kill yous'.

Recognizing that the days of explosive mobile industry growth are over, T-Mobile International strategically decided to use segmentation as a part of a strategy to increase revenue from existing customers. The first step was calculating customer equity. 'We wanted to go to a customer value focus, but we realized we didn't know how valuable our customers are,' said Andras Kondor, vice-president of CRM at T-Mobile International. 'We had to determine acquisition and retention costs because we consider them investments in the customer.'

The next step was segmentation, based on data on 40 million customers. Analysis determined that customer life cycles ranged between 30 and 50 months. 'So, now we have for each customer a value, and then we segment these customers, based on their value,' said Kondor. Segmentation was based on profitable usage. Four segments, based on voice, SMS (short message service) and data content, emerged: top 2 per cent; next 18 per cent; next 30 per cent and the bottom 50 per cent.

T-Mobile developed retention branding programmes to retain and increase the profitability of the top three segments. And the bottom segment? 'Nothing. They are low value. We are trying to get rid of them. We want to give them to the competition,' said Kondor.

As T-Mobile realized, customer equity-based segmentation generates improvements in four areas:

- *Profitability:* Customer equity segmentation allows companies to pick the best targets; optimize retention of the most profitable customers;

dedicate spending to the best customers; and determine which activities produce the most profitable customers. The impact on profitability can be dramatic. According to Garth Hallberg in *All Consumers Are Not Created Equal* (1995), high-profit customers generally deliver 6 to 10 times as much profit as low-profit customers. Other studies indicate that, typically, 80–90 per cent of profits are generated by 10–20 per cent of customers. *Harvard Business Review* reported that, as a rule in the financial industry, 20 per cent of customers will be very profitable, 20 per cent will cost money to retain and the middle 60 per cent will pay for themselves while generating marginal revenue. Chase Manhattan Bank said that 20 per cent of its customers generate the bulk of its profit.

Just as importantly, equity-based segmentation allows firms to identify unprofitable customers. A study of retail banks by accounting firm KPMG found that 140–170 per cent of profits come from 20 per cent of customers while 80 per cent of losses are attributable to 20 per cent of customers. Vendor Unity Solutions reported that 5–15 per cent of customers generate 100 per cent of net profit. As many as 60 per cent of all customers are unprofitable, and unprofitable customers consume 25–55 per cent of resources. Additionally, 'bad' customers are harder to deal with, potentially increasing employee dissatisfaction and profit-sapping turnover.

- *Resource allocation:* Companies must only spend on customers what they are worth or risk profitability. Customers with higher profitability should receive more frequent service or other value than low-profit customers. Spending on high-profit customers produces greater returns than spending on low-profit customers. Union Bank of Norway (Gjensidige NOR) leveraged a data warehouse to launch a programme that focused on the investment preferences and financial goals of its most profitable customers. The response rate to customized offerings totalled an eye-opening 70 per cent.

- *Organizational focus:* Segmentation succeeds because it focuses the resources of the firm on a specific target of similar customers. It gives a firm deep experience within a segment. Segmentation drives capital and resource allocation to areas that provide the greatest profitability and enhanced customer experience.

- *Acquisition branding:* Segmentation allows companies to learn characteristics of profitable and unprofitable customers. How were they acquired? What products or services do they demand? Who is the decision maker? What is their life cycle? This knowledge is vital for effective acquisition branding. Rather than spending to make any prospect a customer, resources can be focused on markets that yield profitable customers. Efforts that result in price-sensitive or unprofitable customers can be avoided.

Segmentation based on profitability pays off. In 2001, the BOC Group, a UK supplier of industrial and medical gases, divided its customers into 'service buyers' and 'price traders'. For the 20 per cent of customers who were classified as service buyers, BOC first negotiated volume purchasing commitments that locked long-term customer equity. At the same time, BOC added flags and other mechanisms to its corporate systems to respond promptly to priority demands from 'service buyers', who required complex supply chain services and immediate information.

Since price traders were concerned with price and little else, BOC reduced available services. It also lowered expenses by using the web to automate sales, marketing and service capabilities. The result: the international branch where BOC piloted this segmentation grew 10 per cent faster than the rest of the company.

SEGMENTATION STRATEGIES: RIGHT VALUE TO THE RIGHT CUSTOMERS

Customer equity-based segmentation involves three steps: identify and rank profitable segments (within a product line or channel); segment services and costs based on each segment's requirements; and reshape acquisition and retention branding around the most attractive customers. Segmentation programmes must also seek to make profitable customers more profitable while addressing the issues raised by unprofitable customers.

Putting such a strategy into action pays off. For example, a large distribution company realized that operating profit per order was a primary profitability driver. To increase profitability, the company identified high-profit accounts. To help sales representatives gain a more systematic understanding of their accounts, the company reduced the number of customers each representative was required to handle. At the same time, customer interviews were required so representatives could identify decision makers, competitors and customer goals. The representative then had to develop an account penetration strategy.

The second initiative involved segmenting customers and matching sales resources to relative profitability. High-profit customers received intensive direct-sales attention. About 600–750 mid-size accounts were serviced by an inside sales group, which supplemented sales calls with occasional face-to-face meetings. The smallest customers, called 'house accounts', were serviced through an inside telemarketing group.

The third initiative reduced sales costs. 'House accounts' were told that future service depended on a minimum number of orders and size. Instead of defecting, many of these smaller customers consolidated orders. The results: the number of products per order increased by 33 per cent, operating profit per order increased by more than 80 per cent and net profits rose by more than 50 per cent, all without capital investment.

A successful segmentation strategy includes the following steps.

Step 1: Segment identification

The first step is to identify and segment customers according to sales or profitability. A variety of segmentation calculations include the following.

Decile (or sales volume) analysis

The simplest segmentation is a decile analysis. Divide all customers into 10 equal groups, or deciles, based on annual (or other period) sales. (Ideally, segmentation can be done on actual profitability.) Include inactive customers. Total sales for all customers in each decile. Divide by the number of customers in that decile to determine the average sale. Identify an attribute that can be linked to sales volume in all deciles. For hospitals, for example, it might be the number of beds. For service stations, it might be the number of bays. Divide the average sale by the number of the relevant attribute.

This analysis has two benefits. It quickly identifies high-profit (or high-value) customers. It also illustrates the 'value' of a relevant attribute. This demonstrates the potential for each customer in a decile, and illustrates the potential for each prospect. More complex analyses are also possible. What about customer life cycles, retention or means of acquisition?

Related to decile analysis is sales volume segmentation. While decile analysis arbitrarily segments customers into 10 groups, sales volume segmentation divides customers into corporate-specific 'buckets'. See Table 5.1.

Calculate total revenue for each customer in a selected period (month, quarter, year). Segment these customers into appropriate sales ranges (eg >US $10,000, US $7,500–US $9,999, US $5,000–US $7,499, etc). The

Table 5.1 Sales volume segmentation

	% of customers
> $1,000	5
$750–$1,000	11
$500–$749	25
$250–$499	13
$1–$249	26
$0	20

number of groups will vary, but should total no more than 10. Analyse these groups as well. What attributes characterize each segment? Why are some customers spending a lot with you, and why are some spending a little? What were the sources of the most- and least-attractive segments?

Additionally, calculate the percentage of customers in each segment. Are the preponderance of customers in the lower segments? This is troublesome, since generally the greatest profits result from those with the greatest sales. Run this report at the end of each period. Seek to increase the percentage of customers in the highest sales segment while decreasing the percentage of customers in the lower segments.

Sales by customer longevity

Generally, customers become more profitable over time. To encourage retention, the relative contributions of new, older and oldest customers must be understood. For this report, calculate total revenue (or profitability) for each customer in a period. Also calculate the percentage of total revenue that customer represents in the same period. Combine those data with the retention period. This report reveals the percentage of total revenue that was generated by customers who just signed up, joined two periods ago, etc. See Table 5.2.

Since existing customers cost less to serve and help generate brand profitability and sustainability through referrals and other contributions, the goal is to increase the percentage of revenue coming from customers who have been with you the longest. Track over time, and be alert for declines in the percentage of long-standing customers.

Increases in the percentage of revenue coming from the newest customers over time may be good or bad news. It is good if it reflects an increased number of new customers; bad if total revenue has remained constant. That indicates older, more valuable, customers are defecting.

Table 5.2 Sales by customer longevity

	% of total customers
Customers beginning current period	25
1 period ago	15
2 periods ago	10
3 periods ago	25
> 4 periods ago	25

Revenue

Revenue segmentation illustrates how high-equity customers contribute to profitability. For a point of comparison, start by calculating the average revenue per customer. Divide the total number of customers into total revenue.

For the first phase of revenue segmentation, customer revenue by period is required. In a spreadsheet, enter customer name (and identification number) and total revenue for a selected period. Sort the customers in descending order by revenue. The biggest revenue source is number 1, second biggest number 2, etc. (Again, ideally, customers are ranked according to actual profitability.) Customers without any activity during the period ('inactives') are at the bottom. Total revenue from all customers. (Most accounting systems sum product revenue to calculate total revenue; a more useful perspective is to sum customer revenue to calculate total revenue.)

In the next column, do a running total of cumulative revenue. In other words, if customer 1 generates US $100,000 in revenue; customer 2 US $90,000; customer 3 US $80,000, the running total would reflect US $100,000, US $190,000 (US $100,000 + US $90,000), US $270,000 (US $100,000 + US $90,000 + US $80,000). Spreadsheets provide several methods for creating running totals (eg =SUM(A1:A1)).

In the next column, calculate the running total of the percentage of total customers each customer represents. For example, if there are 200 customers, customer 1 would represent 0.5 per cent (1/200), customer 2 would represent 1.0 per cent (2/200), and so on.

In the next column, calculate each customer's percentage of total revenue. For example, if customer 1 represents sales of US $100,000 against total corporate revenue of US $1,000,000, then customer 1's percentage of total revenue would be 10 per cent (US $100,000 / $1,000,000), and customer 2's sales of US $90,000 represents 9 per cent of total revenue.

In the next column, also do a running total of revenue percentages so that customers 1 and 2 represent 19 per cent of total revenue, customers 1, 2 and 3 (US $80,000) represent 27 per cent of total revenue, etc.

Now, it is possible to segment customers into four groups. Draw a line on the spreadsheet that separates the top 20 per cent of customers based on the total number of customers. These are most likely the most profitable customers. At a minimum, they are generating the bulk of sales. These customers are golden. When these customers say 'jump', everyone in the firm must ask 'how high?'.

Next, segment the next 60 per cent of customers. These are mid-tier customers. The goal must be to increase the revenue/profitability of these customers. Finally, draw a line that divides the bottom 20 per cent of active customers. Unprofitable customers will be found in this segment.

Finally, note the number and type of inactive customers. Reactivation of customers with the greatest potential will be discussed later. See Figure 5.1.

(Segmentation can be more complex. Customers can be, for example, divided into the top 1, 4, 5, 10, 20 and so on percentiles. The top 1 per cent of customers are more than golden; they are diamond-encrusted platinum, especially if the segmentation was based on profitability. The four-tier segmentation is adequate for initial segmentation.) Calculate the percentage of total revenue from the top 20 per cent of customers. Do the same for mid- and bottom-tier customers.

Divide the total revenue from the top 20 per cent of customers by the total number of top customers to get the average revenue per top-tier

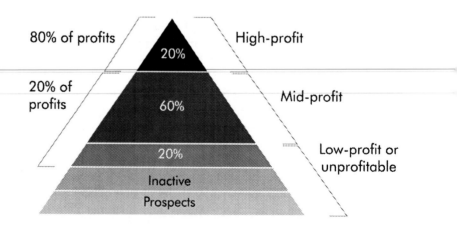

Figure 5.1 Customer profitability segmentation

customer. Do the same for the mid- and bottom-tier customers. Note how much higher the average revenue is from top-tier customers compared to the average revenue per customer that was calculated as a first step. Undoubtedly, the truth of the adage will be seen: 20 per cent of customers are generating 80 per cent of the profits.

It is possible to stop the analysis here, if the costs of goods, service, etc are roughly equivalent for all customers. If that assumption is true, then this segmentation, which identified your highest-revenue customers, also identifies your most profitable customers.

For further value, however, costs must be allocated across each customer segment to get a truer picture of profitability. Primary areas of costs include product (COGS), service and support, sales, marketing, returns and, ideally, overheads. Determining these costs can take time. As discussed previously, traditional accounting cannot easily ascribe costs to particular customers.

But accounting systems can generate data about COGS, SG&A (sales, general and administrative expenses, representing salaries, commissions, marketing and travel expenses) and overheads. Allocating these data among customer segments requires negotiation among sales, finance, manufacturing, marketing and senior management. Remember that inactives and prospects must be allocated a portion of sales, marketing and even overhead costs. Although necessary and illuminating, this negotiation can be difficult. Departments are motivated to shift costs to other departments while claiming revenue.

Allocated costs are then subtracted from total revenues to determine profitability for each segment. Profitability will be greatest for the top 20 per cent, while inactives and prospects will show losses (reflecting overhead and marketing expenses without revenue). Note the difference in relative profitability between the top and bottom segments.

Once companies understand their customer-related costs, they can make informed decisions about areas in which to boost investment or cut costs. Resources used by low-profit customers can be outsourced. Or more sales representatives can be dedicated to high-profit customers.

After segmentation, develop profiles for each segment and, ideally, each customer. What are the product, service and communication preferences? What are the purchasing patterns? Do retention or customer life cycles differ? How about responsiveness to promotions? Are there any product affinities (products or services that are often purchased together)? Sales forces with a clear understanding of their accounts may segment customers based on loyalty (secure, complacent, at-risk, etc).

Segmentation analyses must be run periodically to identify trends.

Step 2: Match offerings to segment

'Exceed customer expectations.' 'Delight the customer.' 'The customer is always right.' Each of those platitudes can destroy a brand.

How? Customers cost money to acquire, service and retain. If you spend more money 'delighting' customers than they are worth, eventually your brand is out of business. That seems obvious, but many companies have a one-size-fits-all strategy based on satisfying – or even going the extra mile for – all customers. They believe, as IBM once did, that every customer is important. Customers are important. But treating customers equally despite differences in profitability and potential wastes resources. Worse, resources that should be reserved for high-profit customers are usurped by low-profit customers. This increases the risk of defection by valuable customers.

Segmenting customers by profitability answers key questions. Does customer profitability justify the level of support? Or do price sensitivity and / or support intensity cost the firm more than a customer is worth? What do valuable customers value most? How were the most profitable customers acquired?

Once customers have been segmented, the next step is to allocate services and offerings based on profitability. In addition to profitability, this segmentation requires understanding customer characteristics, requirements, priorities and processes. Matching requirements of 'first', 'business' and 'economy' customers also requires having 'first', 'business' and 'economy' classes of service. Customers in the top percentile can receive personal support, while bottom-tier customers are restricted to e-mail. Top customers get overnight deliveries; less profitable customers get postal delivery. See Figure 5.2.

For example, the Global Treasury Services, a US $4 billion unit of the Bank of America (BOA), conducts foreign exchange and other transactions for institutional clients. Traditionally, the group segmented customers by asset size. All customers got the same level of service and access to expensive services.

'We tried to be all things to all clients,' said Lisa Margosian, senior vice-president. 'We were underserving some clients, but we couldn't always identify them. And we knew we were overservicing some, and it was too costly. What we built for the most demanding clients dominated everything we did. Too much energy and resources were offered to all clients indiscriminately. Some clients commented on how costly our service model must be. Yet others told us that routine tasks took 45 days to get done.'

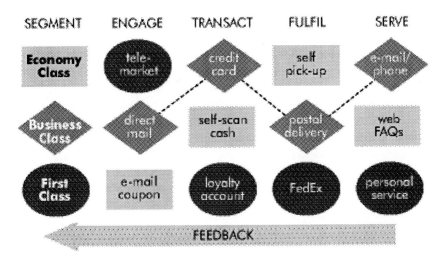

Figure 5.2 Customer planning

Wanting to deliver more to profitable clients and less to others, BOA segmented Global Treasury clients according to service needs: *basic* (essentially self-service); *steady* (ongoing relationships with specific customer service representatives); and *strategic* (consultative services with trained bank specialists). All segments were encouraged to use the web and other self-service options as much as possible.

The result was that 60–80 per cent of customer transactions used the self-service option. About 20 per cent of customer service representatives were eliminated, while client satisfaction levels remained high. To provide segmented service, all customer 'touch points' must know how customers are classified. It is not necessary to provide exact data on customer profitability. Instead, a classification system can be used. UK banks are famed for categorizing customers as 'cherries', 'pears', 'apples' and other fruit. Each category must have guidelines for service, fees and privileges that customers receive.

Policies must also change to reflect segmentation. Instead of 'the customer is always right', the policy must be 'some customers are more right than others, depending on profitability'. Rules can be bent for the best customers, while it is by the book for everyone else.

Despite the benefits, Forrester says only 43 per cent of 60 global companies offer better service to profitable customers. More need to follow the example of the consumer credit company Providian, which uses statistical analyses to segment pricing and service levels to maximize profitability or encourage defection.

Step 3: Reshape branding

Once customers have been placed into their respective segments, analyse each segment. The low-profit segment may only care about price. The high-profit segment may treasure on-time deliveries. Find out how customers in each segment were acquired. Were high-profit customers acquired through telemarketing, while direct mail brought in the unprofitable? Through surveys, customer interviews or other methodologies, determine performance and other metrics important to each segment.

Apply those analyses to acquisition and retention branding. For acquisition branding, stop casting wide nets that generate 'wrong', unprofitable customers. 'Wrong' customers continually utilize a disproportionate amount of corporate resources, hurt employee morale and disparage the company via word of mouth. As a result, each 'wrong' customer destroys shareholder value. By contrast, the 'right' customers can be served profitably.

More focused branding efforts on the 'right' customers will save money. Apply branding resources to target audiences and media most likely to supply look-alikes of your profitable customers. Prospects who look like your most profitable customers represent the highest potential value.

For retention branding, focus on keeping top-tier customers. Do business on their terms. Provide the service and offerings they desire. Communicate frequently according to their wishes. Provide other 'members-only' benefits, such as invitations to special events. Give them dedicated websites, telephone numbers and support representatives. Monitor their purchases, and quickly determine the reasons behind declines in RFM, sales volumes or longevity. Encourage referrals. Referrals by loyal customers often generate more loyal customers who generally are more profitable than those that are acquired by other means. In the retail automotive industry, for example, prospects who rely on recommendations from others take less time making purchase decisions, consider fewer dealerships and are less price-sensitive. Set up a warning system. A profitable customer who goes is cause for concern.

For the mid-tier customers, concentrate on increasing their profitability. This can result from increasing your share-of-wallet through up- or cross-selling, lowering costs of service or finding other means to increase profitability.

SEGMENTATION RISKS:
PAINTING YOURSELF INTO A CORNER

While segmentation is key to branding, there are risks. The biggest risk results from concentrating solely on high-profit customers while neglecting the mid-profit segment. Such 'creaming' opens the door to competitive poaching. Xerox's problems began when it began focusing on big-ticket buyers – those who bought expensive, high-performance copiers. Service to other markets declined. Their resultant dissatisfaction created an opening for Japanese competitors.

Another risk results from evaluating customer profitability with incomplete data. Profitability must be based on the entire customer relationship. A bank customer can be unprofitable based on checking account activity, yet profitable if mortgage, safety box accounts and other activities are included. It's especially important to consider cost-to-serve in customer equity calculations. A customer may order low-margin products, but profitability may still be good if service demands are low.

A common issue concerns customers who are not profitable now, but who may become so later. To address this issue, equity calculations must be complemented by an understanding of customer segments. If a prospect is acquired through a medium traditionally associated with low-profit customers and hasn't passed a purchase threshold associated with profitable customers, then it is unlikely that the leopard will change its purchasing spots and become a high-profit customer.

Remember strategic goals when making decisions. For example, international customers may have lower equity. But the long-term importance of establishing an international presence may outweigh the initial lower equity. While segmentation is valuable, it can suffer from the law of diminishing returns. ROI suffers the more finely an audience is segmented. The direct mail industry, which lives and dies by data analyses and segmentation, has found that more sophisticated segmentation increases response by only tenths of a percentage point. Additionally, the cost of collecting and analysing data required for detailed segmentation reduces profitability.

Consider catalogue merchant Eddie Bauer. After studying the ultimate in segmentation – one-to-one marketing – Eddie Bauer rejected the concept. 'One-to-one marketing is a beautiful vision. But it is a vision,' said Michael Boyd, Eddie Bauer's CRM director. 'The complexity it brings to your business is overwhelming.' Part of the complexity results from constantly updating and generating new customer profiles.

Like Capital One, Eddie Bauer uses only two segments: 'professional shoppers' and 'too-busy-to-shop'. For professional shoppers, the company showcases the latest trends on its website and in its catalogues. 'Too-busys' see complete ensembles. Such segmentation increased sales 10 per cent. Eddie Bauer does not plan additional segmentation.

Similarly, office products retailer Staples stopped tracking purchases of individual consumers through membership cards. Database and other maintenance costs were too high. 'We also came to realize that the most valuable information was to organize buying patterns into "clusters", rather than focusing on individuals,' said Jeffrey Levitan, senior vice-president.

CONCLUSION

Some customers are profitable; some not. The key to brand profitability and sustainability is maximizing the former and minimizing the latter. Customer equity enables companies to measure customer value, and segmentation is how that knowledge is applied. Firms that properly segment customers and penetrate profitable segments will be much more profitable than those that market and serve everyone in the same way. It's not enough to say that 'the customer is number one' to establish a ProfitBrand. You also have to know who is actually number one... and who are numbers two, three, four and five.

A common branding mistake is equating sales or market volume with success: 'We're selling a lot, so we must be making money.' Danger! Danger! If a product or segment is unprofitable, then every new customer hurts the bottom line. Why pursue and serve the unprofitable? It is a hard concept for some to grasp: profitability can be greater with fewer customers. But profitability growth is always more important than sales or market share growth.

Segmentation deepens understanding of profitable and unprofitable customers. It is vital for strengthening relationships with the best customers and targeting acquisition branding. It is the foundation for deeper, more profitable relationships with the 'right' customers while eliminating the customer black holes who drain profitability. Segmentation improves acquisition branding not only by identifying who is likely to become a profitable customer, but also by avoiding the capture of unprofitable ones. And trends within segments provide critical feedback on the effectiveness of branding and operational strategies.

The right segmentation powers a 'fewer, deeper and more profitable' strategy. Brands will grow more – with more profitability – if they focus on fewer, more profitable customers. Such customers represent the highest pay-offs from branding investments. Service can drive to make profitable customers more loyal. Sales can concentrate on expanding share-of-wallet, not share-of-market. Companies can develop deeper understandings of customer requirements. Customer-driven metrics and accountability will be easier to achieve. As always, remember that the goal is not just to brand. The goal is to brand profitably.

Takeaways

- How are you segmenting customers? What is the basis for this segmentation? Are the most valuable customer segments known? What characteristics do they share? How were they acquired? What makes them more profitable? Is it the products they buy, or the services they use?
- Have offerings and services to various customers been segmented? Are there, for example, different web pages for customers and prospects? Is services segmentation based on relative cost and customer profitability? Are customers offered self-service to increase the options available for profitable customers while lowering costs for low-profit customers?
- What steps are you taking to increase the profitability of mid-tier customers? How can you eliminate, or increase the profitability of, unprofitable customers? Can you raise prices or reduce services?
- Does the sales team target prospects based on the characteristics of existing profitable customers? What are you doing to ensure that unprofitable customers are not acquired?
- How is the long-term profitability of prospects and new customers evaluated? Are these assessments tracked to determine accuracy?

6

Winning strategies to increase customer profitability

'If you don't sell, it's not the product that's wrong. It's you.'

Estée Lauder

The principles are clear. Retention branding is more critical to success than acquisition branding. Retention is key to profitability. Customer equity is how to calculate the relative value of customers, and segmentation is how profitable customers are separated from unprofitable ones.

Increasing brand profitability and sustainability requires three strategies. Retain high-profit customers. Increase profitability of low- to mid-profit customers. Stop programmes that acquire the unprofitable, and deal with existing unprofitable customers.

Two factors enable these strategies: organizational commitment and understanding and, more important, rigorous metrics relevant to CEOs and CFOs. Effective branding measurement is critical for setting objectives, planning strategy, tracking progress, rewarding results and ensuring profitability. Without metrics, there is no accountability. Without accountability, there is no management.

Companies must leverage their knowledge about customer equity with customer planning (also called sales planning or account management). Customer planning applies finite sales and marketing resources, including sales force time, towards where it can generate the greatest potential return in customer profitability. It also adds accountability to sales.

Most firms do a terrible job of customer planning. Once senior executives lay down sales goals, they leave the task of increasing revenues from customers in the hands of the sales force. At first blush, that seems logical. Who knows customers better than the sales force?

However, unless the sales force understand customer profitability, they risk wasting resources on unprofitable customers. Leaving customer planning up to the sales force is especially unwise for commission-based staff. They will sell where it is easiest, or where commissions can be maximized, regardless of customer or corporate profitability.

Effective customer planning depends on using customer equity to devise strategies that increase the profitability and/or remove the costs associated with customers. The first step is customer evaluation, primarily based on the profitability-based segmentation described in Chapter 5. Special attention must be paid to 'golden' – the top profitable 1–5 per cent – customers. Inactive or lapsed customers must also be incorporated into sales planning.

Customer planning initiatives inevitably encounter sales force resistance. 'Are you telling me how to manage my customers??!!' But customers do not 'belong' to any salesperson; they belong to the firm. Relationships and sales must be based on the greater good of firm and customer profitability, not the individual good of salespersons. (However, with the right compensation structures, commissions will inevitably grow as customer equity increases.)

CUSTOMER PLANNING: MINIMIZE BRAND SPENDING, MAXIMIZE CUSTOMER SPENDING

Three factors are used to evaluate customers – actual worth, potential worth and the probability that such potential worth can be achieved. Actual worth refers to current and/or historic revenue from the customer. Potential worth reflects anticipated revenue. Probability is a judgement call that indicates the likelihood of achieving a customer's potential. Judgement is based on relationships, chemistry, financial condition and sales skills.

The second step is sales and marketing resource analysis. Given existing or planned budgets, how many trade shows will the company exhibit at? How many personal sales calls can one account representative make annually? How many calls can an inside sales representative make?

How many catalogues will be produced? Be sure to align all contact with customer preferences and requirements for value.

Finally, grow customer profitability. Three penetration strategies generate such growth – customer, account and product. Customer penetration is 'share-of-wallet'. What percentage of a customer's total purchases in a category is being spent with you? How can a greater share be achieved? Account penetration refers to brand presence within an account. If one division is buying, why not another? Product penetration consists of the number of products being purchased. If a customer is buying two, the goal is to generate three or more purchases.

Step 1: Find, keep and grow high-profit customers

Once more, with feeling. The surest way to increase profitability is to acquire and retain high-profit customers. These customers are golden; manage them for maximum retention through special services, loyalty programmes and other activities. Flag high-profit customers in systems to alert employees. Give them priority phone numbers. Set up separate websites for service and information. Process their orders first.

IBM knows how to treat high-profit customers. At IBM, only the top 10 per cent of customers qualify for the IBM Software Premier Club. Benefits of the Premier Club include customer-to-customer collaboration as well as priority access to industry research and IBM experts.

Special service pays off. In one study, the top, most profitable 20 per cent were almost 10 times as responsive to changes in service quality. IBM has seen the benefits. Premier Club members account for about 90 per cent of total revenue for the software group. In 2002, 35 per cent said membership motivated them to purchase IBM software that they otherwise might not have considered. Members spent 80 per cent more on software than similar companies.

Often, technology is key to customer differentiation. One telephone company has segmented its top 10 per cent of customers. If one of those customers calls on a mobile phone, and the call gets dropped, the call centre immediately receives a message. A customer service representative then either calls that customer back or sends a text message. In both cases, the message is the same: 'We understand you have a dropped call. You are a valuable customer. We are going to credit you 60 free minutes of service to keep your business. We are sorry for the inconvenience.'

Of course, one way to increase customer equity is to cut costs. Yet, this may negatively impact a brand's value to the customer. If customers defect, what good did it do to increase profitability temporarily through lower costs? All decisions affecting costs must be looked at in terms of consequences to retention and long-term customer profitability.

Step 2: Align costs to profitability

Alignment consists of investing in customers based on their profitability, and optimizing costs and resources to increase that profitability.

The first alignment step is to identify the highest-revenue customers. In most companies, the costs of servicing each customer are roughly equivalent. This makes it likely that those customers who write the largest cheques are also the most profitable. In other organizations, costs should be allocated to generate a more accurate picture of customer profitability.

The second step is a global understanding of costs and resources. More business from more customers does little good if that business comes with greater costs and reduced profitability. Companies must understand the fully burdened costs to sell and serve each customer, which can range from field sales calls to e-mail communications. Activities can also be ranked for effectiveness in either converting leads or increasing customer profitability.

These costs must be put in the context of the sales and marketing budget (although other departments, such as support, manufacturing and delivery, also carry branding costs). In other words, how can activities limited by the size of the budget be applied most effectively? Often, budgets are determined by a percentage of total sales or gross margins. (Percentages can vary from 5 to 50 per cent, depending on industry and product life cycles.)

In Table 6.1, the fully burdened costs (including allocated overheads) of a phone salesperson is US $125,000. Each phone salesperson is responsible for 25 calls a day, which represent 5,000 calls a year (200 workdays, subtracting holidays, vacations, training and administrative time). As a result, each call costs US $25. Similar calculations are done for each resource, such as direct mail or e-mail.

Once resource costs are understood, the next step is to optimize the limited availability of resources to each customer segment (high-, mid- or low-profit). In general, high-cost resources, which are generally more effective, are dedicated to high-profit customers to ensure maximum return.

As Table 6.1 illustrates, 4,000 field sales calls can be made a year at a cost of US $300 per call. So, those 85 'segment A' customers with the

Table 6.1 Determining available resources

	Resources	Total cost*	Total no. of contacts (yr)	Cost per contact
Field sales	8 staff	$1,200,000	4,000	$300
Phone sales	2 staff	$250,000	10,000	$25
Mail	1 staff	$125,000	12,500	$10
E-mail	Outsource	$13,500	13,500	$1
Total costs		$1,588,500	40,000	

*Fully burdened plus related costs like phone, postage, etc

greatest revenue/profitability will be apportioned 36 field sales calls a year while those 'C' customers who generate less than US $100,000 annually get none. A total of 25 sales calls annually are reserved for high-potential prospects. The primary means of contact for those billing less than US $100,000 a year is phone (17 times a year), mail (26 times a year) and e-mail (24 times a year). Some resources are reserved for inactive customers or prospects. In other words, the more valuable the customer segment is, the more that is spent on retention branding.

Aligning brand resources with customer revenue potential results in more sales at less cost. However, this is not an exact science. Within each segment, customers can get greater or fewer contacts, depending on an evaluation of individual customer potential. However, the segment contact plan remains a master touchstone for sales management accountability. To ensure accountability, call records and other documentation can be reviewed regularly to ensure that benchmark contacts have been made.

Table 6.2 Segment contact plan

Customer revenue/ profitability	Profitability segment	No. in each category	Field (@ $300)	Phone (@ $25)	Mail (@ $10)	E-mail (@ $1)	Contact cost/ customer
> $500,000	A	85	36/yr	6/yr	6/yr	12/yr	$11,022
$100,000– $499,000	B	150	6/yr	12/yr	12/yr	18/yr	$2,238
< $100,000	C	200	0	17/yr	26/yr	24/yr	$709
	Inactive	200	0	20/yr	22/yr	12/yr	$732
	Prospects	100	25 (total)	300 (total)	600 (total)	100 (total)	$211

The next step is to allocate resources within each customer segment to achieve three goals. The first, obviously, is to retain the most profitable customers. The second is to make less profitable customers more profitable. Between 5 and 30 per cent of customers can be migrated 'upward' to increased profitability. If only 2 per cent migrate upwards it can mean 10 per cent more revenues and up to 50 per cent more profit. The third goal is to restore inactive customers to the fold, especially if they have been profitable in the past.

Current and future profitability depends on three factors: customer penetration, or the percentage of total category spending; account penetration, or the number of divisions or other purchasers within a company; and product penetration, or the number of products purchased by a customer. Not only does increasing reach within each category increase profitability, it is also a primary sign of loyalty.

Knowledge about customer equity, account potential, and sales and other resources provides input for a customer plan. The customer plan determines how existing resources are applied to maximize profitability from each customer. It allocates resources to each customer (or, alternatively, each profitability segment) based on both current and potential profitability. For example, high-profit customer 'A' may get 14 personal sales calls, three invitations to industry events and four telemarketing calls during a year. By contrast, low-profit customer 'B' will never enjoy a high-cost sales call, but will get 22 telemarketing calls. However, customers targeted for upward migration can receive additional marketing efforts.

First, the existing revenue and potential revenue, based on customer penetration, account or product penetration, are recorded. Sales goals then are based on both the account's own spending growth and your projected ability to capture a larger share of total spending. Goals must reflect current and projected customer, account and product penetration.

Table 6.3 Contact potential

Customer	Profitability segment	Existing revenue	Existing penetration	Current customer spend	Planned customer spend	Target penetration	Target revenue
Acme	A	$750,000	50%	$1,500,000	$2,000,000	65%	$1,300,000
Beta	A	$715,500	95%	$750,000	$750,000	95%	$712,500
Certus	B	$400,000	25%	$1,600,000	$2,500,000	50%	$1,250,000
Dogtech	C	$125,000	10%	$1,250,000	$1,300,000	10%	$130,000

If, for example, you already enjoy 90 per cent penetration, or share-of-wallet, and the customer will not increase category spending, it is unrealistic to expect a substantial revenue increase.

In Table 6.3, customer Acme and customer Certus represent excellent potential not only because the customers are increasing category spend, but also because the company believes it can capture a greater share of total category spending. Growth for Beta is not as great, because the company is already capturing 95 per cent of customer spend. Minimal growth is anticipated for Dogtech.

As a result, the customer contact plan will focus the bulk of resources on Acme and Certus to achieve their growth potential. Fewer resources will be devoted to Beta and Dogtech.

Part of aligning services to customer requirements means remembering that it is impossible to be all things to all customers. Losses result when you try to do something you are not skilled at. If customers request a service outside your competency, either refuse or outsource it to a specialist.

Step 3: Expand customer, account and product penetration

Companies focused on sales or market growth concentrate on prospect and market penetration. But just as compound interest is the secret behind great wealth, customer (also called share-of-wallet), account and product penetration are the secrets to increasing customer equity.

Customer penetration

One key to increased customer profitability is greater share-of-wallet, known differently in different industries. The food industry calls it 'share-of-stomach'; the car business, 'share-of-garage'; and the clothing industry, 'share-of-closet'. Whatever it is called, customer penetration

Table 6.4   Customer contact plan

Customer	Profitability segment	Field contacts	Phone contacts	Mail contacts	E-mail contacts	Contact cost
Acme	A	38	7	7	12	$11,657
Beta	A	34	6	6	12	$10,422
Certus	B	8	14	14	18	$2,908
Dogtech	C	0	15	22	24	$619

consists of deepening the relationship so that the customer is spending a greater share of category spend with you. The difference in what customers spend now and what they could spend is called 'headroom'.

No one understands the importance of customer penetration better than Tesco. Customer penetration represents the backbone of its phenomenally successful Clubcard loyalty card programme. Based on data from its loyalty card, Tesco uses customer penetration analysis to understand the amount of headroom. By knowing household demographics and past purchases, Tesco can estimate existing customer penetration. Data are analysed to find out how many customers are spending more with Tesco than a year ago and in what categories.

As Clive Humby, chairman of dunnhumby and one of the architects of Clubcard, said, 'It is not about winning new customers, like in the credit card market. It is about winning a few more dollars in the wallet. There is a lot of money to be gone after among your existing customers... If you could understand that, and understand that intimately, that is how you are going to make your real gains.'

Disney believes in customer penetration. When CEO Michael Eisner joined Disney, the focus was on divisional profitability. Then Eisner asked: 'How much of what families spent on vacation does Disney capture?' The answer was a disappointing 25 per cent; airlines, taxis, hotels and restaurants accounted for the remainder.

So Eisner started building Disney hotels and Disney stores. Airline partnerships produced Disney travel packages. Tourists travelled in Disney buses to Disney hotels where they watched Disney TV. Thanks to these so-called 'toll booths', Disney increased customer penetration to about 75 per cent, substantially boosting profitability.

For those without Tesco-like capabilities to generate detailed information on customer spending, other methods can estimate customer penetration. The simplest and best way? Ask customers, 'How much are you spending in this category?' and compare it to current revenue from that customer. Many companies find that customers like talking about themselves, and often offer suggestions for generating more business. In a customer survey, semiconductor manufacturer Atmel asks, 'What is your total expected level of business with Atmel next year?'

Market research can supplement such data gathering. Telindus, a Belgian systems integrator, assists its top 20 clients with IT budget allocation, which provides insights on spending plans. To estimate customer penetration for the rest of its customers, Telindus relies on a local market research firm, which estimates annual IT budgets and identifies major new IT projects for more than 600 actual or potential clients.

Go beyond simply asking about spending plans. Technische Unie (TU), a Dutch distributor of electrical, plumbing and heating products, starts with customer field interviews. Two employees go to one of 35 TU branches and select a random sample of 30 customers, stratified by customer size. The employees visit about 500 of these customers each year for a two-hour interview.

During interviews, customers reveal the total amount of material purchased in each product segment. They also communicate the number of their mechanics working in specialized areas, which provides a rough indication of how much material will be ordered. The customer also relates the percentage of material bought from wholesalers versus direct. Customers cooperate because they believe that TU will use the information to improve its operations on their behalf. Customers also use these interviews to argue for specific offerings.

The information is input into a program that shows sales, margin and other information for each customer. Knowing its product acquisition costs, TU adds the cost of customer sales calls as well as logistics, credit and other costs to determine actual profit margin. The program then generates a customer contribution analysis. This analysis is used to develop profitability goals and customer contact plans.

In some cases, information exchange unlocks customer spending plans. Lubrizol, a lubricant and fuels additive supplier, provides specialized reports to customers contributing data. These reports are worth up to US $50,000 if purchased.

To gain estimates for customers unwilling to provide data, indirect methods work. Sometimes industry research is available. Lubrizol uses American Petroleum Institute studies. Honeywell Performance Fibers uses multi-client studies from the Fiber Economics Bureau. The Bank of America collects annual reports and other public documents to research capital acquisitions, business loans and securities trading for each account. From these data, managers can calculate interest payments and bank fees. Dividing the actual amount of a customer's business by the estimate of a customer's total banking business provides managers with an approximate penetration measure.

Once penetration is known, work toward a higher, specific penetration goal. One strategy is to penetrate an account with a particular speciality, and then use that penetration as a beachhead to move into other activities. For example, rather than seek sales from multiple customers that might be marginally profitable, Seghers Better Technology Group, a Belgian design, engineering, fabrication and maintenance company, uses a four-step process to capture 100 per cent of a customer's business.

The first step consists of providing bolt tensioning, on-site machining or another special service where it has a distinct advantage. After its performance builds trust, Seghers then proposes a higher level of service involving ongoing plant maintenance. Such maintenance provides in-depth knowledge about customer issues. Maintenance issues lead to step three in Seghers' penetration strategy – high-profit equipment overhauls. Finally, when customers become fully confident in its capabilities, Seghers pursues the fourth level – total shutdown service. For Seghers, this is very profitable. And at this stage, Seghers has achieved its goal of 100 per cent customer penetration.

Another customer penetration strategy involves incentives to increase current spending or transactions. The Canadian hotel chain Delta Hotels segmented its customers into three classes: 'green' (guests who want to participate in a loyalty programme); 'gold' (stay 5 or more times a year); and 'platinum' (stay 15 or more times a year).

Delta wanted to move customers from lower segments into the next higher segment. After identifying 'green' customers who had stayed with the hotel chain at least twice, Delta sent a mailing inviting them to stay three more times in a five-month period to achieve 'gold' status. 'Gold' members were invited to stay three more times for 'platinum' class. About 9,000 customers achieved the next level by staying extra nights, increasing customer equity.

Avoid discounting to achieve customer penetration. This may increase penetration, but it wrecks profits. Additionally, customers who value price above all quickly defect for a lower price. Track customer penetration trends. It is a warning sign if the customer's total category spend is increasing faster than purchases with the company.

Product penetration

A single purchase can occur because of convenience, promotion or luck. Second, third and more purchases indicate trust and loyalty, and lead to greater profitability.

Three activities drive product penetration, or expanding the breadth or depth of offerings purchased. The first two are the time-honoured methods of cross-selling – selling complementary products – and up-selling – selling an upgraded or enhanced version. Up-selling and cross-selling increase loyalty and customer equity. Sprint has found that customers who subscribe to two or more services are 25–50 per cent more likely to stay loyal than those who use only one service.

Table 6.5 Penetration analysis

	Customer	Product	Account
Account	Current sales Total customer category spending Probability of growth Planned customer and category spend Headroom	Type of products (new, dated, according to product life cycle) No. of products purchased Bundled offerings Product profitability	Percentage of existing buyer groups being sold to compared to total available Recency of sale to new dept, etc Internal customer referrals

Another product penetration strategy is to provide an offering unavailable elsewhere. For example, KLM Cargo, part of KLM Royal Dutch Airlines, has moved away from providing commodity cargo space to specialized solutions not offered by other airlines.

KLM studied the requirements of importers and large retailers who dealt with perishable goods. Their main issue was rapid, consistent delivery without spoilage. To meet this demand, KLM began offering a dedicated, three-level service that ensures unbroken 'cool' handling in temperature-regulated containers from producer to delivery. KLM now delivers orchids from Thailand to the world's largest flower market in The Netherlands. KLM also provides cool transport of salmon from Norway to Tokyo, Osaka, Sapporo, Hong Kong and Beijing within 48 hours. Since a premium price is charged, all customers are profitable. In fact, KLM is unable to meet all demand.

Despite the advantages of product penetration, too few make it a part of their branding strategies. A study of the top 100 Asia Pacific banks found that 85 per cent did not try to cross-sell or up-sell related banking products while talking to customers. By contrast, consultant Booz Allen reported that customers were 20–30 per cent more likely to be sold product bundles, which were 30 per cent more profitable, after a bank client instituted a product penetration campaign.

Remember, however, that all cross-selling and up-selling must be based on customer requirements, not an across-the-board script ('would you like fries with that?'). If the customer does not see a benefit, the effort can be annoying. To ensure appropriateness, know preferences and needs before making recommendations. A bank, for example, must never make a home equity loan offer to renters. Various software programs can analyse a customer's profile to suggest products to up-sell or cross-sell.

Account penetration

Account penetration means selling elsewhere within a customer, such as additional departments or divisions or even different national or international locations. If a customer has 10 manufacturing plants, what percentage of each plant's purchase requirements can you supply? If human resources is buying an offering, why not marketing?

Account penetration can substantially boost customer equity. In 2001, Bank of America shifted its strategy from growth through acquisition to delivering shareholder value through enhanced profits. To execute the new strategy, Global Corporate and Investment Banking (GCIB) targeted 375 clients for growth. It sought to expand its sales of funds collection, forecasting services and other cash management services. At the same time, GCIB worked to reduce the high-risk and low-profit loan business it had with these customers.

Revenues in 2002 declined 4 per cent, which resulted from dropping unprofitable business, even with such major firms as Wal-Mart and IBM. But because GCIB successfully expanded its account penetration, profits increased 12 per cent and shareholder value nearly doubled within two years. Revenue per strategic client jumped 54 per cent from 1999 levels.

One way to increase account penetration is to reduce the account load for each sales rep without reducing responsibility for sales outcomes. This forces representatives to penetrate high-potential accounts more deeply and form relationships with more decision makers.

Once customer, product and account penetration have been determined, analyse them in a matrix. Categories under customer penetration include current sales from the customer, total current customer spending in that category, planned customer spending, headroom and target sales. Under product penetration, look at the number of products, the type of products (new, dated, according to product life cycle) and the profitability of these products. Account penetration must compare the number of existing locations, departments or individuals being sold to the total universe available to sell to.

The matrix may reveal surprises. Is there an over-reliance on one or two top customers? Are many customers buying only one or two products, indicating a lack of cross-selling? Is there a lot of revenue from products approaching the end of their life cycle? Do some customers just buy products on sale? Are sales representatives gaining referrals from internal customers?

Often technology assists penetration. For example, Nykredit, a Danish financial institution, wanted to diversify beyond mortgage services.

However, customer information was scattered among multiple data-bases, depending on products purchased. Customers were unhappy because they had to repeat information each time they were shuttled among Nykredit representatives. Because of this silo-based handicap, Nykredit not could obtain an integrated view of customers.

So Nykredit automated 48 local offices, customer contact centres and sales centres. The effort included consolidating multiple databases containing 450,000 private and 80,000 business customers. Separate tele-phone numbers for each product were replaced with one number for all enquiries. Now, when a customer calls that number, the consolidated database enables a Nykredit customer representative to see a complete customer profile, including services being used, recent mailings and outstanding service issues. Representatives use this information to resolve enquiries quickly and suggest additional products. Sales oppor-tunities are easily transferred to branches near the customer. Since the system was introduced, 40 per cent of Nykredit customers have bought more than one product. Customer loyalty has increased 10 per cent.

Track customer, product and account penetration over time. The bank First Tennessee has a 95 per cent retention rate, averages five products per household and claims a 31 per cent share-of-wallet.

INCREASING PENETRATION: TACTICS TO EXPAND PROFITABILITY

Increasing obstacles to acquisition branding (telemarketing restrictions, e-mail spam filters, opt-in requirements, etc) increases the importance of customer, product and account penetration. To ensure brand sustain-ability, companies seek penetration during all customer engagements (service requests, order placement, etc). This is when customers are most receptive to sales efforts.

Tactics to expand penetration include the following:

- *Ongoing communications:* Newsletters, appropriate e-mails and phone calls strengthen loyalty bonds. In 1996, Microsoft targeted 30,000 small office/home office customers with a newsletter as part of its Microsoft Advantage programme. In 12 months, Advantage customers generated 111 per cent more revenue than a control group. Encourage pass-alongs of messages, and always ask, 'Is there anyone else we can talk to?'

- *Guarantees:* Guarantees encourage both trial and loyalty. Hampton Inn Hotels estimated that its service guarantee increased revenue by US $11 million and earned it the industry's highest retention rate.
- *Stress total cost of ownership:* Consumers and businesses often value how much an offering costs over its lifetime, in terms of service, support and maintenance, more than its initial costs. In car sales, for example, incentives that save money in the long run, like free oil changes, are prized much more than such incentives as a cruise vacation.
- *Sell services, not products:* Global firms like IBM and GE now view services as the heart of their business models. Products can be copied and manufactured cheaply around the globe. Services, on the other hand, strengthen customer relationships, are tougher to copy and generate greater profitability.
- *Special offers:* Invite the best customers to special showings or events. One of Tesco's most popular programmes was reserved supermarket time for top-tier customers. Exclusive jeweller Henry Birks & Sons threw a 'Swiss watch' party. Watchmakers such as Montres Rolex SA, Cartier SA and Baume & Mercier shared a private evening with several hundred invited customers who were timepiece aficionados. Luxury furniture retailer Robb & Stucky hosted seminars that ranged from aquarium design to an all-day feng shui class using Robb & Stucky furniture.
- *Customers first:* Never make an offer to new customers without first offering it to existing profitable customers. A primary reason that magazines and mobile telephone firms suffer high churn is because prospects get better deals than customers.

UNPROFITABLE CUSTOMERS: IDENTIFY, UPGRADE OR 'FIRE'

Customer equity analysis and segmentation inevitably uncovers unprofitable customers. *Harvard Business Review* estimates that, on average, 15 per cent of all customers are unprofitable. According to the book *Angel Customers and Demon Customers* (Selden and Colvin, 2003), in most industries the worst 20 per cent of customers typically lose money equal to 75 per cent of profits. Unprofitable customers can include 'price grinders', 'constant complainers' and those who require services that cannot profitably be supplied. Look for warning signs that signal likely unprofitability, such as late payments, excess service calls, numerous returns or frequent complaints.

Unprofitable customers require one or more of the following strategies: raise revenues; decrease costs; or, as a final alternative, 'fire' them. The right strategy depends on a key question: are customers unprofitable because of their behaviour or your costs?

Raise revenues

Raising prices is often the best option. If the customer accepts the higher price (or lower discounts), revenues (and usually profits) rise. McKinsey & Company estimates that a 1 per cent increase in price leads to an 11 per cent increase in customer equity. It is estimated that 60–70 per cent of customers accept price increases. If the customer rejects the higher price, then an unprofitable customer is lost and overall profits improved. Chapter 7 discusses pricing.

Reduce costs

Cost reduction often involves the internet or other automation. Fidelity Investments uses an automated phone system that identifies unprofitable customers and routes them into longer queues. This allows Fidelity to serve more profitable customers faster. If the unprofitable customers switch to the internet, they become profitable. If they go to a competitor, Fidelity smiles.

Cost reductions can also result from policy changes. Consumer goods giant Procter & Gamble (P&G) realized that direct LTL (less-than-load) shipments raised costs. So P&G changed its policy to ship goods in truckload volumes only. As a result, smaller, less-profitable customers had to use distributors, and P&G was able both to lower its costs and to differentiate services to larger, more profitable customers.

Costs can also be reduced by bundling or unbundling offerings. However, care must be taken that cost reduction does not result in the attrition of profitable customers.

Fire customers

Every customer must have the opportunity to increase profitability before being 'fired'. Strategies to improve customer profitability include encouraging more purchases, reducing service, unbundling features or changing the speed of service or compliance. But when these do not work, profitability must be protected by firing the customer.

In 1998 FedEx unveiled a new e-commerce system for customer sites. It had two advantages. It helped customers become more efficient, and it allowed FedEx to calculate profitability for each customer. Sales representatives then either negotiated price increases with unprofitable customers or closed their accounts. Understanding that profitability was more important than volume, FedEx ultimately waved good-bye to customers who shipped a total of 150,000 packages per day.

Yet the call to 'fire customers' causes protests. 'We worked hard to acquire that customer.' 'That customer will be profitable tomorrow.' 'Volume is important, so even unprofitable customers help cover production costs.'

All valid points. That is why the decision on firing a customer must incorporate managerial judgement. This judgement reflects the intangibles that might not be seen within a customer equity calculation. For example, customers can become more profitable over time. The key determination is customer, account and product penetration. If the penetration percentage is great, and the customer is still unprofitable, how likely is it that profitability will improve?

Keep your eye on the prize – profitability. Is the potential greater than current profitability? How long do you want to subsidize unprofitable customers? Companies drop unprofitable products all the time. Why not unprofitable customers?

If customers must be fired, do so gracefully. An unhappy ex-customer can generate negative word of mouth. Ideally, get customers to fire themselves. Keep raising prices, slow service or make processes more complicated. Other steps include not renewing contracts or not accepting orders.

Remember that brands may be 'fired' as well. Several years ago, Unilever, wishing to reduce brand redundancy, shrunk its brand portfolio from 1,600 brands to 400. Japan's cosmetic giant Shiseido cut its brand portfolio by 75 per cent. Recognizing that its top 10 brands account for half its sales, P&G is now focusing on 14 of its approximately 300 brands.

CUSTOMER RECOVERY: GETTING THE PROFITABLE BACK

One UPS customer was the chairman of several banks. He was also an avid map collector. To add to his collection, he sent a die-cut map of the lunar surface to each of the nine astronauts who had walked on the moon, asking them to sign at the spot where they had walked. It took many months, but eventually all of them, including Neil Armstrong, signed the map. After Armstrong signed it, he shipped it via UPS back to the bank chairman... and UPS lost the package.

The package loss meant a major customer loss for UPS. But a UPS customer service manager bought another die-cut map of the moon. After many months, he too got the signatures of each astronaut. He sent the finished map to the customer, who was obviously delighted. UPS had its customer back.

That illustrates a customer recovery programme, or effort to bring profitable customers back into the fold. Companies cheer when a customer is acquired. Who notices when a customer, or worse a profitable customer, is lost?

Customer loss is commonly underestimated. The usual guess is less than 10 per cent. Actually, every year, the average company loses 20–40 per cent of its customers. Such customer loss wastes acquisition branding investments. It reduces customer equity. It may indicate operational, service or other problems. It opens the door for negative word of mouth. Yet it is estimated that only 3 per cent of businesses have a 'lost customer' recovery programme.

Customer recovery, which addresses customer loss resulting from dissatisfaction or other issues, seeks to maintain the investments made in customers and ensure continued profitability. Customer recovery can be more important than acquisition, especially when the lost customer represents substantial equity. Additionally, unhappy defectors can tarnish reputations among potential buyers.

Just because customers are gone does not mean they are gone for ever. If customers have been profitable in the past, it is likely that they can be profitable again, if recovered. Research firm Marketing Metrics found the average company has a 60–70 per cent chance of selling again to regular customers and a 20–40 per cent probability of successfully selling to lapsed customers. By contrast, companies enjoy only a 5–20 per cent probability of selling to a new prospect. Studies indicate that customer recovery investments yield returns of 30–150 per cent. In fact, British

Airways finds that 'recovered' customers give the airline more of their business.

Recovery programmes can be the basis for successful direct mail campaigns. To promote its new 'V-Power' petrol, Shell sent out US $2 discount coupons to nearly 10 million customers. The majority of these customers had purchased Shell petrol two or three times and then switched to another brand. Companies must develop systems to signal departing customers, or customers who have not purchased for an extended period. Encourage re-engagement or repurchase.

Unhappy customers typically include those who were satisfied until a single poor experience. If a company can successfully make amends, customer faith in the brand is both restored and deepened. Such actions help create advocates who spread the good word to potential customers. However, be wary about trying to purchase renewed loyalty with significant discounts. Customers who defect for lower prices will do so again.

Even if the customer cannot be persuaded to buy again, a lot can be learnt from an 'exit interview'. Find out through surveys or 'exit interviews' why subscriptions aren't renewed, replacement products aren't purchased or upgrades installed. For example, wireless carrier BellSouth Mobility (now Cingular) was winning 2,500 customers each day. On the other hand, it was losing 500 customers daily. Recognizing this profitability drain, Cingular sought to win back 10 per cent of lost customers. Defection interviews revealed that customers liked Cingular's call coverage, customer service and billing. However, they had changed carriers because they were denied credit for dropped calls or were denied promotions available to prospects.

Solicit complaints. No one likes to hear complaints, but they are really opportunities to improve loyalty, especially since only about 5 per cent of customers who are unhappy (more in business-to-business) take the effort to complain. Anyone who takes time to complain is offering both a suggestion for improvement and a chance at recovery. Ireland's Superquinn supermarket constantly asks customers to 'complain' about their experiences. Customers who uncover 'failings' receive a 100-point deposit in their loyalty programme. In essence, Superquinn is enlisting hundreds of thousands of quality control inspectors. Customers must be easily able to complain via e-mail, letter or well-publicized hotlines. Capturing such feedback gives companies a chance to address sources of dissatisfaction, improve the chances for recovery and salvage customer equity. Insurance giant USAA scans every complaint into its database. Complaint causes are analysed, and processes examined to avoid similar complaints in the future.

If profitability justifies recovery, follow a four-step process. The first step consists of both apology and accountability. Say 'I'm sorry' and take ownership of mistakes. Next, involve the customer in the resolution. Ensure that employees have enough authority to satisfy reasonable demands. Marriott International employees can spend up to US $2,500 without authorization to compensate customers. Schedule a resolution. In one Citibank experiment, specifying time frames for next steps increased customer satisfaction by 40 per cent. Resolve issues quickly. British Airways found that about 50 per cent of complaining customers defected if it took the company longer than five days to respond.

Finally, deliver and follow up. Determine whether customers have received promised remedies. The effort will pay off. One study indicated that a follow-up call to a once-unhappy customer boosts satisfaction by 5–7 per cent, and intentions to repurchase by 8–12 per cent. Another survey indicated that 82 per cent of customers whose problems are resolved buy again. The research group TARP found that a customer who receives some compensation is usually 10–30 per cent more willing to repurchase than someone who received no compensation. A study by the US Office of Consumer Affairs found that 54 per cent of households would remain loyal if problems were satisfactorily resolved. Only 19 per cent would repurchase if they were unhappy with a problem's resolution.

By instituting a customer recovery programme, British Airways doubled its retention rate among those who complained. It estimated its ROI, based on the value of business saved plus increased loyalty and new business from referrals, to be more than 200 per cent. KeyCorp, a financial services firm that includes a large US bank, also stresses retention and recovery. Using predictive modelling, KeyBank identifies customers at risk of defection. These customers receive proactive calls to address their issues as well as mailings with special offers and incentives four times a year. Branch personnel are trained in retention techniques to help 'save' customers intending to close accounts. Additionally, KeyBank has a dedicated call centre to handle telephone calls from customers seeking to close accounts. Call centre representatives are trained to help these customers and empowered to take action to preserve profitable relationships. As a result, the attrition rate at KeyBank has declined by 2 per cent.

Not all defectors need be retained, however. The unreasonable demands of unhappy customers, or those whose needs do not fit with the company's capabilities, can devour excessive resources and wreak havoc on employee morale. That is why such outstanding service organizations as Nordstrom department store, Sewell Village Cadillac Company in

Dallas, and Southwest Airlines regularly 'fire' customers they cannot properly serve.

CONCLUSION

Essentially, profitable branding comes down to five complementary strategies. Add more new profitable customers. Often the profiles of these customers are similar to those of existing profitable customers. Grow the profitability of existing profitable or unprofitable customers by increasing account, customer or product penetration, raising prices and/or reducing costs. Choice three is to add fewer new unprofitable customers. Again, these are easy to recognize once existing customers have been segmented. The fourth choice is to lose fewer existing profitable customers, either by consistently meeting their requirements for value or by instituting customer recovery programmes. Finally, companies have the option to lose, or 'fire', customers that cannot be made profitable.

To maximize scarce and expensive branding resources, companies must apply them based on customer knowledge and profitability. The first step is segmenting customers by profitability. The next step is allocating branding resources for each profitability segment. Finally, companies must leverage their knowledge about customer equity with customer planning. Customer planning applies finite sales and marketing resources, including sales force time, towards where it can generate the greatest potential return in customer profitability. Individual customer contact plans are prepared, again based on current and potential profitability.

Based on increasing customer, product or account penetration, customer planning adds structure, control and purpose to customer contact, improving retention and profitability. Resources are applied towards profitable segments and away from unprofitable business. Sales accountability improves. At the end of the year, changes in customer profitability can be tracked against the planned and actual customer contact. Other components of a profitability strategy are letting unprofitable customers go and winning back profitable customers.

Takeaways

- Is a contact plan in place? Are strategies being pursued on three fronts – customer, product and account penetration? Is customer, product or account penetration being measured? Is performance tracked against plans regularly?
- What steps are you taking to increase customer profitability and/or reduce costs? What automation initiatives are under way?
- Are resources and services aligned with customer profitability?
- Can you identify customers who have not done business with you for a period? What activities are in place to renew lapsed customers?
- Can you identify unprofitable customers? What are you doing about them? Are you considering price increases or similar strategies?

7

Increasing customer profitability through pricing

'In the factory we make lipstick; in the drugstore we sell hope.'
Charles Revson, founder of Revlon

Customer equity is how companies create value. ProfitBranding is how companies deliver value. Pricing is how companies capture that value.

No company illustrates how pricing can be used to capture value better than Japanese car manufacturer Nissan. In 1999, Nissan was on the brink of bankruptcy, with US $22 billion in debt. Market share was less than 5 per cent. The Nissan brand was in tatters, ripped by ageing products. No new models were on the horizon. That forced it to rely on large incentives, ultimately resulting in low residual values.

Then French car manufacturer Renault bought Nissan and installed Carlos Ghosn as president. One of his first acts was to unveil a 'Nissan Revival Plan' based on the 'number one goal of long-term enduring profit'. The aggressive Nissan Revival Plan sought to generate profitability in less than two years and reduce debt to US $700 billion in three years. To execute the plan, cross-functional teams came up with the 'Nissan 180' programme. The '180' represented 1 million new sales by 2005, an 8 per cent operating margin and zero automotive debt. When Ghosn announced his Nissan Revival Plan, two pricing models dominated the car industry – volume-driven and profit-driven. The volume-driven model, epitomized by GM, seeks to amortize high fixed costs by keeping production lines churning. When cars do not sell, costly incentives are offered to 'move iron', which cheapens brands and slashes profits. By contrast, Porsche and a few others limit production. This keeps prices high, but constrains growth.

To revive its brand, Nissan opted for a new pricing model – value pricing. It would stop incentives in favour of product enhancements and aim for reasonable production levels to keep prices stable. Actual pricing would depend on competitive offerings, other Nissan products, vehicle options and volume objectives.

Nissan's value pricing had four cornerstones:

- *Planning and analysis:* Every successful brand starts with smart questions. What need will the product fulfil? Who will it compete with? What competitive advantages does it offer? What sales goals are reasonable?
- *Customer research:* Customer surveys and other tools were used to confirm the analysis, estimate volume at varying prices and predict market receptiveness.
- *Quantitative value analysis:* How did the offering compare to competitive offerings and other models? How did the value emerge in various configurations of the same model? How did various options affect customer willingness to pay?
- *Better measurement:* Nissan established systems to measure current retail pricing and leasing as well as track competitive incentives or price changes. It also built a new pricing team with members from sales, marketing, finance, product planning, pricing and promotion. The team's marching orders: 'maximize profit!'

With this foundation, Nissan was then able to use price as a weapon in the struggle to rebuild both its brand and profitability. For example, market research revealed that the just-developed vehicle Xterra had no direct competition. Customer research revealed intense interest. Nissan launched Xterra with a sales price of US $1,000 below its potential market price. The result was a 'frenzy' for the vehicle. Sales were twice as great as anticipated, and Nissan ensured profitability through an appealing trim and option mix. Six months after the introduction, Nissan raised prices US $250.

A similar strategy guided the introduction of an enhanced Altima. The old Altima had been too small, forcing Nissan to drive sales with substantial incentives. Nissan raised the price, eliminated all incentives for the new Altima and persuaded dealers to sell on customer value. Sales volume doubled. Nissan has even increased prices since the launch.

Nissan has followed similar strategies for the introduction of the Titan and other vehicles.

'Did value pricing work for Nissan 180?' asks Duane Leffel, director of pricing strategy and analysis for Nissan. 'In 2003, Nissan reported [US] $7 billion in operating profit, and the [US] $22 billion in debt was eliminated 18 months earlier than targets. And we are on track for selling 1 million incremental vehicles.'

Nissan illustrates how pricing is critical to branding. Price affects how offerings are advertised, perceived and received. Since price encapsulates one of the first interactions a customer has with an offering, it affects relationships. Most important, price affects profitability and the ability to offer value to customers.

Despite its importance, pricing does not get the attention it deserves. The topic is ignored in most branding books beyond the obligatory comment about 'brands support higher prices'. According to a member survey by the Professional Pricing Society, only 11 per cent report that senior management is involved in pricing. At many firms, pricing decisions occur at the last minute, the result of compromises between the finance staff, which wants to recover costs, and the marketing/sales department, which seeks sales.

As a result, poor pricing decisions are common, resulting in money left on the table, unprofitable sales or an open door to competitors. A common mistake is using pricing as a tool to achieve sales or market share. (Penetration pricing for a new market entry must only be a short-term tool.) While market or sales share may increase with lower pricing, profitability usually suffers, ultimately hurting the brand. Worse, market share-driven pricing attracts the worst kind of customer. Customers who buy on price frequently defect for lower prices elsewhere.

Admittedly, pricing is complex. It involves costs, channels, product life cycles, operations, competitors, support and other factors. Psychology and emotion further complicate the issue. Adding to the complexity is the fact that consumers have access to pricing information in the customer economy that they never had in the mass economy. Progressive Insurance provides competitive pricing as part of its branding strategy. Bizrate.com and other online sites make it easy to compare prices. Wireless capabilities will soon make such comparisons easy while shopping in retail aisles. No company looking for an edge wants to raise prices in such an environment. Yet, at the same time, pricing is the most valuable tool to increase customer equity. A McKinsey & Company study points out that raising prices 1 per cent increases customer equity by 11 per cent.

PRICING BASICS: A 60-SECOND PRIMER

Pricing is at the intersection of supply and demand, which is driven by economic, experiential or emotional value. Simple formulas allow companies to measure price elasticity and the comparative profitability advantages of price increases/decreases based on varying levels of supply. (These formulas are detailed in the excellent *Strategy and Tactics of Pricing* (1994) by Thomas Nagle and Reed Holden.)

A core concept in pricing is the 'contribution margin'. The contribution margin is the difference between the unit sales price and the variable costs involved in producing that particular unit. In other words, the contribution margin is the profit resulting from an additional sale, or the amount above what's necessary to recover the incremental, variable cost of the sale.

The 'best' price maximizes profitability yet also matches customer perceptions of value and price sensitivity. In general, pricing seeks to achieve maximum contribution margin, not maximum sales or market share. Increased sales or market share may even hurt profitability, if they are achieved through low pricing. If higher margins at low volume result in greater profits than low margins at high volume, then throttle back the production engine.

If pricing isn't right, companies give away their value – the only thing they have to sell. Even brilliant branding cannot salvage the effects of poor pricing or lack of price discipline. Companies often concentrate on cost cutting (Six Sigma (see page 127), etc) to increase profitability. Cost cutting that does not affect customer value must be complemented by strategic pricing that seeks to maximize profitability. Strategic pricing rests on a foundation of '4 Cs': comprehend customer value; create segment-based value solutions; convince target customers to pay for value; and capture value with pricing discipline and other tools.

Comprehend customer value

Companies roughly understand their own costs. However, they are much less knowledgeable about the emotional, experiential or economic value of brands to customers. For consumers, value is defined in terms of time, certainty (reliability, effectiveness, etc), economy, image or other benefit. For businesses, value comes from productivity improvements, revenue improvements, new market entry, cycle time reduction, quality improvements or reduced error/defect rates. Businesses also seek an enhanced ability to deliver value to their own customers.

Quality, technical or sensory superiority, service, delivery, training, packaging or other aspects of operational excellence are only means to deliver a brand's value. This value must be above its cost to the customer. It must also be above what competitors could deliver or what customers could achieve by themselves.

Understanding a brand's value to customers requires understanding customers. Not many have such understanding, believes legendary consultant Peter Drucker. 'What the people in business think they know about the customer and market is likely to be more wrong than right... The customer rarely buys what the business thinks it sells him.'

Understanding customers requires knowing the answers to these questions. What do customers care about? Why are they purchasing from you and not from a competitor? What is the value of the brand from their perspective?

The answers are essential to profitable pricing. All companies have to sell is their value to customers. If they do not know – or cannot communicate – that value, they cannot recover that value through pricing. They also cannot focus the organization on increasing that value. Additionally, ignorance of customer value gives the upper hand to customers in negotiations. This often means lower pricing and profitability than what is possible.

If customer value is understood, higher prices can be justified. Furniture Medic, a Canadian mobile furniture restoration company, based its prices on what shop-based competitors were charging, even though it performed work on-site. ServiceMaster took over the struggling firm and raised prices substantially. '[Furniture Medic] didn't understand that the customer values service and is willing to pay more for it,' said the franchising director. Since then, sales and profits have risen dramatically.

Determining customer value is a two-step process. The first step is translating features into performance benefits. It is not enough to say 'this offering increases productivity'. ProfitBrands must be able to answer these questions. Whose productivity will be increased? How much will productivity be increased? How soon will it be increased? How certain will the productivity increase be? And so on. Even 'soft' features like service and responsiveness must be translated into hard performance data that reflect costs saved/avoided, revenues realized or even psychological benefits ('first in your area...'). For example, consistent on-time delivery justifies higher prices, especially when plant shutdowns can cost large sums of money per minute.

The second step is comparing these benefits to a 'reference value', determined by the benefits of the next best alternative. The customer value is in the difference between the ProfitBrand's benefits and the next best alternative, which could be a personal or 'home-grown' alternative. Pricing is based on this value. No matter how difficult determining this value and the appropriate price may be, the effort must be made. At worst, the effort will keep organizations focused on delivering maximum value to customers. At best, it results in pricing that offers the greatest competitive differentiation, is sustainable for the longest time and is achievable at the least cost.

Create segment-based value

A common, across-the-board price can lead to lost profits and sales opportunities. Costs, price sensitivity and competition can vary significantly among customer segments. Variable pricing can charge segments that are relatively price insensitive, cost more to serve or are poorly served by competitors more than those that are price sensitive or well served by competitors.

In general, there are four price-based segments: loyalty, convenience-driven, price-sensitive and value-sensitive. Since each segment may need a different pricing strategy, this requires knowing contribution margins at varying levels of production. It also requires knowing the price sensitivity and other characteristics of a segment. Such understanding, combined with variable pricing, can bring in profitable, incremental revenue. The classic example is the airlines, which sell discount tickets after they have sold the expected number of full-fare tickets. To support higher pricing to various segments, differentiation can include location, time of purchase, volume, services and design. Because of the variables involved, segmented pricing is the most difficult strategy to implement, although the pay-offs can be immense.

Many attempting to compete on pricing offer lower prices across the board. But such across-the-board pricing hurts profitability by benefiting those who would have bought anyway at a higher price. One benefit of segmentation is to identify price-sensitive customers and what they buy. Prices can be lowered on these items to generate increased volume – without affecting the profitable purchases by other customers.

Convince customers to pay for value

Effective pricing is based mainly on customer value, not costs or competitors. Companies create value for customers with the experiential, economic and emotional power of brands. If brands cannot understand and communicate their value to customers, customers will neither value the item nor purchase it at a price that maximizes profitability. So the issue becomes, how do you determine exactly what that customer value is and then convince customers to pay for that value? The first step is to identify the value that customers place on a solution to their issues.

In the dream world of economists, humans make logical decisions based on self-interest. While purchasing processes can be logical, the ultimate decision rarely is, even in the business world. The emotional and other factors that drive purchases are strongly influenced by perceptions of value, which vary according to knowledge, convenience and substitute availability.

Customer value and price sensitivity vary according to knowledge of substitutes. Companies can get higher prices when offerings are innovative or when access to alternative information is limited, such as when offerings are sold over the phone. Customer value also depends on the costs of switching to an alternative. Even a steep price advantage won't cause customers to defect if the potential risk of failure is high or the status quo is below a 'threshold of pain'. That is why Microsoft continues to command vast market share. Value also depends on immediacy of need, the size of expenditure relative to budgets/revenues and 'shared cost' – whether someone else is picking up the bill.

Value is sometimes determined by price sensitivity, which is driven by access to information or psychology. For example, a US $20,000 order for parts would not be renegotiated if a competitor offered the same parts for US $19,600. However, a purchase order for US $1,000 would quickly be cancelled if a competitive offering was available for US $600, even though the US $400 savings is the same in both cases.

Prospect price sensitivity is affected more by comparative price levels than by actual price. For example, three items offered at US $300, US $600 and US $900 would attract the same segments they would if the goods were priced at US $200, US $250 and US $300. This means that introducing a premium-priced offering above a profitable segment can pay off. The new 'middle' segment is then presumed to have greater value because it is priced below the premium offering. Nokia, for example, often introduces luxury mobile phones. Sales of the new offering may be minimal, but overall profitability increases because purchasers in search of 'value' buy more of the middle segment.

This strategy represents a competitive tactic. In one case, a competitor directly targeted a profitable offering from a spirits vendor. At first, the company considered dropping its price and/or spending more on promotion. Ultimately, the firm raised the price of its existing product, introduced a new brand at the original price and added a low-cost offering as part of the product family. The line extension strategy increased market position and profits.

A primary ProfitBranding goal is to change customer perception of value, and shape the willingness to pay for that value. The product can be compared to a more costly substitute. Economic or other value can be explained more effectively. Emotional value can be enhanced through differentiation. Buyers are less sensitive to price when they value a differentiator. Heinz commands a premium because US consumers like thick ketchup. Black-bodied cameras usually cost more than their metal-finished counterparts, even though production costs are the same. An 'image' of exclusivity, individuality or safety can justify price. Look at Nikon in cameras and Harley-Davidson in motorcycles.

DuPont provides a good example of changing a perception of value, and then capitalizing on it through improved pricing. DuPont introduced irrigation pipes made from its Alathon 25 resin. These pipes lasted 5 per cent longer than competitive products. Despite an initial series of price cuts, the Alathon 25-based product made little headway in the market. So DuPont began advertising its value by illustrating the long-term savings in labour and crop damage associated with replacing worn-out irrigation pipe. The advertising enabled DuPont to increase the price of Alathon by 7 per cent. More important, sales doubled the next year.

In general, the more differentiated an offering, the less price sensitivity. Even commodities can be differentiated with services, quality control, financing, etc. A University of California study showed that mark-ups for commodity foodstuffs ranged between 8 and 20 per cent. More than 40 per cent of this variation was due to sales expertise or more effective 'adaptation' (read: differentiation) to the local market. Consultant Booz Allen studied more than 100 customers in a commodity market. In some cases, prices at similar volumes varied by as much as 300–400 per cent.

Older offerings at the end of their life cycles also represent a differentiation opportunity. These can be used to appeal to price-sensitive buyers or those who just require minimal functionality and support.

Capture value through pricing

Pricing discipline is key to capturing the value customers place on an offering. It makes little sense to determine customer value or calculate segmented pricing if profit can be given away through discounts or lower prices in a misguided attempt to win sales or market share.

A division of ServiceMaster first surveyed customers, asking 'What are the key drivers of satisfaction?' Answers included 'service people who show up for appointments' (58 per cent); 'provides trained specialist who can fix the problem' (57 per cent); and 'service people fix the problem the first time' (49 per cent). By contrast, the sales force had a firm belief that the only issue that mattered to customers was price, and that discounts were needed to drive sales growth. Examining data from more than 60 branches and thousands of customer accounts, the study also found huge variations in pricing.

The study fuelled two initiatives. The first was sales force education to support pricing discipline. ServiceMaster illustrated the impact of discounts by showing how discounting required many more sales to hit profit targets. They also showed the managers the results of the customer survey, which indicated performance was more important than price.

Another initiative involved focus groups. The focus groups revealed that, if on-time performance was achieved and the technician made the repair the first time, price was rarely an issue. This became the basis for the company's 'on-time service guarantee'. If a technician was late for an appointment, the customer received a US $50 rebate.

Focusing on what customers valued and ensuring pricing discipline paid off. ServiceMaster enjoyed US $4 million in incremental net profit in 2003, and a projected US $8 million improvement in margins in 2004.

As ServiceMaster learnt, misunderstanding the role of customer value can warp pricing decisions and decrease profitability. Other common pricing mistakes include the following:

- *Cost-plus pricing:* Although cost-plus pricing is routinely criticized, its beguiling simplicity still attracts. Just add up costs, tack on an acceptable profit and fill in the price tag. This approach has three problems. First, common accounting systems do a poor job of capturing such 'hidden' costs as process or inventory-carrying costs. (Activity-based costing (ABC) is required to capture these costs.) That means that cost-plus pricing will fail to capture all costs, hurting profitability. Another problem is that setting prices based on costs reduces incentives to cut costs, since the higher costs appear to be recovered through higher prices. Finally, cost-based pricing also ignores the role that competitors and customers play in pricing. As Chrysler Group CEO Dieter Zetsche said when explaining corporate losses, 'You cannot price a car based on your costs. You have to price it to the market, and we ignored that principle.'

- *Competitor-driven pricing:* This also has appealing simplicity: match the price of a competitive offering. But what if competitors also lack knowledge about the market? Companies assume that pricing below a competitor provides an advantage while pricing above it leaves them out of the running. That is not necessarily true. Pricing below a competitor only provides a short-term advantage at the cost of lower margins. Competitor-based pricing fuels price wars, hurting corporate and industry profitability. And price is just one of many factors considered when purchasing.

- *Customer-driven pricing:* Companies bow to customer pressure for lower prices because of the ceaseless search for sales or market share growth, and because they do not understand their value to customers. Compensation schemes also motivate sales forces to emphasize volume instead of profitability. It is easiest, from the sales force perspective, to keep cutting prices – and profitability – until contracts are signed. The issue with customers must never be 'what price are you willing to pay?' Instead, it must be 'do you need the competitive values we offer?' Sales forces, understandably, resist price discipline since it means a willingness to walk away from price-sensitive sales. But losses in profitability can never be made up with sales or market share.

Customer-driven pricing also risks that customers will learn about lower prices elsewhere. Insurance firm USAA 'persuaded' a vendor to cut a price from US $7 million to US $2 million after learning that the vendor had sold the product to another at the lower price.

PRICE HIKES AND DROPS: MATCH CUSTOMER VALUE

Pricing is often discussed in terms of sales. However, pricing is only a means to an end – increased profitability. Prices should only be cut if it drives additional demand that leads to increased contribution margins. By the same token, there's nothing wrong with raising prices, as long as the probable drop-off in demand does not decrease overall profitability.

A low price won't drive sales unless prospects can appreciate the value, and a high price is not a barrier to sales as long as ProfitBranding can communicate customer value. According to McKinsey & Company, companies often overestimate the risk of price increases. They also sometimes overestimate competitive reactions. Accenture found that 80 per cent of corporate buyers believe that brand and customer service are more important than price.

Price is always more significant in the mind of the seller than in the mind of the buyer. Companies fear raising prices because of potential customer loss. But the issue is the amount of money that falls to the bottom line, not the number of customers. Pricing doesn't make customers more or less loyal, according to The Gallup Organization. In numerous studies ranging from cars to current accounts, Gallup has found that price often plays no significant role in building repeat business. While price may stimulate trial, it is rarely a reason for loyalty. On the other hand, loyalty supports price increases. For example, personal insurance premiums go up about 8 per cent a year as families upgrade their cars and homes.

Buyers, especially in B2B, do not judge prices simply in monetary terms. They judge them in terms of their economic and other value. ProfitBrands win when their differentiation value – the value delivered by those services or capabilities not offered by a competitor – is greater than the cost. Convenience, payment terms and service are often more important factors for making or breaking sales.

Pressures to cut prices run strong. When customers threaten to take their business elsewhere, sales decline or competitors reduce prices, the knee-jerk reaction, especially from sales forces, is 'Cut prices!' The hope is that increased volume will make up for decreased margins. As ServiceMaster learnt, that is not always true. Alternative strategies must be explored before price cuts. For example, will customers asking for a price cut be satisfied by unbundling a service or other differentiator?

Serial price reduction usually leads to cuts in quality, service or other factors that affect the brand's value to customers. It also leads to even greater pricing pressures and harms the brand. If managers price offerings like commodities, then inevitably customers will see the offering as a commodity.

Prices are often set low during product introductions, when it is considered critical to entice 'triers' and penetrate markets. But studies indicate that people seldom buy a new offering just because the price is low. Initial pricing must always be related to an offering's value and equal to what a satisfied buyer would pay again. Branding must focus on educating prospects about that value and the certainty that it will be delivered. More effective for capturing those first key purchasers are 'try-before-you-buy' promotions, coupons and bundling.

Discounting can be a valuable tool. But it generally should not be used to increase sales volume. Instead, discounts must be used as a tool to reward and influence profitable behaviours. For example, discounts can give customers incentives to increase purchasing volume or to switch to more profitable products.

Discipline and analysis are vital. That is because price cuts, for whatever reason, are like cocaine. Yes, they provide a quick sales boost, but the long-term profitability consequences can be debilitating. A low-price strategy to 'buy' loyalty often only buys disloyalty, since price-driven customers will defect for lower prices elsewhere. Low-price strategies only reward customer promiscuity, not customer loyalty.

Price cuts can spark price wars, like the one in retail security systems that almost destroyed both Checkpoint Systems and Sensormatic. Another disadvantage of price cuts is that existing customers, not new ones, often take advantage of them. Only companies blindly pursuing sales or market share growth would institute a strategy based on attracting disloyal, price-sensitive buyers.

Rather than responding with knee-jerk price cuts, companies should first defend themselves with branding that limits price sensitivity or add greater or more certain value. Examples include longer service contracts, faster deliveries or extended warranties. That's not as easy as cutting prices, but it's a lot more important to sustaining financial health.

Other tactics include bundling or unbundling products or services. Pricing often covers both product and service. Over time, customers lose sight of what they're paying for. Unbundling lets customers receive the core offering at a lower cost and illustrates the value of accompanying services. Another unbundling benefit is that often higher prices can be charged for services. Bundling can lower cost-to-serve or change the profitability of the product mix. For example, PC manufacturer Gateway offers a warranty plan for US $99 per year that guarantees support calls will be answered in 30 seconds. Otherwise, a refund is given.

A successful pricing strategy can also be built around retention branding. Film rental firm Netflix, Microsoft and other technology firms that offer frequent upgrades, and others, seek profits through subscription-based offerings. Each transaction might be less, but costs are generally lower and long-term profitability higher.

Instead of price cuts, companies can reduce or increase product quality, change discounts or migrate price-sensitive customers to less expensive channels, such as the web. Companies can also extend their lines with 'value' offerings to appeal to the price-sensitive. For example, Pella, a maker of custom windows and doors, saw sales of its high-end offerings decline dramatically. Instead of cutting prices, the firm launched a lower-priced line. This extension offered buyers the same quality, but with a limited range of sizes and without any design services.

Avoid 'sucker pricing' that reduces loyalty. Companies lock in customers through contracts or proprietary implementations, and then keep prices unfairly high from the customers' perspective. Look at the wireless industry, where companies offer deals to new customers that are unavailable to existing ones. As a result, expensive 'churn' in the wireless industry reaches 25 per cent as customers jump ship at the first opportunity. Sucker pricing also generates bad word of mouth.

Setting prices is like setting a screw – a little resistance is a good thing. If prices cannot be raised directly, end discounts and incentives. Whenever prices are raised, be sure that service, value and other operational fundamentals remain strong.

Price cuts must always be the last resort, unless they are backed by sustainable decreases in costs that do not affect customer value. Price decreases hurt profitability, and may even harm the ProfitBrand image. Rather, other alternatives to increase customer value, decrease costs or alter customer price sensitivity must be explored. Prices must never be cut just to get business or meet sales objectives, especially if it hurts profitability. Price cuts only become necessary during the mature and end phases of an offering's life cycle, when customers are price-sensitive, and competitive alternatives plentiful.

CONCLUSION

Pricing is a complex issue, but the right price will never be found if the strategic goals are based on sales or market share growth. The temptation to cut prices – and profitability – in pursuit of growth will always lead to poor pricing decisions. ProfitBrands understand this. Hong Kong-based Cafe de Coral Group, which operates more than 510 outlets and is the largest Chinese quick-service restaurant group in the world, has recorded double-digit growth in profits for the past seven years in a row. According to chairman Michael YK Chan, better customer value comes through taste and service, not price. 'Being more creative and offering better food, service and ambience at a stable price is more important than lowering prices to attract customers. I refuse to win market share by price cutting.'

For maximum profitability, ProfitBrands must optimize pricing according to the economic, emotional or experiential value received by various segments, based on costs, price sensitivity, image or differentiation. Branding tactics then communicate value, change price sensitivity or optimize differentiation. If knowledge of customer value exists, and branding techniques are effective, price hikes can hold. In almost every case, price cuts are a last resort, unless cost reductions can be sustained.

It is also important to remember that pricing strategy and discipline are not enough. Companies must truly understand all costs, even process and other 'hidden' costs. Operational policies, rewards, organizational structure, information systems and control systems must also be dedicated towards maximizing the extraction of customer value.

Takeaways

- How is pricing determined? Does pricing start from an internal perspective by adding up costs or margin goals, or does it start from an external perspective based on an understanding of current or potential customer value? What research concerning costs, competitors and customers is involved?
- Can customer value be quantified? How does the value from your offering compare to the value from competitors, or even to a 'do-it-yourself' option by the customers? Is customer value reflected in pricing?
- Is the price sensitivity of segments known? Does branding concentrate on changing price sensitivity? Have pricing strategies been built into offerings and even customer life cycle plans?
- Why do you cut prices? How do price cuts affect profitability? What do you do if price cuts do not generate anticipated sales?
- Have you tried raising prices or bundling/unbundling offerings to increase customer equity? Did the increased profitability make up for probable customer loss?

8

ProfitBrand principles for brand communications

'It is difficult to launch a product through consumer advertising because customers don't really pay attention as they did in the past. I look at the money spent on advertising and it surprises me that people still believe they are getting returns on their investments.'

Howard Schultz, CEO, Starbucks

The mass economy made it easy to build brands. With sufficient frequency and reach as a battering ram, mass marketing could generate the awareness that opened the door to brands.

It's not easy any more. Continuing reliance on mass-economy models has led to brand communication oversaturation – in schools, on aircraft overhead compartments, in retail floors. Even cars are wrapped as ads now. It is worse online. JupiterResearch forecasted that each online consumer will receive nearly 1,600 retention-based e-mails in 2007, up from 800 such messages in 2003. No wonder a Yankelovich Partners study found 65 per cent feel 'constantly bombarded' by ads; 59 per cent feel that ads have little relevance; and, worst of all, almost 70 per cent said they would be interested in offerings that would help them avoid marketing. Research shows that viewers watch 20–30 per cent more television after getting a personal video recorder (PVR), but they use it to skip about 70 per cent of ads. Customers even pay not to see ads on websites like Slashdot.

Why has mass marketing lost its impact? Part of the reason is jaded, more sophisticated consumers who are faced with a cornucopia of options. Lack of creativity is sometimes blamed, but creative pixie dust rarely translates into magical results. How often are creative ads remembered but not the advertiser? The second most popular ad during the 2003 US Super Bowl featured a fictional football player who tackled anyone violating company policy. More than a third of viewers (38 per cent) thought it was a McDonald's ad. How the actual advertiser – Reebok – felt about spending money on someone else's behalf is not known.

Oversaturation and lack of impact contribute to lack of ROI. Deutsche Bank looked at the effectiveness of TV advertising on 23 new and mature packaged goods. Although sales volume increased, companies received a positive cash return on that investment only 18 per cent of the time. In other words, companies were losing money on 82 per cent of their branding efforts – not good news for the CFO. The study concluded that 'increased levels of marketing spending were less important than having new items on the shelf and increasing distribution'. Other studies have reached the same conclusion. In a Wharton business school study, a large retailer did not generate enough revenue to offset the cost of its extensive advertising programme. Another analysis of 45 brands concluded that, on average, every advertising dollar returns just US $0.54 for consumer packaged goods and US $0.87 for non-consumer packaged goods.

Not just advertising is suffering from ineffectiveness. After analysing its US $600 million trade promotion programme, packaged foods firm Kellogg's found that 59 per cent of its events lost money. *The Economist* has concluded, 'Some of the traditional methods of advertising and marketing simply no longer work.'

Companies are responding to this lack of ROI. Starbucks spent less than US $10 million advertising during its first 10 years, small change for a national brand. The Body Shop has never advertised. Zara, the fastest-growing retailer in the world, does no advertising except for two sale ads a year. Linux has 99.9 per cent name recognition in the high-tech community without any advertising. Other well-known brands such as Ben & Jerry's, eBay, Krispy Kreme and In-N-Out Burger spend little on advertising. Amazon.com has dramatically scaled back its advertising, preferring to spend the funds on service.

In many ways, this is unfortunate. Brand communications will always be critical. It turns prospects into buyers, shortens sales cycles, raises competitive barriers and communicates new and ongoing value. But what is required to make brand communications effective for the CEO and cost effective for the CFO?

Start by recognizing that brand communications can no longer be driven by the elementary need to 'get your name out there'. When the average consumer is carpet-bombed with 3,000 messages a day, 'awareness' is as difficult to find as an open lane during rush-hour traffic. Even awareness is not enough. Think of all the companies you are 'aware' of, but would never establish a relationship with. Yes, 'awareness' must precede action, just as a key must go into the ignition before driving, but that is much too low a threshold to justify the high cost of brand communications. As many companies have sadly realized after much expense, greater 'awareness' can still fail to contribute to profitability. General Motors has announced that building 'awareness' is no longer enough to award sponsorship money: all efforts must bring in at least 500 sales leads.

Effective brand communications rest on three foundations. First, all communications must incorporate one or more brand adoption goals: attraction; retention; and/or advocacy. The second involves constituencies, or audiences for the brand. Finally, brand communications must be targeted and integrated.

COMMUNICATION GOALS:
STRIVING TOWARDS ADOPTION

In the mass economy, the goal of most brand communications was *dissemination* to help build awareness. The goal in the customer economy has evolved into *persuasion*, or using logical or emotional appeals to encourage belief or purchase. Persuasion is a stepping stone toward the ultimate goal of *adoption*. Adoption occurs when profitable customers incorporate an offering into either their business operations or personal lives. Adoption enables a ProfitBrand to be seen as the best – if not the only – choice, based on its economic, emotional or experiential value. Adoption is not an event. It is a process, built on the back of operational excellence and reinforced by the ability to deliver solutions on customer terms. Without adoption, there can be no long-term relationship.

Adoption involves three stages:

- *Attract:* To attract, brand communications must use an offer and relevance to project a vision of a relationship. The key, however, is that the relationship must be seen as one that pays off for the customer. Communications without an offer or even the promise of a relationship is sometimes justified on the basis of 'brand building'. That's mass-economy thinking, and a wasteful luxury amid intense competition for time and attention. Without a direct or implied offer to drive an action, such vague advertising is almost always wasted on everyone but the advertiser's sales representatives. The offer must be relevant, based on economic, emotional or experiential customer value. Relevancy is established through targeting and communications on customer terms. Relevancy also requires timing. Much brand communications is wasted, not because offers are wrong, but because the timing is off. The most effective advertising is 'event based'. Prospects receive a message just as a desire or need emerges. For example, new car advertising has the most impact when leases are about to expire.

- *Retain:* Brand communications must focus less on acquisition and more on increasing customer, account and product penetration among profitable customers. The mutual fund company The Vanguard Group, whose brand communications are focused on retention, has grown 30 per cent annually even though its communications spending is only 10–15 per cent that of large competitors. PR, advertising, direct mail and other brand communications are vital both to reinforce the purchase decisions of existing customers and to inform them about new offerings. Brand communications are integral to loyalty programmes and even customer recovery.
- *Advocacy:* Brand communications must make it easy for customers to promote offerings. To brand Clean & Clear, a teenage skincare product, Johnson & Johnson gave girls the online ability to send one another electronic postcards. The postcards offered a free skin analysis and product sample. The response was several times higher than other online campaigns. Encourage pass-alongs of e-mails, catalogues and other material. Ask customers for the names of others who might be interested. Use promotions like pens and cups that serve as employee and customer gifts. Incentives can generate referrals. Myfamily.com gave away vacations when six or more family members signed up.

Encourage word of mouth, also called 'buzz' or 'viral' marketing. Word of mouth made Hotmail the most popular e-mail program in Sweden and India, even though it was never marketed there. eBay owes its success to word of mouth. Instead of launching with ads and PR, the founders demonstrated eBay's capabilities at collector shows, asking that friends tell friends. Collector newsgroups spread praise. Later, celebrity fans like Barbra Streisand boosted the site. eBay became not only a ProfitBrand but a cultural icon. Until the company went public, advertising was minimal.

However, word of mouth can also work against a company. Coke's experiment with New Coke remains a classic lesson. After spending US $4 million and interviewing 200,000 consumers, Coca-Cola introduced New Coke. In large-scale taste tests, New Coke swamped classic Coke, 63 per cent to 37 per cent. But after the introduction, Coke's brand zealots swamped the airwaves and other media with a 'good story' about Coca-Cola's 'betrayal'. Coca-Cola surrendered to the outrage, putting 'Classic Coke' back on the shelves. Coca-Cola ultimately let New Coke sink beneath the waves, despite spending almost US $50 million on the reformulation.

Despite hype, word-of-mouth marketing is not 'free' or 'easy'. It takes labour-intensive work to generate and sustain word of mouth. Targeting is hard, timing difficult and testing virtually impossible. Efforts may peak in a month or, as with eBay, take years. You don't know who is going to receive a message when, or even what they will say about it if it is passed on. Leads generated by word of mouth are often unqualified.

Another element of advocacy is 'seeding the vanguard'. Getting offerings into the hands of industry or consumer influencers – so-called prosumers – can pay off. Retailer Abercrombie & Fitch recruits students from popular fraternities to work in its stores, hoping that other students will mimic the discounted clothes the employees purchase.

CONSTITUENCIES: COMMUNICATING WITH COMMUNITIES

Brand communications often speak in terms of audiences, but that implies one-way, mass-economy communications, where the brand plays upon a stage and a homogeneous audience either cheers or boos. In the customer economy, those audiences no longer exist. Audiences have evolved into the constituencies familiar with every politician, who must consistently meet constituency demands for responsiveness and interactivity or lose the next election.

Every communications plan must be tailored to six constituencies: prospects, customers, media/analysts, investors, employees and, to a lesser extent, competitors. Even though these constituencies are critical to ProfitBranding, they have often been treated as antagonists.

Customers are kept on hold. Corporate contacts cannot be found on websites. Journalists receive responses after deadlines. Employees are the last to know. Investors have to use divining rods to find information buried in balance sheet footnotes. ProfitBrands cannot be built upon such antagonistic relationships.

Constituent communications has four goals: strengthen relationships by helping each constituency meet its own imperatives; solicit, collect and channel feedback; provide experiential, emotional or economic value; and ensure accountability. Constituency programmes must generate relevant information, ensure two-way dialogues, monitor communications and feedback, and measure outcomes. Responsiveness is vital. Each constituency must quickly be able to get the information it needs, in the form that it requires, in the time frame that is important. Remember that each constituency is not independent, but is instead characterized by networks with thriving, interconnected links. For example, journalists regularly talk to customers and investors.

Tools available for constituency communications include dialogue automation (e-mail, virtual press rooms); interactive communications channels (chat and discussion lists, blogs, intranets/extranets, IM); communications media (e-zines, newsletters, content syndication); and data collection and analysis (online surveys, online clip tracking/analysis, data mining). These are in addition to traditional tools like bulletin boards, press releases, speeches, community involvement, etc.

Prospects

Prospect dialogue starts with content. Content, once hailed as sovereign, is now in the dungeon. That's because the high costs of content development, combined with customer unwillingness to pay, made betting on content a losing proposition. But just because content cannot support a business does not mean it loses its importance in ProfitBranding. Content provides credibility, the first step toward trust and loyalty. As advertising legend David Ogilvy said, 'I do not regard advertising as entertainment or an art form, but as a medium of information.' Much brand communications fails because it lacks content or actionability.

Content encourages action. For example, purchasers of Bruce Springsteen concert tickets received a confirmation e-mail. Prior to the concert, ticket holders also received e-mail updates on Springsteen's tour, pre-concert activities near the arena, driving directions and even a view of the stage from their seats. Immediately following the concert, they received an e-mail from The Boss himself. Ticketmaster also sent out a concert play list at the same time, with links for buying CDs and concert items. Such content pays off. The day-after e-mails generated a 47 per cent response rate.

Converting prospects to customers requires responsiveness. Every website, direct mail, advertisement and even letter must provide a phone number or e-mail address. Prospect communications must be answered promptly. The second biggest ProfitBranding sin is not following up on a qualified lead. (The biggest sin, of course, is losing a profitable customer.)

Customers

How many companies still seek to 'position' offerings, even though passive audiences willing to accept corporate messages uncritically died with the mass economy? Now, two-way dialogue, fortified with content, credibility and responsiveness, is required. Despite lip service, companies shy away from dialogue because it often means responding to criticism. But if companies provide no avenues for dialogue, customers will create them elsewhere. Just look at blogs and the numerous websites devoted to discussing corporate activities.

Conversations about a brand are going to happen, with you or without you. Generating loyalty and trust requires involvement in the conversations. Recognizing the importance of dialogue, Procter & Gamble redesigned its site to encourage feedback. The site even encourages complaints about corporate products or activities. P&G understands it is better to hear customer criticism directly than to let them vent to other consumers. By the same token, Cisco reports all product bugs on its public web page. Not only does this help its customers, but it also provides an employee incentive to improve quality.

Companies are missing a prime branding opportunity by failing to solicit dialogue. According to a survey from Harris Interactive, based on interviews with 7,900 shoppers and 75 firms, 74 per cent of US consumers are willing to provide feedback on websites and 50 per cent are willing to answer questions about product preferences. However, only 38 per cent of consumer goods manufacturers ask for this feedback.

Media/analysts

The splintering of the mass media in the customer economy means public relations has to work harder at reaching media influencers, which range from vertical publications to blogs. But the efforts of many are lacking, wasting valuable opportunities to build brands. Just a third of corporate websites provide the press releases, contact information and corporate information that journalists seek, according to a Vocus study. Three out of five journalists surveyed said the lack of information affects coverage.

Measurement can occur through public relations audits or various sophisticated strategies to measure the effectiveness of outcomes, not just the efficiency of outputs (calls, press releases, etc).

Investors

A good investor relations (IR) programme offers content on multiple levels. The website offers current stock price and stock history, current and archived financial news (quarterly earnings, annual reports, key management changes, etc), event calendar (conference calls, stockholder meetings, etc), conference call transcripts, webcast replays and relevant contacts. Additional information can include officer and board information as well as lucid explanations of business strategies.

In addition to regular conference calls and investor conferences, dialogue can occur through e-mail. Dell offers an opt-in reminder service tied to its financial calendar. Customers can specify which financial events they want reminders for, and even how many days in advance they'd like to be notified for each selected event. Don't reserve dialogue just for mutual funds and other large shareholders. Respond to individual investors as well – quickly. In the customer economy, a single committed investor – aka 'gadfly' – can impact a ProfitBrand.

Monitoring financial communications is even more important than for other corporate communications. Commentary – or rumours – on various financial commentary sites can dramatically affect share value. Financial institution commentary should also be closely monitored. An imperfect measurement for financial brand communications is, of course, the share price. Although fundamental forces are at work, financial brand communications can contribute to improved share performance.

Employees

'Always the last to know.'

That common employee complaint indicates that companies are failing at one of their most important branding activities – employee communications. News on bulletin boards stays up for ever. Rumours fly along corridors. Ultimately, this hurts a ProfitBrand. Customers are poorly served by poorly informed employees. Change management is complicated. Dissatisfied employees generate negative corporate news or, worse, sabotage corporate efforts. Unless employees believe in the ProfitBrand, and understand the importance of customer relationships and retention, customer interactions will suffer.

Employees must always be the first to know information that affects them. Keeping employees informed generates numerous benefits. Knowledgeable employees are more loyal. Numerous studies indicate that the greater the employee loyalty, the greater the customer loyalty. For example, consulting firm Bain & Co surveyed a national car service firm. It found that outlets with the highest employee retention also had the highest customer retention. Not surprisingly, these outlets were also highest in productivity and profitability.

Effective tactics include appointing communication leaders to relay information from upper management, providing communications on employee terms (e-mail, voicemail, meetings, print, etc) and putting corporate decisions in the context of customer, supplier or regulatory requirements. Feedback solicitation is vital. Every company should have an open-door policy, online and offline suggestion boxes and hotlines for critical issues. Such programmes can be measured by readership and other surveys, 'grapevine studies', behaviour versus vision comparisons, etc.

Competitors

Brand communications toward competitors can ward off price wars, dampen competition and fight regulation. Companies reflexively hide information from competitors. But sometimes 'leaking' competitive plans can support industry pricing discipline and keep companies from being ambushed by negative customer reactions. For example, companies in the airline industry routinely pre-announce price increases. If competitors join in, the price hike holds. If not, the higher price is rescinded, without affecting market share.

Brand communications can also signal to competitors about intentions and capabilities. After Chrysler established the minivan market in the early 1990s, other car manufacturers thought about jumping in. In a speech well covered by the press, a top Chrysler executive announced that the company planned to build a low-price minivan. 'If it ever comes to a price war in minivans, I am convinced that we can win it,' he said. Message to competitors: destabilize the market, and you'll lose the price war.

In other cases, explaining advantages can encourage competitors to abandon a market. For example, Goodyear built a new tyre plant that allowed it to cut prices. It conducted highly visible plant tours and analyst briefings, outlining the cost-cutting automation. Weaker competitors soon withdrew from the market.

COMMUNICATION PRINCIPLES: ETERNAL VERITIES OF BRANDING

Billions of words have been written about advertising, PR and other brand communications. All the advice boils down to eight principles, which are discussed in the following sections.

Set objectives

Accountability is impossible without objectives. Set quantitative and qualitative objectives before beginning any programme. Use the right metrics. Metrics must relate to either the retention of profitable customers or activities that create customer value.

Target

Targeting improves response by about 10 times compared to a 'one-size-fits-all' approach. Better targeting has substantially increased Procter & Gamble's advertising ROI. In 1998, P&G spent 10 per cent of sales on advertising to increase unit sales volume by nearly 4 per cent. In 2003, P&G spent US $4.4 billion, or 10.1 per cent of sales, on advertising, yet achieved a 9 per cent jump in unit sales, thanks to improved targeting.

Mass media are dying a death of a thousand cuts, as companies turn to segmented media for targeted brand communications. A study by the

Wall Street firm Sanford C Bernstein & Co predicted that, by 2010, companies will spend more for advertising on cable (US $27 billion) and the internet (US $22.5 billion) than on network TV (US $19.1 billion) or in magazines (US $17.4 billion). Even *Time*, the prototypical mass magazine, now runs as many as 20,000 ad-customized versions of its national edition. Household targeting is already possible. The libertarian monthly *Reason* customized one issue so each of its 40,000 subscribers received a copy with a close-up satellite photo of his or her local area on the cover. Online ads can be targeted more precisely than almost all offline media. Such targeting enables contextual advertising, where ads can be placed within closely related editorials or timed to respond to prospect action. The online edition of the *Wall Street Journal* used 'behavioural targeting' to pinpoint frequent flyers based on how much time readers spent on travel articles. These readers were then presented with American Airline ads whenever they logged on. As a result, the number of business travellers who saw the ads more than doubled.

Targeting is also critical to PR. Unfortunately, that is a sermon frequently made, seldom heard. A survey of 1,750 journalists by the Council of Public Relations Firms indicated the top five pet peeves concerning PR professionals were irrelevant story pitches (80 per cent); annoying phone calls (74 per cent); not understanding the publication (63 per cent); not understanding a reporter's beat (54 per cent); and e-mail attachments (45 per cent). Targeting eliminates such PR sins.

Leverage interactivity

Digital media are blessed by three advantages over mass media. First, they are interactive. This capability enables personal information to be collected so that offerings can be adjusted. Online media can engage viewers and enable them to view offerings from multiple angles, get questions answered or customize experiences. Data collection is easy. Applications can track conversion, click-throughs and other actions, and analyse profitability, buying patterns and preferences, seasonality and returns. Finally, this interactivity and analysis enable accelerated marketing velocity. For e-mail campaigns, for example, about 90 per cent of results are available within 48 hours, allowing rapid tailoring and fine-tuning of subsequent campaigns.

However, interactivity only works if companies take advantage of it. Market researcher AMR Research reported that 38 per cent of marketers failed to e-mail regularly to customers. Worse, companies are failing to meet customer expectations for responsiveness. Customers expect e-mail answers within eight hours, yet the average corporate response time is roughly three days.

Integrate

Integrated unity is vital. Differing messages in differing media – or even different looks – dilute brand communications. Themes, colours and even copy must echo each other throughout all media. This reinforces messages, avoids confusion and significantly boosts response. Integrated unity also leverages growing cross-channel habits. Consumers read while watching TV. They listen to radio on the internet. They research online and buy in stores. In one study, 62 per cent of marketers integrated traditional and interactive efforts. In that group, almost two-thirds reported a 5–10 per cent increase in response. Furthermore, 16 per cent saw an increase of 11 per cent or more.

Track

Track leads, campaigns, customers and operational execution. Tracking starts with sales representatives asking 'How did you hear about us?' and continues beyond the last service call. Every ad, brochure, white paper, coupon or even press release must have a tracking mechanism (special phone numbers, mailing codes, URLs, etc). Every database program must have a field for identifying the lead source. The lead must be tracked all the way through to sales conversion, to account and customer pene-tration and even to defection. That reveals which branding is producing profitable customers. Especially track leads and sales to existing customers to measure customer, account and product penetration. Brand communications are primarily thought of in terms of acquisition branding, but they are also a significant retention branding tool.

Test

Testing takes two forms. Pre-testing assesses effectiveness before material is distributed. First show brand communications to existing high-profit customers. If the communications do not resonate with them, they will either not attract prospects or, worse, attract the wrong types of customer. Focus groups are also useful. Focus group testing can vary widely, from simple discussions to Orwellian set-ups where participants are wired to test emotional responses. However, be aware of pitfalls. For example, care must be taken that the focus group does not become a 'jury', simply picking a creative 'winner'. Although testing is expensive, it is extremely important, and saves money in the long run.

The second form is alternative testing. The same ad or direct mail is run in different media, at different times, or in the same publication via split runs. Test target segments, headline, copy or offer. Ideally, just change one variable at a time. This makes cause-and-effect analysis easier. Source code tracking is vital.

One advantage of online branding is that iterative testing can be done rapidly. As soon as early responses come in, the e-mail or advertising can be improved. Similar testing offline can take days or even months. Post-testing is valuable to measure results and fine-tune future programmes.

Measure

Measurement is common, but it is commonly measurement of the wrong things. Measurement is not about activities or such intangibles as 'brand equity'; instead, it is centred around profits. No longer are numbers-driven CEOs and CFOs content with spending billions on branding without knowing its contribution to profitability. A survey by the American Advertising Federation (AAF), an organization of major corporate advertisers, found that only 10 per cent of business executives surveyed agreed that ad departments were essential contributors to corporate performance. Only 16 per cent felt that PR departments were important to success. By comparison, 29 per cent felt that product development was essential.

At one time, it was believed that the internet solved branding measurement. That was because, for the first time, PR- or ad-inspired changes in behaviour could be tracked. It was even easy, if tedious, to measure results from specific campaigns.

The variety of data that can be captured via the web includes demographics from opt-in registrations, click-through tracking, demographic, location and other data from site traffic, chat room and bulletin board monitoring, etc. Debate about web measurement quickly gets arcane and technical. While collecting data is relatively easy, extracting meaning is not. Popular sites generate gigabytes of data daily. Extracting, analysing and archiving so many data is an expensive headache. It is not always clear which data are the most relevant, or how they relate to the retention of profitable customers.

However, the internet added a new level of accountability to brand communications. Look at the growing success of pay-for-performance (PFP) metrics such as pay-per-click. Instead of paying for an impression (ad view), advertisers pay for an action (sale, request for information, etc). PFP metrics are typically based on cost-per-action (CPA), including cost-per-conversion, cost-per-lead/enquiry and cost-per-sale. Some of the demand for PFP is due to unhappiness with the common cost-per-thousand (CPM) model, linked to the number of potential impressions. CPM is just a tool for media cost comparison. It does not reflect targeting or relevancy.

The demand for accountability has led PR organizations to generate output measurements – editors contacted, releases generated, pages viewed, etc. According to a survey of 4,200 PR professionals by a consortium of PR groups, more than 80 per cent provide clip books and tapes to prove 'success'. Such 'by-the-pound' measurements result in news releases sent out without news, or 'smiling-and-dialling' editors, all in the name of volume.

Recognizing the issue, PR groups have turned to various measurement alternatives. One is 'advertising value equivalency' (AVE). The value of the coverage is calculated by multiplying the column inches or seconds of air time by the advertising rate. Some multiply the AVE by three to account for editorial credibility, although this practice lacks statistical justification. AVE has been justifiably criticized on multiple grounds. One argument is that equivalency between advertising and editorial content has not been proved. A better, more sophisticated measurement is media content analysis. This uses computer algorithms and content analysis experts to produce data illustrating coverage value. The analysis evaluates whether media coverage reached target audiences, and whether it contained the organization's messages. It also measures 'share-of-voice' compared to competitors.

The customer-economy measurements that actually matter, however, are those impacting customer equity. Especially useful measurements detail the source of customer interest or acquisition. Was it a print ad, reference from a friend or an article? These measurements can be collected via lead tracking, before-and-after surveys, split testing, focus groups and other attitudinal or behavioural measurement techniques.

Analyse

Brand communications analysis often revolves around CPM or other measurements of efficiency. But even the cheapest advertisement or PR programme is no bargain if it does not result in profitable customers. Other common analyses are the number of enquiries or lead-to-sale conversion. Both are valuable, but are short-term measurements. What is more important is to track the number of enquiries converted into profitable customers. Monitor over time. Analyses are handicapped without historical data. Parse your data. Analysis is key because it not only enables results to be measured but also, just as importantly, provides lessons for product development, service and brand communications. Analysis must also address ROI. By combining goals and benchmarks with testing and/or results, companies can determine the cost-effectiveness of campaigns. Again, lead tracking and quantification are critical.

Numerous companies can help with brand communications analyses. These companies can provide media values for TV, radio, print and web exposure. Additionally, sophisticated software is available for such activities as intelligence gathering, content development and distribution, contact management, activity tracking and measurement.

CONCLUSION

In the light-hearted film *Weekend at Bernie's*, two eager young executives prop up a corpse. They seek to save their own skins by getting everyone to believe that the corpse, Bernie, is still alive.

Like Bernie, traditional brand communications died with the birth of the customer economy, but it's still being propped up by many agencies and corporate communications departments. In the mass economy, the media were primarily used as one-way funnels to prospects. Brand communications became a numbers game – the more releases distributed or ads run, the better. Outputs were stressed more than outcomes.

Such acquisition-focused brand communications no longer work. Because of oversaturation and various mental and technological filters, brand communications must expand from an overwhelming emphasis on acquisition to a focus on attraction, retention and advocacy aimed at customers, prospects, media/analysts and other constituencies.

Effective brand communications are based on time-tested principles. Although so much of the discussion about brand communications revolves around process – creativity, 'positioning', placement, flights and so on – it is vital to remember that the only thing that matters is outcomes. For ProfitBrands, the only outcome that counts is the attraction, growth and retention of profitable customers.

Takeaways

- Are brand communications more focused on acquisition branding or retention branding? Why?
- Are there specific communications programmes with benchmarks for each constituency? Is there a two-way dialogue with these constituencies?
- What brand communications measurements are being collected? Are measurements based on outputs or outcomes? Who is accountable for results?
- Are all brand communications integrated with the same visuals, messages and benefits? Are brand communications checked against operational 'ability to execute'?
- Is it easy for advocates to spread the word about your ProfitBrand with e-mail links, promotions, group offers, etc?

9

Establishing accountability through branding systems

'People don't cause defects. Systems do.'
W Edwards Deming, quality management guru

Customer relationships must be sown, nurtured and profitably harvested. To ensure efficiency and accountability in this process, systems are required. Systems ensure consistent methodology, rules, measurement and analysis. Yet how do most organizations handle customers? E-mail, Word, Excel and sticky notes. These are tools, not systems.

Brand profitability, accountability and sustainability require moving away from tools to systems. Systems, which the International Technology Education Association defines as a 'group of interacting, interrelated, or interdependent elements that function together as a whole to accomplish a goal', are vital for translating brand initiatives into results. Systems add structure, uniformity, discipline and measurement to processes. Routine activities are easily replicated, increasing efficiency. They institutionalize customer knowledge. Systems can automate data collection. Such capabilities are becoming increasingly important in an era of accountability and regulatory oversight, such as the US investor-protection Sarbanes–Oxley Act.

ProfitBranding requires two types of systems. The first is strategic, providing a panoramic overview of operations and objectives. Common strategic systems include scorecards, which involve a matrix of interrelated goals, activities and measurements, and the well-known Six Sigma, which seeks to reduce defects through measurement and the elimination of variability.

The second type is tactical. Tactical systems, which range from account management to territory management, enable managers to handle effectively the 'blocking-and-tackling' activities involved in generating leads, converting leads into customers and increasing customer profitability. The tactical systems most useful to branding are campaign management, lead management and CRM. Lead management systems track leads from prospects to customers while campaign management systems increase the effectiveness of acquisition and retention branding. Sometimes, these are stand-alone systems; at other times, they are part of complex CRM systems, which enable companies to capitalize on integrated customer and even operational views.

STRATEGIC SYSTEMS: EYES ON THE BIG PICTURE

Brand sustainability requires strategic systems. These systems ensure the capabilities to provide customer value, measure progress and generate profitability. Such systems need to be closely integrated with corporate strategic objectives. Several types of strategic systems are available, but all require top-level executive backing and long-range commitment.

Keeping score through scorecards

Developed in the early 1990s by Drs Robert Kaplan and David Norton, the Balanced Scorecard (BSC) is a framework that links business strategies with day-to-day activities. According to *Harvard Business Review*, BSC represents one of the most important management advances of the past 75 years. It is estimated that at least 40 per cent of Fortune 1000 companies, including Honeywell, Federal Express, GE and Wal-Mart, use some form of BSC. Other well-known scorecards include the Baldrige Award assessment model, and the EFQM (European Foundation for Quality Management) model.

The strengths of BSC and other scorecards derive from interlinking financial and non-financial indicators, tangible and intangible measures, internal and external aspects, and performance drivers and outcomes.

Scorecards organize disparate data and provide organizational benchmarks. By highlighting inevitable trade-offs, they help managers understand the interrelationships of activities to short- and long-term objectives. They identify areas for improvement and required investments in people, systems and organizational alignment. Scorecards can be used to communicate corporate and branding strategies, align departmental and other goals to the corporate mission, and generate feedback and measurements.

In a three-year study of UK firms, the Chartered Institute of Personnel and Development analysed why Tesco, Selfridges, Nationwide and other firms consistently outperform their peers. Several common themes emerged. One was a clear direction and purpose, well communicated and well understood. Another was usage of some form of scorecard. Selfridges, for example, regularly measures key benchmarks for shoppers, investors and workers. Other studies point out that many of the companies that have adopted some form of scorecards have outperformed their peers.

For example, the BSC has four interrelated components, all vital to branding. These include:

- *Customers:* Analyses customer relationships. Measures include retention, customer profitability, customer satisfaction, service levels and win-back levels.
- *Internal business processes:* Tracks operational excellence. Measures include productivity rates, conversion rates, lead handling, quality rates and responsiveness.
- *Financial:* Looks at financial health. Measures include revenue growth, earnings, return on capital, cash flow, customer equity and customer, account and product penetration.
- *Learning and innovation:* Encompasses not only knowledge improvements but also relationships. Measures include employee retention, supplier relationships, IT capabilities, production quality, percentage of revenue from new products and even community involvement.

Scorecards require vision and strategy, objectives that support the vision and strategy, and relevant measurements that can track progress. Systems must collect relevant data for analyses. Rewards are matched to objectives. Feedback is incorporated into future efforts.

Scorecards can be challenging. Many companies cannot fully articulate their strategy and mission and link them to specific objectives. It is also tough to identify the processes that facilitate or block progress toward objectives. Metrics are ambiguous (eg 'excellence'). Executives make the common mistake of attempting to drive scorecards from the top instead of incorporating input from the rest of the organization. Finally, extensive change management issues, ranging from performance metrics to compensation to interdepartmental teamwork, can muddy waters.

Why should brand executives care more about scorecards than blue-lines? Short-term, they unite the brand around common goals and mutual understanding. Longer-term, they unify the organization around delivering value to customers, increase efficiencies and add accountability.

Six Sigma measures... and measures again

Six Sigma is a disciplined, data-driven methodology that seeks to measure, analyse, control and improve processes until they are near perfection. Six Sigma gets its name from continuous improvement until products and processes are 99.999966 per cent perfect. To put it another way, playing two rounds of golf a week, two sigma would mean missing six putts per round. Six Sigma means missing a putt every 163 years.

Six Sigma is a working practice at Motorola, GE, Sony, Telstra, Airbus and even in the kitchens of restaurant chains. Results have been impressive. Motorola estimates that Six Sigma has saved US $16 billion over 15 years. Dow Chemical put its savings at US $130 million over two years; Kodak, US $50 million. At GE, no manager gets promoted without Six Sigma training.

Six Sigma has primarily been applied to manufacturing, where defects, cycle times and inventory levels can significantly impact costs, quality and customer value. However, Six Sigma was never based on 'quality in everything built'; it's 'quality in everything done'.

As a result, Six Sigma represents a strategic branding system. Six Sigma can ensure that branding has a clear customer focus, structured measurement and minimal waste. It allows managers to structure projects around the best tasks, tools and deliverables. It can eliminate such branding 'defects' as leads not converting, visitors leaving websites, order-entry errors and inaccurate customer data. Once the causes of those defects have been identified, then processes – and the branding – can be improved.

The customer-focused, data-driven methodology is spreading to services. Raytheon applied Six Sigma to its legal department and saved US $20 million. Dow is expanding its programme to marketing. The Canadian firm Bombardier has shifted its Six Sigma emphasis from cost reduction and efficiency improvement to projects that increase sales volume and margins. DuPont is using Six Sigma to find the link between advertising and price premiums.

Honeywell Aerospace used Six Sigma to improve customer relationships. Since customer data were stored in more than 160 systems scattered across 16 lines of business and 11 business units, Honeywell lacked an integrated view of customers and requirements. With 40 product lines to market, several salespeople would contact the same customers during the same week or even the same day without knowing it. Large customers had as many as 50 points of contact with the company. Customer relationships suffered as a result.

Recognizing the problem, Honeywell adopted Six Sigma. Its Six Sigma initiative identified four key branding processes: customer service request and issue tracking, sales and lead management, campaign management and customer satisfaction.

The first step was consolidating customer databases and enhancing tracking capabilities. Sales representatives, field service engineers, product personnel and others could then see customer products, outstanding service issues and potential sales opportunities. Additionally, service requests could easily be routed to the right engineer.

Since implementing the new system, Honeywell has increased on-time problem resolution from 45 per cent to 83 per cent and reduced response time by 27 per cent. Customer satisfaction improved by 38 per cent. In the first year, the system was credited with a rise in revenues from US $45 million to more than US $100 million in one division.

Using monthly and quarterly measurements, GE Appliances applied Six Sigma to its PR department. Results included a 16 per cent decrease in 'cost per positive media impression', an 8 per cent increase in the number of positive media impressions and a 20 per cent decrease in negative media impressions.

Briefly, Six Sigma is based on the following steps:

- *Define:* A team identifies a project based on business objectives and 'voice of the customer' (VOC). The team also identifies 'critical to quality' (CTQ) characteristics.
- *Measure:* The processes that affect CTQ are identified. Defects related to those processes are measured.
- *Analyse:* Teams study why defects occur, and the key variables in each process.

- *Improve:* The effects of the key variables on each process are quantified. Then a system for measuring and enforcing deviations from an acceptable range is developed. If necessary, the process is modified.
- *Control:* Efforts continue to ensure that key variables remain within acceptable ranges.

Six Sigma has detractors. Some argue that it is best for repetitive processes, and cannot effectively be applied to services, which have a lot of unstructured functions. That is a valid argument, yet every service has numerous repetitive processes, ranging from filling out forms to sending out follow-up information. How often has a customer been lost because a standardized process wasn't followed? Six Sigma is not meant to measure or limit creativity, but only to improve the processes that affect customers and provide data for accountability. Some dislike Six Sigma because of its statistical emphasis. Yet spreadsheets and other software can do the heavy lifting, and everyone in business today must understand basic concepts like median and standard deviation.

TACTICAL SYSTEMS: IDENTIFYING, MONITORING AND MEASURING

Once strategic systems are in place, tactical systems are required to ensure effective execution. Lead management, campaign management and CRM systems support both acquisition and retention branding. However, other systems such as warehouse management, procurement, human resources, etc are also required to deliver customer value.

Lead management keeps leads from being a lost cause

According to the Center for Exhibition Industry Research (CEIR), 9 out of 10 companies attend trade shows to generate leads. Yet about 80 per cent of those leads are not followed up. Horror stories about opening a booth for a new trade show and finding leads from the last one abound. A survey by Response Direct Publishing in the UK found that an astonishing 50 per cent of advertisers did not respond to requests for information from consumers who viewed the ad within 10 weeks.

What sad statistics, yet so symbolic. The success of branding efforts is frequently measured in terms of leads, but many leads are lost, ignored or forgotten until long after the customer has made an alternative purchase. Generating a lead is less than half the battle. It does not count until a lead has been converted into a profitable customer. Leads represent the great divide between marketing and sales. 'Sales never follows up on the leads we give them,' says marketing. 'That is because we never get any good ones,' retorts sales, which justifiably loses time and faith when given unqualified enquiries.

The problem is not a lack of good leads. It is a lack of process. A lead-tracking process starts with knowing the source of a lead. Every ad and direct mail piece must have a code. Every call-in prospect must be asked 'How did you hear about us?' The tracking of leads is critical not only to determine which efforts generated the most prospects but, more importantly, which efforts resulted in the most profitable customers.

The process continues through determining who is a qualified current or future prospect. That takes work that neither marketing nor sales enjoys doing. Responsibilities and resources for qualification must be clear and constantly underscored.

Other issues affect lead handling. Timing is critical. Call a prospect immediately, and a sale is made. But call in two weeks, and that sale has gone to a competitor. Or call a lead without contextual information, such as industry knowledge or even whether the lead may be an existing customer, and the sale may be lost.

How do leads become prospects? First, determine what information is required to qualify a lead. Get input from sales as well as other parts of the organization. Train call centre representatives and other employees to capture relevant information. Then qualify the leads. Qualified leads consist of those with the 'right' answers to questions about need, readiness and ability to purchase. This qualification can occur through research, or by answering questions on a web or other form or during an initial interview. A continuing dialogue communicates where prospects are in the purchasing process as well as relevant issues. Issues can include decision makers, requirements, competitors, budgets and timelines. Ensure that processes match customer steps to a sale.

After qualification, convert prospects into customers or nurture those not ready to buy immediately. Such nurturing can be done with calls or e-mails at appropriate times. Systems must also be able to drop prospects after events such as a competitive purchase. However, be alert to lead recovery. One company found that 56 per cent of its leads that were six months old were still in the market for its offerings.

Lead management (also known as opportunity management) systems, which automate tracking, management and measurement, help transform caterpillar leads into customer butterflies. They help weed out the unqualified, and track prospects until purchase or disqualification.

Lead management systems can consolidate leads from across an organization, enforce sales and other standards, ensure timely routing to appropriate professionals and enable ROI calculation by linking leads to sales and branding investments. Lead management systems can also help qualify prospects, respond automatically to informational requests and alert professionals to follow-ups and other required events. For example, ESRI, which specializes in geographic information systems, asks prospects to fill out online questionnaires. Depending on the responses, ESRI sends sales materials or forwards information to its lead management system as a pre-qualified lead. The system increased ESRI's sales conversion rate to 30 per cent.

Lead management systems show the status of each lead (new, qualified, lost, etc), track the sales process, provide alerts concerning slow-moving leads or windows of opportunity and often include data useful to closing the sale, such as competitive data, timing and expected budgets. Such information increases sales representative productivity and allows representatives to take advantage of buying windows. By seeing how leads are moving through the pipeline and knowing conversion/win/loss data, managers can better guide and coach sales forces. Forecasting improves, too.

Poly Hi Solidur illustrates what a lead management system can do. The polymer producer generated 8,000 leads per year from ad, web, direct mail, trade show and other brand communications. However, a manual lead management process handled these leads poorly. Marketing took a week to qualify and relay leads to sales. Many leads fell through the cracks. Sales resulting from leads were not tracked. The company was unable to calculate marketing ROI.

Poly Hi Solidur then automated lead management. The new system instantly routes data when prospects complete a web form. Trade show leads are scanned into the system, eliminating the mistakes common to manual data entry. Based on time to buy, budget size, materials requested, request for call by salesperson and other business rules, the system automatically ranks each lead as 'hot', 'qualified opportunity' or 'closed'. Using industry databases, the lead is enriched with such data as numbers of employees, revenue, branch locations and additional contacts.

Once qualified and enriched, the lead is routed to the sales force via web browser, e-mail, pager or other device. Leads are tracked to confirm that sales representatives accept leads. If a lead is not accepted after 72 hours, sales managers are notified. The system also tracks leads routed to distributors. This enables Poly Hi Solidur to track the status of every lead throughout its life cycle and measure the ROI of each marketing programme.

Key reports include the number of leads accepted in each sales territory, lead-to-sale closure rates and the average time from lead acceptance to closure. Plans can be compared to actual data. Analysis showed Poly Hi Solidur that its website and trade shows generated the most profitable leads.

Some systems also automate how leads are provided to the channel, or resellers. Systems let companies track sales performance against targets and create scorecards to measure partner performance. Computer distributor Avnet lets resellers view pre-qualified leads online. The system also helps resellers evaluate leads and resulting business. The system allows Avnet to measure better the efficiency of its branding investments on behalf of resellers.

Campaign management creates branding order out of marketing chaos

Marketing often is the four-year-old in the organization. It frequently jumps up and down, yelling 'look at me!' It shouts out with direct mail, calls or e-mails, hoping for attention. It relishes its independence. But exuberance and energy do not excuse a lack of focus, quality or execution. ProfitBranding requires coordinated, focused campaigns for various segments with well-targeted messages that communicate value.

That is logical, but difficult. The choices are immense (ads, PR, sponsorships and more), resources are limited and the permutations among channels, messages, audiences and frequency are infinite. The problem is compounded when the goal is elevated from response to profitability. The solution is campaign management. Campaign management identifies which segments are most likely to respond profitably to an offer, executes the offer through the most appropriate channels and evaluates and refines the effort. Campaign management seeks to increase customer, account and product penetration while increasing retention as cost-effectively as possible. Currently, the complexities of campaign management are often handled with spreadsheets and tickler systems, but more companies are turning to automated systems.

For example, FBTO, a Netherlands-based insurance company, turned to campaign management software to optimize its direct mail, telemarketing and web marketing. The software helps FBTO determine to whom to send offers, which offers to send, when to send them and which channels to use. One capability includes cross-campaign optimization, or the ability to enhance customer targeting across multiple campaigns. While traditional campaigns seek the best prospects, FBTO's system matches the most appropriate campaign for each prospect. Such campaign analysis evaluates all the potential offers for a prospect or customer, and selects the one with the greatest potential for profitability.

Benefits to FBTO have been substantial. Campaign volumes have been cut by 40 per cent, saving postage and other costs. Response rates have doubled. The first campaign using the automated system generated 29 per cent more profit at the same cost as previous campaigns. Other companies have reported similar results with campaign management systems. The Australian bank BankWest commonly achieved response rates of more than 35 per cent with less waste with its system.

Branch offices and even distributors can get involved with customizing campaigns for specific requirements. For example, Sharp Electronics LCD Products Group used campaign management software to differentiate its marketing efforts within its dealer network. The system reduced marketing costs by 400 per cent in six months.

In addition to running campaigns with greater savings in postage, labour and other costs, campaign management systems improve marketing velocity, or the time required to conceive, execute, measure and alter subsequent initiatives. More campaigns can be run in less time. Results from one campaign can be rapidly incorporated into future campaigns, making them more effective more quickly.

Campaign management systems are most effective when used in conjunction with databases and analytical business intelligence tools like predictive modelling. A mobile telephone company analysed its database to select customers in the ninth month of 12-month contracts. This is when most customers weigh renewal or defection. This group was further refined by only selecting profitable customers whose spending averaged more than US $125 a month. Each of these customers was then offered a free phone or other valuable offer to renew.

While targeted, this approach wasted money. Free phones went to customers who would have renewed without any incentive. Predictive modelling would have identified profitable customers most at risk of defection. The campaign management system could then have executed a special renewal offer just for these customers. The software could also track the success and profitability of this campaign.

Although campaign management tools have been used since the mid-1990s, capabilities have substantially advanced in the last few years. Now, campaign management systems enable firms to anticipate how customers will respond to specific direct mail, e-mail and call centre campaigns, and calculate which campaigns will provide the greatest revenue. Business rules and optimization algorithms determine the best matches among segments, product offers and marketing channels. As a result, customers receive timely and relevant offers that address actual needs. Campaign management systems can help prevent such gaffes as when UK bank Abbey offered a loan via direct mail to an applicant just after the same bank had turned him down.

Systems can track multiple campaigns across multiple media, and successful campaigns can easily be modelled and reproduced. Campaign management systems are particularly valuable in customer retention and penetration efforts. Campaign management systems are linked to resource management, also known as production management, tools. These systems manage and track the myriad details associated with a campaign, ranging across design, copywriting, workflow and sign-offs. They are also used to track expenses and monitor budgets across multiple projects and teams.

CRM must be more than technology

CRM, which can include lead and campaign management capabilities, tracks customer responses throughout the sales cycle and synchronizes operational and other customer-related activities. Armed with this knowledge, companies can better coordinate interactions with customers, match service levels to profitability and understand customer value for more effective sales. Benefits include increased retention, faster sales cycles, lower sales and administrative costs, and more productive sales staff. Forecasting also improves.

CRM is so popular that even telephone headsets are sold as CRM tools. Because of the difficulty in monitoring and responding to customers, companies understand that systems are needed for end-to-end customer care. Companies also realize the costs and lost opportunities resulting from the lack of information integration. Customer information trapped inside multiple databases results in inconsistent service and incomplete customer views. Customers are treated like strangers when they want to be welcomed as family.

CRM promises to solve these issues. A common CRM goal is an integrated, or '360-degree', view of customers. CRM also promises to handle all interactions as a single, complete process instead of separate, isolated activities. With these capabilities, business can be done on customer terms. CRM has numerous trophy successes. After Collectibles.com, an online venture of broadcaster Shop At Home, built a CRM application, monthly revenue increased from US $125,000 to more than US $2 million. Gross margins rose to more than 30 per cent. A study by research organization IDC showed CRM projects yielding an immediate 8 per cent increase in revenues for large companies. Other companies have demonstrated revenue increases up to 42 per cent and margin improvements of 2 per cent from CRM.

Yet CRM often fails to live up to expectations. McKinsey & Company reported that only one in five US retail banks had increased profitability as a result of a CRM implementation. A study by the Cranfield School of Management in the UK cites surveys showing that 50 per cent of CRM projects do not produce results and, even worse, damage customer relationships 20 per cent of the time. Anecdotal horror stories abound. One Fortune 500 company tried four times to implement CRM. One reason for such difficulties is that CRM is used mainly as a technological tool. But the ability to deliver customer value rarely comes packaged in a box. CRM can do little unless companies design and align processes to do business on customer terms. For CRM to succeed, business rules must be standardized, workflow optimized and organizational data consolidated. Installing CRM as a technology without altering processes and organizational capabilities almost guarantees failure.

Successful CRM is not based on identifying who is most vulnerable to a sales pitch. Neither is it about improving transactional efficiencies, such as enabling service representatives to make more phone calls. Nor, finally, is CRM a technological lever to offload customers to automated systems to reduce costs.

Successful CRM systems share two characteristics: end-to-end customer care and institutionalization of customer knowledge. End-to-end customer care involves accurately and effectively handling customer orders from the initial sale through to the last day of support. It builds customer equity by facilitating coordinated, consistent responses, speeding problem resolution and giving customers insights into order, shipping and service processes. It makes interactions more effective, not transactions more efficient. According to an Accenture study, the five

CRM capabilities that consistently produced the highest impact were service, employee motivation, turning customer information into insight, attracting and retaining people, and strong selling and service skills.

The need to institutionalize customer knowledge is great. Many divisions in large companies do not even know if they share a customer with another division. Ideally, CRM systems collect and integrate relevant customer information from across an enterprise. This allows the company consistently to present one face to the customer, no matter how many 'touch points' – or areas of interaction – are involved. Transactions are more complete; interactions, more strategic. Retention and customer equity improve.

Once customer knowledge has been institutionalized, analysis can provide valuable insights into acquisition and retention strategies as well as resource allocation. Are processes supporting customer profitability? How is the company performing against customer expectations? What are customer costs-to-serve? What are the most frequent customer demands? CRM can also play a role in pricing. CRM can capture price sensitivity among customer segments, transactional histories for rules-based discounts and, of course, customer input for the differentiation that leads to increased pricing and profitability. CRM, in conjunction with business analytics, can also uncover customers who are relatively price insensitive, or cost more to serve, or are poorly served by competitors.

CONCLUSION

Anyone in branding is familiar with haphazard execution, missed deadlines and lack of coordination. Inevitably, the brand suffers. So agencies are fired or new gurus found. Sometimes, a new 'strategy' or 'positioning' is developed to erase all past sins. Such treatments rarely result in cures.

Problems remain because much of branding lacks accountability to measurable goals and process repeatability. This makes it difficult to determine what worked or not, and ensure that mistakes made once are not repeated. As a result, strategic and tactical branding systems are required. By establishing, measuring, managing and improving processes that affect customers, systems lead to better acquisition and retention branding as well as optimized customer relationships. Systems help meet customer requirements for value-based service, quality or experience.

Both strategic and tactical systems are required. Strategic systems like scorecards and Six Sigma not only give the organization common, customer-focused goals but also lay out the roadmap and milestones for achievements. Tactical systems, including lead management, campaign management and CRM, gain much of their strength from a common prospect and customer database. Branding is often associated with creativity, presentation and emotional impact. While these are important, it is critical to understand that branding is a collection of processes that produce customer value. Processes have metrics. Metrics can be improved. And systems provide structures and tools for improving those metrics.

Takeaways

- How complete, accurate and integrated are customer and prospect data? Are customer data 'owned' departmentally or shared organizationally?
- What strategic systems are in place to improve operations, processes and customer profitability? What are their objectives and measurements? Are the systems understood and shared throughout the organization?
- Is lead management automated? Can leads be linked to specific brand investments? Are leads tracked through conversion into profitable customers? Does the system help nurture prospects that may buy in the future? Does it provide the enriched data and timely alerts that help close sales?
- How are customers or prospects selected for campaigns? Are targeted offers based on either segmentation or previous behaviour? Are communications and campaigns relevant to targets? Are results incorporated into future efforts?
- Are your processes capable of doing business on customer terms? Does the CRM system support those processes? Does CRM help provide better, more timely services and information to customers or just increase sales efficiency?

10

Establishing accountability through effective metrics

'There is measure in all things.'

Horace

'Make the numbers.'

Organizations run on metrics. Sales numbers. Inventory turnover. Machine availability. Hold times. Defect rates. Measures are vital for setting goals and ensuring accountability. But, for too long, branding professionals have been exempt from the rigour demanded from their organizational peers. ROI is unquantified. Branding activities are pursued as acts of faith. For example, Willott Kingston Smith and the PACE Partnership asked 20 UK agencies to score their performance in 14 client management areas. The agencies rated themselves highest in the area of 'media neutrality' and 'good work' (surprise). But few agencies had measurement systems and even fewer were paid based on results. In an age of internet collaboration, few had sites that enabled clients to track projects, share information or measure outcomes. How can such agencies help clients brand when they are not involved in activities that deliver customer value?

It is not just agencies. In 2004, the CMO (Chief Marketing Officers) Council surveyed more than 1,000 CMOs at technology firms representing more than US $400 billion in annual revenue. Even though nearly 70 per cent of companies with annual revenues greater than US $500 million considered measurement a top priority, fewer than 20 per cent had meaningful metrics. More than 80 per cent were dissatisfied with their ability to quantify the value of branding campaigns.

The CMO Council survey delivered two important findings. First, companies with measurement systems had significantly greater performance. 'Specifically, companies with a formal comprehensive MPM (marketing performance management) system significantly outperformed companies that had not even entered the consideration phase, with mean performance ratings 29 per cent, 32 per cent and 37 per cent better in relation to sales growth, market share and profitability,' according to the study, entitled *Measures and Metrics: The marketing performance measurement audit*. That is not surprising. Measuring what works and what doesn't enables executives to do a better job at acquiring, retaining and growing profitable customers. Not surprisingly, those companies that did have formal brand measurement programmes reported superior financial returns and greater CEO confidence in branding.

The other finding was that CEOs, boards and other executives are demanding quantification that proves branding investments pay off. Additionally, research firm IDC has reported that 50 per cent of CMOs are under mandates to provide better measurement. As the CMO Council report noted, 'CEO satisfaction with the marketing function varied in a statistically significant manner with adoption of MPM. Generally the greater the adoption of MPM, the more satisfied the CEO.'

What brands require more than 'personality' or other nostrums *du jour* is accountability. Once, mass media were so powerful and measurement tools so primitive that branding accountability was not an issue. But as the mass economy fades and customers begin to reign in the new economy, measurement must be at the heart of all branding. Otherwise, the brand will be hurt by an inability to link and measure goals, activities and outcomes.

Measurement generates numerous advantages besides accountability. These include more effective branding, ROI tracking, cost justification for branding programmes and cost-effective resource allocation. They enable consensus building by focusing discussion on data instead of individual agendas. US retailer Best Buy spent more than $50 million on a 'customer-centric' programme after a 32-store pilot demonstrated that sales improved 7 per cent and its close rates – the percentage of shoppers who made a purchase – improved by 6 per cent compared to the remainder of its 600 stores. Training included teaching store associates about the importance of such metrics as ROI for measuring results.

Admittedly, measurement is more difficult for branding than for other corporate activities. It is easy to examine incremental costs and revenues associated with a new machine and calculate ROI. Multiple systems can track output per hour and other productivity barometers. Numerous soft factors and hard-to-track pay-offs complicate branding measurements. But such difficulties do not mean that companies should absolve marketing of the duty to measure investments and progress toward quantifiable goals.

FINDING THE RIGHT METRICS: FINANCIAL, CUSTOMER AND OPERATIONAL

What type of metrics are required for branding? They are financial, customer and operational measures that are aligned with corporate strategic objectives. They are reliable, unambiguous and, ideally, predictive. Metrics must be understandable to change behaviours. They are standardized and repeatable to enable trending over time. They are actionable, with a direct and demonstrable impact on customer value and corporate performance. And they must be widely accepted. If no one agrees on the numbers, everything else is irrelevant.

Accountability requires goals linked to metrics. Examples include 'increase lead conversion rate by 5 per cent', 'reduce the number of unprofitable customers by 8 per cent' and so on. Metrics also apply to operations: 'reduce order turnaround by 24 hours', 'reduce complaints by 15 per cent' and so on. Metrics must be as specific as possible, with steps, timetables and expectations. 'Improve customer satisfaction' is a wish, not a goal incorporating accountability. For example, the Radisson hotel chain uses such metrics as franchise sales and retention, room rental percentage and average rates, and the number of guest stay extensions. It also looks at guest willingness to return and to refer. It measures complaints per 1,000 occupied rooms. It also quantifies the customer equity of its Gold Rewards loyalty club members.

The right metrics are empowering. They lead people to work smarter, not harder. With the right metrics, managers and employees are empowered to maximize profitability. Remember that firms become exactly what they measure. Customer-focused organizations start by focusing on metrics that benefit customers.

Table 10.1 Key branding measurements

Objective	Metrics
Financial growth	
Maximize margins	Profit (contribution margin)
Maximize customer equity	Customer equity, cost-to-serve
Lower costs	Materials, labour, cost-to-produce, etc
Increase efficiencies	Marketing and sales costs as a percentage of revenue
Customer growth	
Grow revenue per customer	Annual growth in total sales
Increase customer penetration	Share-of-wallet, percentage new business, average order size, recency/frequency of purchase
Increase account penetration	Number of divisions, sites and divisions buying per customer
Increase product penetration	Number of product lines per customer, number of new products per customer
Grow customers	Number of new customers
Increase retention	Retention/attrition rate, number of contract renewals, repurchase intent
Reduce defections	Number of defections, win-backs
Create advocates	Referral rates
Employee growth	
Increase satisfaction	Satisfaction rates
Increase retention	Retention rates
Improve skills	Education/training
Absenteeism	Absenteeism rates
Performance	
Increase sales productivity	Lead conversion rate per channel, cost of sales per channel, cost of proposals, pre-sale engineering, etc, proposal win ratio, sales cycle length, lost sales
Increase marketing effectiveness	Number of qualified leads per channel, trial-to-adoption rate
Improve service quality	Service level per segment, service cycle time complaints, fill rates delivery times etc, performance by customer-based metrics
Improve support	First-call resolution, hold times, e-mail response times, calls-to-resolution
Improve operations	System uptime
Brand communications	
Maximize internet	Website traffic, content viewing, e-mail click-throughs
Maximize advertising	Qualified leads, recall
Maximize PR	Cover, recall, media audits
Trade shows	Qualified leads

Next to profitability, service metrics are the most important organizational benchmarks. Organizations must continuously track service levels, deliveries, response times and other customer-centric metrics. Lack of quality, integrity or performance must never be allowed to threaten customer value. Metrics must be based on issues important from the customer perspective.

Some measurement is easy. Most call centre and related applications generate extensive reports, ranging from the calls handled by a single representative to operational overviews. Results may surprise. One mystery shopping service called the help desk of a software company. The 'customer' asked questions posted in the online FAQs. Unbelievable but true: the help desk couldn't answer its own FAQ questions. Examples of the right metrics are in Table 10.1.

Companies establish measurement systems to track successes – new customers won, revenue increases, etc. Systems also must track complaints, warning signs and defections. Loyal customers wave warning flags before they exit. Product returns, slow payments, falling revenue and even silence can all be signs that a customer is about to leave.

Not all metrics are good. The wrong metrics either do not link to customers or put a premium on efficiency at the cost of effectiveness. Wrong metrics lead to the wrong behaviours. A well-known example concerns call centres. Representatives are judged on the easily measured number of calls answered per hour or the number of times customers are put on hold. Such metrics rapidly transform call centres into places that process lots of calls quickly. Unfortunately, customers are much more interested in accurate and complete answers than quick calls. Brand loyalty declines.

Wrong metrics also include measurements for measurements' sake, or measuring just what is easy to measure. The wrong metrics take too much time to collect, measure and analyse. The wrong metrics are too broad (satisfaction) or too vague (awareness).

Without quantifiable metrics for customer value, departments use benchmarks that highlight their own value or role. Shipping concentrates on trucks filled; PR boasts about releases distributed; R&D discusses patents. While these reflect needed accomplishments, they must be linked to customer value and standards for accountability.

VOICE OF THE CUSTOMER: LEARNING CUSTOMER VALUE

One reason that Six Sigma is so successful is because its metrics are based on what is termed 'voice of the customer' (VOC). Without knowing VOC, companies cannot develop the metrics that reflect economic, experiential or emotional value from the customers' perspective. VOC-based metrics can range from hold times to quality levels.

VOC can also spur innovation. In an effort called 'Customers Do the Darnedest Things', Grace Performance Chemicals, a division of WR Grace, asked sales representatives to uncover innovative uses of its products by customers. The sales representatives captured 134 ideas. Seven of the ideas potentially represented new markets worth millions in sales. Black & Decker exhaustively talked to customers about what they wanted in a utility light. The result was the 'Snake Light'. The product was so successful that demand exceeded supply by almost 50 per cent for a year after introduction.

VOC must capture such information as product/service performance and importance, competitive offering performance, attributes needing improvement, likelihood to repurchase or continue purchasing, likelihood to recommend and complaints, expressed and unexpressed.

Five activities can capture VOC:

- *Customer interviews:* Brands fail when they do not know, or forget, what customers value. Question customers about current and future requirements. What would result in more business more often? Faster delivery? Electronic billing? Better-trained personnel? Since intent to repurchase is a prime indicator of customer loyalty, regularly ask customers about intentions to repurchase. Ask: 'What do we do you wish we didn't?' 'If you were in charge of this relationship, what would you do differently?' 'What does nobody in our business do that you think everybody should?' Visit customers frequently. The software firm Red Hat conducted a world tour to seven cities on four continents to meet with customers and prospects. Other input results from complaint monitoring and 'mystery shoppers', or undercover 'customers' who obtain snapshots of actual service and fulfilment.
- *Market/competitive research:* Track market trends and industry imperatives. Establish a competitive intelligence (CI) programme. In many organizations, CI does not receive the attention it deserves. CI is not

about cloak-and-dagger rummages through rubbish bins. Rather, CI seeks a beyond-the-headlights look at emerging forces to identify opportunities, minimize surprises and speed reactions. A CI programme collects not only information about competitors, but also information on industry, technological, legal, regulatory, political, economic and international trends. About 90 per cent of needed information is available internally or through such public sources as annual reports. CI includes buying competitive products, and calling competitors for information or service. Such information can lead to better product development or uncover factors that can lure competitive customers into your camp.

- *Feedback:* How are customer comments, complaints and questions captured? Are there comment cards, freephone numbers and other channels for feedback? How are e-mail and other feedback analysed? Brands must provide easy and multiple ways for customer feedback. Front-line personnel must be trained to listen effectively and make the first attempts at amends when customers have poor experiences. More importantly, company feedback must be incorporated into processes and products.
- *Customer interactivity:* Find ways, in addition to user groups and similar events, to involve customers in operations. Most employees of MTV are in the cable music channel's target demographic of 18- to 24-year-olds. Southwest Airlines sometimes invites frequent flyers to its first round of group interviews with prospective flight attendants to get their reactions to candidates. Customers of financial software firm Intuit participate in product-development sessions. Harley-Davidson, whose ability to capture the voice of the customer is legendary, has executives talk with customers at motorcycle rallies.
- *Entrance and exit interviews:* Question customers early in the relationship ('How did you hear about us?', 'Why did our proposal win?', 'What influenced you to try us?') and again when they leave. Exit interviews, which provide an opportunity for recovery, must address reasons for defection. A common answer will be 'price'. Probe deeper to find out why customers feel they are no longer receiving value.

VOC is critical to ensuring that brands deliver customer value, bolster profitability and generate other pay-offs. According to *Harvard Business Review*, more than 80 per cent of successful new products come from customer suggestions. A popular advertising campaign for Coca-Cola in Malaysia ('Chupp!!') resulted from a customer suggestion.

SATISFACTION VERSUS ACCOUNTABILITY: WHICH METRIC FOR SUCCESS

Few gods rank higher in the branding pantheon than 'customer satisfaction'. According to *Inside Research,* a marketing research newsletter, US spending on satisfaction measurement in 2003 exceeded US $600 million. Companies tout satisfaction ratings. Companies are urged not just to satisfy customers but to 'WOW!' them. Links between customer satisfaction and loyalty are promoted. Often, compensation is linked to satisfaction. According to the European Centre for Customer Strategies, 22 per cent of organizations surveyed even link customer satisfaction to board member compensation. But is satisfaction a worthwhile metric? How is it related to loyalty? Does satisfaction really help companies improve profitability?

Although satisfaction is part of every corporate mantra, the lip service does not seem to have had much effect. Case in point: customer satisfaction has declined almost every year since 1994, according to the American Customer Satisfaction Index, conducted annually by the University of Michigan Business School.

Although the goal of satisfied customers is all well and good, it misses the point in any strategic branding effort for several reasons. First, 'satisfaction' is too fuzzy to serve as a meaningful metric. It reflects a temporary mental state that will shift multiple times during a lifetime of product usage. For example, measurements taken immediately after purchase are likely to yield more favourable responses than later surveys. Definitions of satisfaction vary from customer to customer, or even within departments inside the same company. Age, gender, income (low-income customers generally express greater satisfaction) and other demographics alter definitions of satisfaction. Additionally, criteria for satisfaction vary widely. For example, in a study for a large information-services company, Opinion Research Corporation found that dissatisfied customers were interested in core product attributes such as data accuracy. Neutral customers were interested in account management issues such as service updates. Satisfied customers were motivated by how well services integrated with strategic objectives.

Data collection inadequacies also limit the usefulness of satisfaction surveys. Most surveys are 'self-reported', opening the door to failings. Questions shape answers. Questions posed in positive terms such as 'how satisfied are you?' get more favourable responses than 'how dissatisfied are you?'

Or satisfaction surveys measure everything but what is important. For example, a customer satisfaction survey from Air Canada asked an astounding 54 questions, including 'were the flight attendant's announcements made in a pleasant manner?', 'was the boarding music satisfactory?' and 'was the headrest comfortable?'. Nowhere did it ask a primary criterion for repeat business: 'was the flight on time?'

Such murkiness darkens analysis. Does 'somewhat satisfied' mean that we do a superlative job in most categories but a poor job in others, or does it mean that our performance is adequate in all areas? What does '90 per cent of customers are satisfied' mean? That 10 per cent of customers are impossible to please or that operations are not firing on all cylinders? Are the 10 per cent profitable or unprofitable?

Another problem is that customer satisfaction surveys lack context. They do not measure the customers who left, and often do not incorporate competitive comparisons. What if every firm in an industry enjoys 90 per cent satisfaction ratings?

Companies often misinterpret customer satisfaction surveys. Many surveys are on a scale of 1 to 5. Companies lump '4s' and '5s' together to obtain results. But there is a huge difference between a '4' ('satisfied') and a '5' ('completely satisfied'). Xerox found that 'completely satisfied' customers were six times more likely to repurchase Xerox products over the next 18 months than 'satisfied' customers. A study by the Opinion Research Corporation found that completely satisfied customers were 42 per cent more likely to be loyal than the merely satisfied. Royal Bank of Scotland found that a third of 'satisfied' customers left the bank, compared to 5 per cent of the 'very satisfied' group who left in the same period.

For statistical correctness, satisfaction surveys generally apply across the entire customer base. This means unprofitable customers influence scores. High satisfaction scores from unprofitable customers can warp strategies. For example, a customer survey by one large bank indicated dissatisfaction with long queues. So the bank hired more tellers. While this increased costs, it had little effect on the satisfaction levels of its most profitable customers. They rarely came into the bank and were more interested in process improvements. Why should brands spend to improve the satisfaction of unprofitable customers?

Satisfaction is also a moving target. According to JD Power and Associates, which has studied customer satisfaction since 1981, 'what makes customer satisfaction so difficult to achieve is that you constantly raise the bar and extend the finish line. You never stop. As your customers get better treatment, they demand better treatment.'

Surveys can be manipulated. Since JD Power started measuring car dealer performance, some have offered 'free car washes' or other benefits to customers who give the dealership high satisfaction marks. The problem is compounded when customer satisfaction is tied to compensation. That leads to 'purchasing' customer satisfaction with lower pricing, or resistance to innovation or other changes that could impact satisfaction levels.

Many companies employ satisfaction surveys because they believe in a linkage between satisfaction and loyalty or profitability. The link to loyalty is tenuous, at best. In business after business, 60–80 per cent of customers who defected to a competitor said they were satisfied or very satisfied just prior to defection. *Harvard Business Review* reported that between 65 and 85 per cent of customers who chose a new supplier say they were satisfied or very satisfied with their former supplier. Look at the car industry. About 90 per cent of car buyers say they are satisfied; however, only 40 per cent of them purchase a vehicle from the same manufacturer.

Most importantly, a clear link between satisfaction and profitability does not exist. A study by professors from the University of Southern California, Stanford University and Washington University suggested that improved customer service may raise satisfaction ratings, but this rise does not always mean greater profits. The Juran Institute, a leader in studies of quality management, found that fewer than 2 per cent of the 200 largest US companies were able to measure a bottom-line improvement from documented increases in customer satisfaction. This is partly because the increased services often behind increased satisfaction cost more, and do not bring in additional revenue, especially from smaller customers.

Customer satisfaction is also inextricably linked to price. Customers can be satisfied with a product that performs adequately when the cost is low, yet they may be dissatisfied with adequate performance if they paid more. If price is the weakest foundation for a brand, then why have an objective that varies according to price paid?

Others have noted the failings in customer satisfaction as a metric. Frederick Reichheld, the customer equity and brand measurement guru, spent two years searching for an issue that could be linked to future customer behaviour. Reichheld knew the question would not be found on customer satisfaction surveys. In his words, 'Most customer satisfaction surveys are not very useful. They tend to be long and complicated, yielding low response rates and ambiguous implications that are difficult for operating managers to act on. Furthermore, they are rarely challenged or audited because most senior executives, board members and investors don't take them very seriously. That is because their results do not correlate tightly with profits or growth' ('The One Number You Need To Grow', *Harvard Business Review*, 1 December 2003). He noted that Kmart's sales nose-dived just as its satisfaction ratings improved.

Reichheld's one question had to be based on loyalty, since 'the only path to profitable growth may lie in a company's ability to get its loyal customers to become, in effect, its marketing department'. However, loyalty is not defined as repeat purchases. These may result from inertia or exit barriers. Rather, Reichheld defined loyalty as a willingness to make an investment or sacrifice to strengthen a relationship. Reichheld surveyed 4,000 customers of 14 companies in six industries and analysed purchase histories. He found that the most common question used in survey questions – 'How satisfied are you with X's overall performance?' – was a weak predictor of growth. The one question that did forecast growth was 'How likely is it that you would recommend X to a friend or colleague?' According to Reichheld, 'for most companies in most industries, getting customers enthusiastic enough to recommend a company appears to be crucial to growth'.

Reichheld found that enthusiastic referrals generate profits. 'In most of the industries that I studied, the percentage of customers who were enthusiastic enough to refer a friend or colleague – perhaps the strongest sign of customer loyalty – correlated directly with differences in growth rates among competitors,' he says.

That is what Enterprise Rent-A-Car has found. Enterprise Rent-A-Car abandoned a long customer satisfaction survey because the results were not actionable. Instead, Enterprise adopted a two-question survey: 'How was your rental experience?' and 'Would you rent from us again?' Analysis showed that customers who gave the highest rating to their rental experience were three times more likely to rent again than those who gave Enterprise the second-highest grade.

Instead of finding out whether customers are 'satisfied' or not, it is better to determine how your company performs against the competition. Atmel asks customers to assess whether the semiconductor manufacturer is 'leading the competition', 'slightly better than the competition', 'slightly worse than the competition' or 'lagging the competition' in such areas as product technology, innovation and shipment accuracy. It also asks about declines or improvements in service and support over the previous 12 months. Most illuminating, the survey also asks 'Why has your company chosen to do business with Atmel?' The final point: 'List three items that Atmel must focus on in order to gain a larger share of your business.' Do satisfaction surveys have any value? They provide an opportunity to communicate with customers. Other than that, not much. So what is better? Customer scorecards.

CUSTOMER SCORECARDS: BENCHMARKS FOR ACCOUNTABILITY

Customer satisfaction is important, but in the customer economy it is not enough. Satisfaction provides little guidance about what's wrong, how to fix it or even whether a customer is worthy of satisfaction. Worse, it has little relationship to profitability. Essentially, profitability and sustainability depend on how well brands answer these customer questions: in what areas do you require performance, what don't you require, and what are you willing to pay for?

Answers to these questions establish customer experiential, economic and emotional value. Linkages to brand activities are established on 'customer scorecards'. Created with customer input, customer scorecards show the areas where customers hold you accountable. Accountability for some customers might be on-time deliveries. For others, it might be quality, with minimal defect rates. Knowing accountability pinpoints specific areas for improvement and guides investment decisions. It helps align service delivery to customer requirements. And it establishes areas of pricing sensitivity.

Scorecards, which work well with the strategic and tactical systems discussed earlier, have numerous advantages. Based on accountability to customer standards, they focus improvements in operational excellence. If customers seek accountability for on-time deliveries, then resources must be devoted to shipping. Knowing areas of accountability also provides an early warning signal. If customers who hold you accountable for customer support start defecting, it's time to improve support. Additionally, knowing what's vital to customers refocuses relationships away from price-based satisfaction toward value, which enables the most profitable pricing. If customers are being provided with capabilities that meet their standards for accountability, it is unlikely that price will become a reason for defection. A relationship providing value-based accountability is too vital to risk for a few pennies.

In many ways, customer scorecards reflect the trend toward service level agreements (SLAs), especially in the technology industry. Established to provide accountability, SLAs are negotiated agreements

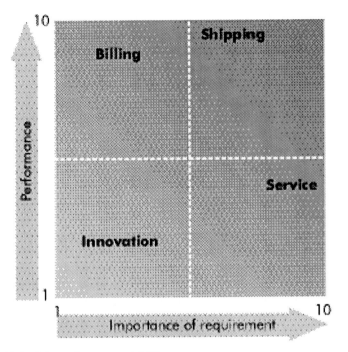

Figure 10.1 Measuring accountability

between a vendor and its customer. An SLA details expected performance and associated metrics. For example, all e-mails concerning support must be answered within 15 minutes, or uptime must exceed 99.8 per cent. Most SLAs have penalties if benchmarks aren't met and/or rewards if benchmarks are exceeded.

Customer scorecards start with three questions. In order of importance, what are the areas where you hold us accountable? Suggestions may be offered (support, delivery, R&D, etc). Next, what are your specific benchmarks for those areas (time, quality, quantity, etc)? On a scale of 1–10, how are we doing on those areas of accountability according to your benchmarks (performance)? Either aggregated or individual scores are plotted on an x–y axis with a 1–10 scale. The x axis is accountability; the y axis is performance.

The graph produces interesting insights. If, for example, customers hold you accountable for on-time delivery but your performance is poor, then you know specifically what area needs operational improvement. If it is an area like billing where you are doing an exceptional job but it is not important to customers, then you know to reduce resources to that activity or even outsource it. If there is an area like support that both is important to customers and represents an area of operational excellence, then consider unbundling the activity and/or increasing pricing for that service.

Customer scorecards deliver another important benefit. Unlike satisfaction surveys, scorecards communicate desired outcomes as well as the specific customer standards for evaluation. This helps drive operational investments and benchmarks. Is 'on-time delivery' next day or within five days? Is 'quality' one defect per thousand or per million?

Aggregated scores indicate areas of excellence as well as areas of weakness. Individual scores, combined with information about customer, product and account penetration, provide an integrated picture of the strength and profitability of a relationship. All results must be trended over time.

Scorecards allow you to segment customers by the ways they hold you accountable. Customers who demand high support levels can be grouped together to improve operational efficiencies and pricing. Low-equity customers who demand high – and expensive – levels of accountability can choose between leaving and paying more.

CONCLUSION

Branding discussions usually involve more pontification than quantification. Without quantification, resources are wasted. Production has difficulty matching sales. Customer service or other experience suffers. Finance cannot calculate true costs.

Numbers matter. Measurement matters. Without numbers and measurement, there is no accountability, and branding activities are running on a wing and a prayer. Marketers have long chafed under the rule of accountants. But, in the customer economy, the language of accountants must become, in part, the language of branding. Terms like incremental margin, ROI and profitability must rest alongside reach, frequency, 'positioning' and the rest. In addition to enabling accountability, this allows branding to be more closely integrated with the other operational areas that deliver customer value.

Understanding about the importance of metrics is growing. The CMO Council reported that about 60 per cent of respondents intend to increase spending on metrics. But the metrics have to be the right ones to have any value. They must represent areas of performance that deliver value to customers.

Companies believe that 'customer satisfaction' represents branding quantification. But satisfaction has numerous problems. It has little relationship to loyalty or profitability. An emphasis on satisfaction leads to exhortations to 'wow the customer'. Such exhortations are self-defeating. It sets the bar higher for future service. It usually means higher costs. And most customers prefer consistency, not extremes, in service.

Worst of all, satisfaction is a backward-looking metric, reflecting a judgement on what has been done in the past. By contrast, customer scorecards based on accountability look forward to what must be done in the future based on rigorous benchmarks. They illustrate the customer standards and expectations for each interaction. They communicate the desired outcomes for customers on issues other than price. And they avoid misunderstandings and enable better resource alignment by illustrating how customers measure results.

Takeaways

- How do you collect the 'voice of the customer'? Customer interviews? Do you have a competitive intelligence programme? Do you interview defecting customers? Is the 'voice of the customer' being incorporated into branding and operational decisions?
- What do you survey customers about? How often? Do surveys measure what is easy to measure, or what is important? Do survey questions cover areas that are generally meaningless to customers just to generate high scores? Are the results actionable in terms of producing customer value?
- Do you know customer standards for performance? What are they? Have those standards been distributed to relevant areas of the company? Have processes been adapted to those standards? How is your firm doing against those standards?
- Are sales and customer service representatives armed with information about customer standards for accountability and corporate performance?
- Are evaluation and compensation based at least in part on customer standards for performance?

11

ProfitBrand service: owning the customer experience

'We have more than 10 million interactions with customers every day; and more than 100,000 staff in more than 100 countries. Every action and every activity is an act of marketing.'

Sir John Browne, CEO, BP Amoco

Everyone has a service horror story. Look at shameful statistics worldwide. One example: the Customer Care Alliance surveyed 11,000 UK consumers in 2003 and found that more than 80 per cent of British households had had an average of 3.5 service problems during the previous year. Out of these customers, 63 per cent said they were extremely or very upset as a result of the problem, and 85 per cent complained. The poor service put an estimated £12 billion at risk.

The most common problems: the product or service did not perform as promised (41 per cent), poor quality (34 per cent) and unsatisfactory service (29 per cent). It gets worse. After contacting the company, only 11 per cent of customers had their problem resolved within a day. It took more than 14 days for 30 per cent of customers. On average, it took 3.8 contacts to solve a problem. More than a third felt their problem was never resolved.

A survey of more than 1,000 US consumers by Customer Care Measurement and Consulting yielded similar results. About 45 per cent of those surveyed had had a problem during the previous year. One-third of the time the dissatisfaction resulted from lack of performance or quality; 15 per cent of the time it was due to poor service. For some the experience was so bad that 16 per cent wanted revenge. It took an average of 3.5 contacts to resolve problems. Only 22 per cent of respondents resolved their problem on the first call, and for an unlucky 18 per cent it took seven or more calls to address the issue.

No wonder the *Wall Street Journal* reported that 'US companies are driving their customers crazy'. Customer satisfaction has declined every year in the United States since 1994, based on the American Customer Satisfaction Index.

Inevitably, poor service damages brand sustainability and profitability. Research organization Meta estimated that poor customer service causes 68 per cent of customer attrition. It affects word of mouth. In the Customer Care survey, 47 per cent of those who were dissatisfied with how their complaint was handled told more than 25 people about the experience.

Without service, there is no brand. Service starts with quality products and services that are sold with an understanding of customer requirements and a commitment to do business on customer terms. Service includes instruction on how to get the most from offerings, education about the industry or market and incorporating the voice of the customer. Above all, service must match the promises made by marketing.

Why is service so poor, especially since good service leads to retention, and retention leads to profitability and a sustainable brand? With substantial acquisition branding investments at stake, why do companies wash their hands of customers after purchase? Why do companies anger the source of profitability? Companies are exhorted to focus on core competencies. Why isn't service one of them? Why does service – and the relationship with the customer – so often get outsourced?

Good service is not an impossible dream. Look at Amazon, Starbucks, Nestlé and many more companies worldwide that have built brands on service.

One answer is costs. Margins have declined an estimated 5–10 per cent over the past decade. Service has become a cost-cutting target, especially since service is hard to justify with traditional accounting. Personnel and other service expenses are easy to track; the benefits are hard to measure, especially if companies do not know customer profitability.

Yes, personnel and customer-centric processes can raise costs, but the investment pays off in customer profitability. Online stores that enable customers to talk with service representatives see average sales orders increase 15 per cent and abandonment rates fall. One vendor claimed that 35 per cent of visitors buy after chatting with a live operator. In a 2004

Accenture survey, 27 per cent said they would switch providers to gain access to a live customer service representative rather than being forced to use an automated voice response system or website. Retail studies have shown that improved store service creates greater loyalty than special vouchers, a priority customer care line, private sales events or special financing. In almost all cases, service leads to greater intention to repurchase and/or increased usage. It also leads to positive word of mouth.

Just because complaints are few does not mean service is good. Only about 5 per cent (more in business-to-business) of customers complain about poor experiences. Complaining takes time, and customers have learnt from bitter experience that the return does not always justify the effort. So they do what is easiest – defect to the competition.

Companies who invest in service see pay-offs. A pilot 'customer-centricity' programme at the US retailer Best Buy increased expenses, but raised profitability by 7 per cent. At some Washington Mutual branches, tellers and managers stroll the floor to welcome customers, help with deposits and withdrawals, and encourage questions. The branches even have a children's play area with the hottest toys. The result: customers are opening new current accounts at twice the rate of traditional branches. Customers are also taking out more loans and mortgages.

Good service enables higher pricing. According to the Accenture survey, 65 per cent of US consumers are willing to pay more for better service in such industries as managed healthcare, airlines and hotels.

Rather than eliminating service, a better strategy is to eliminate the need for service. This would not only save companies money, but also end customer frustration. When software firm Intuit decided to lower call centre volume by eliminating the need to ask questions in the first place, it started by providing incentives to call centre personnel to record all customer questions and problems. These results were given to software designers to address in the next generation of software. Researchers visited customer homes to observe how customers learnt and used the software. Finally, Intuit took ownership of every issue, even printing problems, whether it was its 'fault' or not. The result was a dramatic fall-off in call centre volume.

Once the process and other operational investments have been made, then ProfitBrands can be backed with guarantees. US Bank offers its customers a 'five star service guarantee'. US Bank guarantees that personal bankers will be available 24 hours a day, seven days a week; no wait in any teller queue will be longer than five minutes; and all questions will be answered on the same day if asked before 3 pm. It also guarantees that current and savings account statements will always be accurate. If these issues occur, US Bank credits affected customer accounts with US $5. Customers just contact a branch manager or call a freephone number to receive the credit.

This guarantee underscores US Bank's commitment to service. US Bank now has a financial incentive to ensure that business is done on customer terms. Additionally, it lets US Bank directly see – and feel – the costs of service failures. It provides a strong competitive branding initiative and adds credibility to its marketing.

ProfitBrand service is based on three core principles – end-to-end customer service, institutionalization of customer knowledge and a service culture.

END-TO-END CUSTOMER SERVICE: 'THE CUSTOMER EXPERIENCE: OWN IT'

Dell's legendary success comes from five words imprinted on the corporate DNA – 'The Customer Experience: Own It'.

'Owning the customer experience' is defined as ensuring a favourable brand experience with products, people and processes. The experience stretches from the time the first ad is seen through to fulfilment to the last contact (and even beyond, through recovery efforts). Each customer interaction represents a potential 'moment of truth' that shapes experiences, affects relationships and either builds or destroys brands. The responsibility for 'owning the customer experience' is in the hands of every employee, whether in accounting or in the warehouse.

End-to-end service means each customer interaction must be backed by required resources, including people, processes and technology. Ordering processes must be simple, without customer confusion. Questions must be answered and promises kept. Not only 'customer-facing' activities but also back-office operations like accounting and R&D must be on customer terms.

End-to-end customer service also means responsiveness. The best form of responsiveness is self-service, or enabling customers and prospects to answer their own questions or initiate transactions. Self-service benefits companies and customers. Companies save money. Forrester found that the cost of a customer sales or support call can run up to US $33, and that even e-mail support can cost nearly US $10 per response. But web-based self-help averages US $1.17 per incident. Dell saves US $8 every time a customer uses its website instead of calling.

Other savings come from reduced contact volume. The Nectar loyalty card is the UK's largest loyalty programme. More than half the households in the UK have at least one card. At one point, member calls were overwhelming Nectar's call centres. In response, Loyalty Management UK, Nectar's parent company, launched a redesigned website in 2004 to improve customer service and take some of the load off call centres. The new site allows members to update personal information and search for answers to FAQs (frequently asked questions). Members can also redeem reward points online. As a result, calls to customer assistance have been reduced by 26 per cent.

Self-service can also increase customer retention. In one programme, mobile phone provider Verizon found that customers signed up for free three-month trials and then defected. After introducing web self-service, three-quarters of the programme-related calls stopped. More important, customers stayed three times longer.

Customers benefit, too. Just as petrol stations realized when they switched to self-service, customers value the control that self-service provides.

To enable self-service, websites must work the way that customers want. That is not always the case. More than 25 per cent of website visitors are unable to find the answers they seek, according to the Software and Information Industry Association. As a result, FAQs must be updated frequently. The updates must be based on actual questions to ensure relevance. Other key self-service capabilities include search, order-status checking, tutorials and, of course, legibility and ease of navigation. Customer knowledge improves self-service. Thanks to its Clubcard, Tesco knows the shopping history of each customer. When customers go to the website for home shopping, a list of purchases made during the last three months appears to simplify online selection.

Extranets, or secure websites only accessible by specific customers, also enable self-service. Extranets are customized to each customer's requirements and contractual arrangements. They can enable purchasing, order management and fulfilment based on customer-specific prices, configurations and terms.

Extranets benefit customers by reducing the costs of doing business. Customers can access centralized, around-the-clock support and other resources, as well as customized pricing and other content based on corporate standards. Technologically advanced customers can integrate these capabilities directly into their own procurement systems.

However, self-service must not be used to avoid service. As one wag has written, 'The most popular use of online customer service is

searching for offline customer service.' Neither is it a way to offload data-entry work on customers. That not only creates a customer burden, but also results in inaccurate corporate databases.

Service responsiveness extends to e-mail and call centre capabilities. E-mail is flooding into companies from customers who do not seem to sleep. Studies indicate that many companies receive an average of 1.1 e-mails for every product they sell. The number of e-mail enquiries to companies exceeds the number of phone calls.

Few companies are coping well with the deluge. According to Jupiter Media Metrix, more than half of all customers expect a response within six hours of sending an e-mail. Only 38 per cent of companies meet that standard. About a third of corporate responses take three days or longer. Half the responses did not answer customer questions. Worse, 24 per cent never reply at all. Ultimately, the brand loses. If customers and prospects do not receive prompt, accurate replies, they assume you don't care about their business. Additionally, frustrated customers turn to the phone to obtain answers, driving up support costs.

Technologically, there is no excuse for poor e-mail handling. E-mail automation now permits about 70 per cent of customer enquiries to be answered automatically, with keywords triggering specific responses to routine questions ('Do you take American Express?'). E-mails can be queued and routed to available or qualified agents. Response libraries and reply templates ensure consistent responses. E-mail can also be stored for later retrieval and analysis.

Call centres are on the front lines of service and relationships. However, most call centres are more focused on cost containment than service. Poorly paid representatives are judged on call quantity, not satisfaction or any other customer metric.

End-to-end service requires transforming call centres from organizational – or outsourced – backwaters into strategic offerings called 'contact centres' (also known as 'customer interaction centres'). Contact centres, enabled by the convergence of voice and data, can provide consistent service to any enquiry, whether by phone, fax, web or e-mail. Representatives have information about the customer and previous transactions. For example, the insurance firm USAA ties every service representative into a database that provides access to integrated customer information and links to order, fulfilment and other corporate systems. Representatives can communicate with customers via internet telephony, regular telephone, e-mail and chat.

Contact centre benefits include better responsiveness, improved sales and lower costs. According to IBM, a contact centre can save 70–90 per cent

of the cost of an inbound call centre. Kellogg's estimates a 13:1 payback from its contact centre. Retailer Lands' End boasts a model contact centre. It lets customers initiate a chat session or phone call with an agent. The customer and agent can parallel-browse and talk simultaneously, either online or through a second phone line. Despite the advantages, few companies have made the investments in bandwidth, training, processing and other technology to enable contact centres. That is unfortunate, since such investments build brands better than most marketing expenses.

Finally, end-to-end customer service includes fulfilment, which involves logistics, warehousing and shipment. Fulfilment can make or break a ProfitBrand. Poor fulfilment is a major cause of customer dissatisfaction. Responsive, accurate fulfilment is the first step toward converting one-time buyers into long-term customers. Consumers, and especially businesses, depend on getting the right goods in the right quantity at the right time. Pricing, packaging and marketing promises mean little if an offering is not in hand when needed.

Fulfilment is not easy or exciting. The benchmarks are unforgiving. As the classic UPS ad said, 'You can't fake early.' Success depends on linking together complex systems and processes. If any link doesn't work, delays or other problems result. But fulfilment is what separates ProfitBrands from the wannabes. As a result, companies must pay significant attention to fulfilment. This ensures that ProfitBrand promises are kept, deliveries are on time – and loyalty enhanced.

Look at Amazon.com. The heart of Amazon.com's ProfitBrand is not books, which are easily available elsewhere. It is responsiveness. This responsiveness is based on world-class fulfilment capabilities that include keeping customers informed along the way. Responsiveness is so important to Amazon.com that it is willing to make two shipments to ensure immediate fulfilment – despite extra costs.

INSTITUTIONALIZATION OF CUSTOMER KNOWLEDGE: INSIGHTS FOR ALL

Currently, customer knowledge is like the proverbial story about the blind men touching an elephant. Information is fragmented. Sales, billing and other departments each see the customer from different perspectives. Obviously, this inhibits doing business on customer terms.

Institutionalization of customer knowledge, or the ability to capture, maintain and access relevant customer information across the enterprise, must be a strategic priority. Customer demographics, purchase history, preferences and other information must be held within a consolidated database. Available to everyone involved in customer responsibilities, the integrated information allows each contact with the customer to benefit from knowledge of all other contacts. One advantage includes facilitating one-call resolution. This helps customers ensure consistent interactions and helps eliminate the 'transfer-and-repeat-the-problem' response that irritates customers. Additionally, integrated information speeds problem identification and resolution. It should never take 3.8 contacts to solve a problem in the UK.

Consolidated databases must include customer preferences, including frequency and type of communication. After customers overwhelmingly indicated that they wanted to 'direct dialogue based on their own needs', IBM's 'Focusing on You' programme reduced the amount of information sent to them. Ritz-Carlton even records which fruit was eaten out of a fruit basket so the next basket contains only customer favourites.

When customer knowledge is institutionalized, companies make better decisions about customer profitability. Appropriate levels of service can be determined for each customer segment. Loyal or high-profit customers can be rewarded. Institutional customer knowledge enables State Farm to reduce insurance rates for profitable customers every three or four years. To boost retention, after 10 years State Farm even guarantees coverage for as long as the customer holds a driving licence.

Processes as well as technology are required to institutionalize customer knowledge. Some companies have sophisticated customer information systems that are running on empty because sales and other corporate personnel do not enter information about customers and interactions.

CUSTOMER CULTURE:
ULTIMATELY, IT IS ALL ABOUT PEOPLE

Until shortly before he died in his 80s, Ray Kroc, the legendary CEO who built McDonald's into a worldwide empire, visited two or three stores each week. He checked the food, toilets and even behind rubbish bins. He also talked to customers, always asking what they liked and what could be done better. He set an example for a customer-focused culture that continues today. Top McDonald's executives must work in a local franchise at least one day a year.

A similar customer culture marks other companies. Car parts retailer AutoZone promotes its WITTGTJDR – 'Whatever It Takes to Get the Job Done Right' – philosophy. AutoZone personnel are dedicated to greeting and helping customers, with an emphasis on helping women feel comfortable. Nordstrom will go to competitors to buy out-of-stock products and deliver them to customers at no additional charge. An LL Bean employee must have senior management approval before saying 'no' to a customer. At the telecommunications vendor Akamai, all customer questions must be answered on the first call or e-mail.

Those are the exceptions, when they ought to be the rule. Too many companies consider efficiency more important than effectiveness in relationship development or customer service. Ultimately, this degrades brand profitability and sustainability.

A customer culture is important because, ultimately, it is not individuals, the marketing department or even the CEO that is responsible for ProfitBranding. The entire organization is responsible for a ProfitBrand. This responsibility extends from the shipping clerk who double-checks an order to the CFO who ensures supplier bills are paid on time. Like all key values, this has to be reinforced time and again.

Building a customer culture requires four elements: leadership, employee loyalty, training/education and a match between compensation and outcomes.

Leaders have a vision that doesn't benefit just employees and shareholders but customers as well. Leaders unite that vision to organizational and individual effort. Leaders encourage imagination and innovation, provide the personal and organizational tools to perform effectively, and nurture the openness required to collaborate across teams, processes and organizations. Leaders use metrics for improvement, not punishment.

Employee loyalty builds customer loyalty. Employees will value customers if the company values them. Studies by consultant Bain & Co showed that companies with the highest employee retention also had the highest customer retention. More importantly, companies with the highest employee retention were the most profitable. A large US bank found that branches whose teller turnover was less than 10 per cent grew their current account base by twice the bank average. The brokerage AG Edwards has a broker turnover rate about half the industry average. Not surprisingly, its return on equity is twice the industry average.

Improving employee retention requires more than money. It also requires empowerment, recognition and the ability to grow personally through training/education or positions of increasing responsibility.

Training and education are the corporate equivalent of tooth flossing – recognized as necessary, but never done as often as required. Even though the American Society of Training and Development reports that the average company spends about 1.8 per cent of payroll on training, every manager knows more is required. Training improves both operational and service skills, and is especially vital for maximizing return from technology. Training teaches employees about their role in delivering customer value, and gives them the required skills and attitude. To help ensure that each employee represents its values, each Ritz-Carlton employee carries a pocket card that lists expected service behaviours.

Cross-training is important to increase customer responsiveness and employee flexibility. Top executives need training, too, especially in statistics and systems management. Statistical knowledge is necessary to guide the data collection and analysis increasingly required to manage effectively.

To ensure accountability, employees must be paid based on customer equity or operational excellence. Sales forces must be compensated not just on immediate sales but also on retention and customer profitability. Since customers easiest to sell to are often the least loyal, some firms even penalize the sales force with commission charge-backs if customers do not remain for a minimum time. To enhance the institutionalization of customer knowledge, other firms compensate according to the completeness and accuracy of the customer data provided.

Service is not limited to corporate personnel. Suppliers and even other customers can be part of a ProfitBrand's customer culture. For example, Cisco customers provide substantial assistance to other Cisco customers.

EXECUTION: SEPARATING PROFITBRAND WINNERS FROM LOSERS

More than 58 per cent of CEOs stay at a company less than four years, according to outplacement consulting firm Drake Beam Morin. The turnover rate is even higher among CIOs, vice-presidents of marketing and other top executives.

According to *Fortune*, 70 per cent of CEO failures are caused not by flawed strategic thinking but by failure to execute. In other words, failure was not caused by an inability to find the big idea or hidden strategy no one else had discovered. It was caused by operational failures to do business on customer terms – profitably.

Sometimes operational failure is due to a lack of resources, inefficiencies or the lack of a customer culture. But when these are not the causes for failure, it's time to look at organizational structures.

Organizational structures based on models born at the beginning of the mass economy handicap branding in the customer economy. Look at most organizational charts – here's marketing, over there are accounting and manufacturing. Employees 'report', like the military, to superiors. Information is funnelled up and down hierarchical levels, not across functional departments, inhibiting coordination. This structure descended from the model pioneered by famed GM CEO Alfred Sloan in the 1920s. While such a hierarchical organization increased efficiency when markets and products were homogeneous and transaction costs high, it hinders at a time when quality, customer focus and service are goals. The disadvantages of this model have been well documented. Fragmented information flows up and down, not among those with a stake in outcomes. Each department focuses on its own issues, breeding bureaucracies and complicating analysis of the trade-offs involved in enterprise decisions. Divergent objectives fuel interdepartmental friction (aka 'politics'), often on issues inconsequential to customers. Information gathering, analysis and other efforts are frequently duplicated.

As a result, maybe executives are not losing their positions because of a lack of strategic vision or personal shortcomings. Maybe it is because their 'classic' organizational structure handcuffs their abilities to execute. In fact, according to an *IndustryWeek* survey of manufacturers, 33 per cent said organizational barriers were the greatest obstacle to growth.

Service in the customer economy requires more than the departmental silos of the past. It requires agility, innovation and responsiveness dedicated to building customer equity. It requires effective and integrated supply chains (discussed in Chapter 13) that can deliver customer economic, experiential or emotional value.

It also requires organization around customers, not products or geographies. A product- or geography-based organizational framework has drawbacks. A single account can receive multiple sales calls. Serial communications among multiple departments can be required to solve a single customer issue. It's difficult to determine customer profitability. It drives an organizational focus on products or geography, not the source of all profits – customers.

ProfitBrands require customer-based organizations. Large companies can even have dedicated teams for specific customers. Other companies can organize around market segments, such as small businesses or just-marrieds, that share similar needs, purchase habits and attitudes. This enables companies to serve customers better, with knowledge of customer standards for accountability. It simplifies the task of matching service to customer profitability. It improves knowledge of customer life cycles. It makes it easier to present 'one face' to the customer and facilitates corporate information sharing.

More companies are organizing around customers. In a sweeping reorganization, Microsoft abandoned its product orientation to divide itself into four customer groups – corporate customers, knowledge workers, consumers and programmers. Coca-Cola is shifting from product categories to aligning many of its brands into lifestyle and life-stage segments. In Canada, Kraft targets emerging families, Asians and empty-nesters.

Sometimes organizations centre on customer-focused processes. Instead of departments, the utility Duke Power has five core processes: develop market strategies, acquire and retain customers, provide reliability and integrity, deliver products and services, and calculate and collect revenues. Focusing on processes lowers barriers to information flow and makes it easier to identify and eliminate bottlenecks. Benefits can be substantial. Texas Instruments changed from a traditional to a process organization. Time for new product launches dropped by as much as 50 per cent, and break-even points were reduced by up to 80 per cent.

Companies also need to look at organizational positions. Positions that adequately met the requirements of the mass economy risk obsolescence in the customer economy. Companies must establish new positions that centre around processes involving service or customer value. Key positions include the following:

- *Vice-president, customer equity:* The marketing department seeks prospects; the sales department turns prospects into customers. But who is responsible for customer retention and profitability? A vice-president, customer equity, strengthens customer relationships, ensures retention of profitable customers, matches service to profitability and facilitates customer recovery.

- *Vice-president, marketing technology:* Marketing has traditionally been a technological backwater. But today's initiatives – CRM, marketing automation, personalization, lead/campaign management – all can involve complex technologies. The vice-president, marketing technology, supports the databases, business intelligence and communications critical to customer relationships and analyses.

- *Vice-president, supply chain:* Currently, supply chain activities tend to be discrete departments – manufacturing, logistics, purchasing, etc. Unless a company can exchange demand, production and other information with others in the supply chain, operational excellence will always be constrained. One executive must have global responsibility for integrating these areas to drive efficiencies and closer ties with customers and suppliers.

- *Vice-president, constituency management:* This position is responsible for orchestrating relationships with key constituencies, including customers, media/analysts, investors and employees, and relaying their feedback to the organization. The executive is also responsible for communications with key partners such as suppliers and retailers/distributors. Duties include managing constituency-centric communications, maintaining relationships and understanding the voice of the customer through complaint monitoring, surveys and other tools.

- *Vice-president, measurements and benchmarks:* Measurement is often haphazard. Benchmarks, time periods and even standards differ within organizations. Without such standardization, accountability is harder. The vice-president, measurements and benchmarks, standardizes and correlates all benchmarks around customer equity and related measurements, using rigorous statistical, financial and other standards.

However, take the advice of Peter Drucker, legendary management consultant, when creating positions: 'Organizational change: it's about creating accountability, not power.'

CONCLUSION

Remember the joke about what a dog does once it catches a car it's chasing? Some companies are like that unfortunate dog. They frantically seek to capture customers, yet don't appear to know how to serve them once captured. Everybody who has hung on hold for a muzak eternity, waited days for an e-mail to be answered or searched in vain for a sales assistant knows how bad service is.

It is hard to understand why service is so abysmal. Service represents the best way for products to become ProfitBrands and for companies to recoup acquisition branding costs. Since it is hard for companies to stand out any more based on distribution, size or even technology, service is the Great Differentiator that keeps companies from sinking into the swamp of commoditization. Good service creates not only competitive barriers to entry but also barriers to customer exit. Without service that matches customer expectations from the first call to the last goodbye, no brand can be sustained.

Companies make the mistake of seeing service as a cost, yet few activities can damage profitability like poor service. The statistics are shopworn, but still provide strong lessons. It takes 12 good service experiences to overcome a single bad one. Poor service causes 70 per cent of customers to switch to the competition. More than 90 per cent of unhappy customers will not buy again from the company that displeased them. Unhappy customers will complain to 4 to 12 associates. How much does that cost a brand?

Executives are focused on building companies that are built to last. That's important, but ProfitBranding requires something more: companies built to serve.

Takeaways

- How are you trying to own the customer experience? How strong is your customer service culture? Is service seen as a prime cost-cutting target?
- Is staffing consistent with customer requirements for service? What are customer service metrics? Are they based on corporate efficiencies or customer effectiveness? What 'grade' would customers give your service?
- How responsive is the organization? Does responsiveness match the expectations of customers, media or other constituencies? What are the benchmarks for responsiveness?
- Can you guarantee your service? Why not? Is marketing making promises the organization cannot keep?
- How much authority do employees have to resolve customer issues? What is being done to reduce employee turnover?

12

Loyalty: the tie that binds

'Clubcard is not just a loyalty card; it is a business system. [Tesco is] way beyond rewarding customers and retention; it is using data to drive business decisions.'

Don E Schultz, Professor Emeritus of Integrated Marketing Communications, Northwestern University

In 1981, American Airlines introduced its AAdvantage loyalty (also known as rewards) programme, revolutionizing branding as much as the jet engine revolutionized air travel. After being copied by almost every other airline, today there are more than 89 million members of airline programmes worldwide, according to the frequent flyer guide WebFlyer.

The concept first spread to hotel and rental car services. Eventually, even the corner sandwich shop offered 'buy six, get one free' loyalty cards. Research firm Gartner estimated that more than 60 million Americans belong to at least one loyalty programme, while McKinsey & Company estimated that 53 per cent of US grocery customers are loyalty programme members. Spending in loyalty programmes totalled US $1.9 billion in the United States in 2003, according to the Industry Trends Report.

Loyalty programmes are also popular worldwide. Supermarket Tesco and coalition programme Nectar are among the largest loyalty programmes in the world, while a De Weaver & Partners 2002 survey revealed that 54 per cent of Australian consumers have at least one loyalty card.

Loyalty programmes, which provide discounts, free offers, special services or other benefits to purchasers, have four goals: reward participants for past purchases, increase the number/frequency/variety of purchases, establish closer bonds to customers and collect information for analysis. Secondary goals include competitive defence and partner assistance. Loyalty programmes work best for high-margin offerings that are difficult to differentiate and are purchased multiple times over a lifetime. Rewards must be related to the brand. Additional travel for an airline makes sense; free business seminars do not.

Loyalty programmes are popular among customers and companies. The top three reasons consumers give for joining loyalty programmes are awards, discounts and member-only perks. For companies, loyalty programmes encourage retention, since customers seek to win more awards and hesitate before losing accumulated points. They can be effective. Accenture said loyalty programmes influence the travel decisions of 80 per cent of business travellers. And they enable customer penetration by inducing customers to spend more each time they buy.

Loyalty programmes do more than aid retention. They also provide vehicles for up-selling and cross-selling, reduce marketing costs and assist customer recovery. Tesco, for example, regularly promotes high-margin wines and financial services through its Clubcard. Ohio supermarket Dorothy Lane was able to drop its advertising three months after it started a loyalty programme. Since beginning loyalty programmes, Irish supermarket Superquinn has dropped all its newspaper advertising, and Virginia supermarket chain Ukrops has cut its newspaper advertising in half. Cendant used its database to identify customers who had not stayed at a Cendant hotel for more than a year and then targeted them with promotions and special offers.

Instead of a price reduction, brands with loyalty programmes can offer additional value through points. Typically, such awards have a high perceived value with a low actual cost. Points can also be linked to promotions that drive seasonal or other product sales.

However, the prime advantage of loyalty programmes is the potential to quantify customer relationships. Thanks to its exceptional database and analytical capabilities, Tesco can precisely calculate the profitability of its loyalty programme. It also can magnify marketing impact. Many promotions just rob future sales, but loyalty programme analyses enable Tesco to generate more than £100 million in incremental sales each year.

Loyalty programmes generate valuable information for inventory selection, pricing, store location and even strategic investments. UK pharmacy Boots introduced travel insurance after discovering customers bought lots of suntan oil before going on overseas holidays. Tesco went into banking services after analysing which existing customers might also be banking customers.

TYPES OF LOYALTY PROGRAMMES: FIVE PATHS TO CLOSER RELATIONSHIPS

Loyalty programmes fall into five categories:

- *Membership clubs:* Customers pay an annual fee in exchange for product discounts, specials, priority help or accelerated shipments. For example, members of the Run America Club, sponsored by athletic shoes catalogue firm Road Runner Sports, pay US $19.95 annually. Members get such perks as a 5 per cent discount on purchases, a free subscription to a popular running magazine, product testing opportunities and the ability to 'save an extra 5 per cent when you order online on the fourth Wednesday of every month'. Membership clubs are common in countries like Germany (eg Swatch the Club, Volkswagen Club), where incentive-based schemes are prohibited.

  Although consumers say they dislike membership fees, in practice they can be effective. One loyalty programme involved 'white table-cloth' restaurant chains throughout the United States. Dining at the restaurants earned points that could be redeemed for wine, special desserts and other benefits. Some restaurants charged a US $20 annual fee; others gave away the programme.

  Those who charged a fee only signed up a third as many members as those who gave away the programme. Traffic and purchases were roughly the same whether the programme was given away or paid for. However, the US $20 fee paid for many programme costs. Additionally, those who gave away the programme had triple the overhead costs because of the greater number of members. As a result, all the restaurant chains converted to the paid programme.

- *Incentives:* Programmes award points for every dollar spent, or for the volume of purchases. These can be redeemed for free products, discounts or other premiums after accumulating a specified number of points. Incentives can also involve information access, such as newsletters with product, industry or other information. One innovation is the 'stored-value' card from Starbucks that combines Visa credit card functionality with a Starbucks loyalty programme, allowing coffee drinkers the power to pay, reload, earn and redeem rewards with a single card. Cardholders receive 1 per cent of purchases in 'Duetto Dollars' each time they use the card. These 'dollars' can be redeemed for food, beverages or store merchandise at any Starbucks. The credit card automatically reloads the Starbucks card when the balance dips under a predefined limit. More than four million Starbucks shoppers have signed up for the card. Sometimes, spending thresholds are required. Joining Neiman Marcus's Inner Circle requires spending US $3,000 a year with the upmarket retailer.

- *Volume:* The more that is purchased or the longer the contract, the better the deal. For example, a loyal reader who signs up for a three-year subscription pays less per issue. Volume-based relationships offer the savings to associate(s) of the main buyer. Examples are 'Friends Fly Free' programmes or the classic MCI 'Friends and Family'. Such programmes are ideal for companies with low variable and high fixed costs.
- *Affinity alliances:* Used by universities and non-profit organizations, affinity programmes enable a group favoured by the customer to benefit from purchases. A 1996 *Harvard Business Review* study found that 54 per cent of consumers would pay more to benefit a favourite cause. One successful example is American Express, whose Christmas-season promotions on behalf of favourite charities have significantly increased revenue and the number of transactions.
- *Continuity:* Similar to book-of-the-month or food-of-the-month programmes like those from Omaha Steaks, continuity programmes send scheduled shipments. These programmes reinforce relation-ships and build sales. Related programmes include auto-ship programmes, which automatically send disposables like printer cartridges or medical gloves at regular intervals.

Operationally, loyalty programmes take three forms. The most popular is the 'sandwich shop' model, where points result from using a single vendor, and rewards may only be redeemed with that vendor. Another is a primary operator with multiple partners, offering multiple opportu-nities to earn and redeem points. Examples include airline programmes and Tesco's Clubcard. Coalition programmes, like Air Miles and Nectar in the UK, S&H greenpoints in the United States or SmartClub in China, have contracts with partners either to issue or to redeem reward points. The advantages of coalition programmes are cross-sponsorship, or shopping at other vendors in the programme. Nectar claims that 85 per cent of Nectar members shopped at only one sponsor when the programme first rolled out; now, only 22 per cent do. For consumers, other advantages of coalition programmes include fewer cards to carry, faster point earning and greater choices for redemption.

One of the most successful loyalty programmes is Tesco's. Launched in 1995, Clubcard allows members to earn one point for each £1 spent with Tesco and with Clubcard partners. When members earn 150 points or more, points are converted into vouchers, which are mailed with the programme's quarterly statements and are redeemable at all Tesco-branded partners, merchant partners and for Air Miles.

Today, Clubcard has 13 million members, who redeemed US $364 million worth of Clubcard vouchers in 2003. Members use Clubcard for 80 per cent of their purchases. Each year, members receive an astounding 1 million different targeted offers, each one designed to drive incremental sales.

Clubcard's fundamental premise is not about capturing more customers. Instead, customers are rewarded for past purchases. Additionally, extremely strong database skills help build marketing and communications relevancy and strengthen long-term loyalty. The increased understanding helps drive ever-increasing customer penetration in more categories.

Despite the benefits, the popularity of loyalty programmes is declining. Between 1996 and 2000, membership in US loyalty programmes spiked more than 30 per cent. By 2002, growth had slowed to 4 per cent. Programmes in Canada, Australia and the UK show a similar trend.

One reason for the fall-off is that consumers are jaded, thanks to oversaturation. Americans belong to an average of four programmes each. Another reason is a lack of differentiation. Many see loyalty programmes as interchangeable, with little comparative advantage. Focus groups conducted by loyalty specialist Colloquy revealed that participants could not tell the difference between hotel loyalty programme information once logos were removed. A final reason involves privacy concerns. Tesco received some bad publicity when a shopper was wrongly accused of shoplifting and then tracked down via her Clubcard data.

Corporate disillusionment with loyalty programmes has also grown. It takes at least 18 months to see returns from loyalty programmes. Rewards and administrative expenses cost the supermarket industry 1–1.5 per cent of revenue. Loyalty programmes can cost other industries 2–4 per cent of revenues. Sheraton's frequent traveller programme costs US $30–50 million annually. Programmes can be complicated to administer. Members can receive not only a base reward level but also a multiplier bonus based on their category (silver, gold, platinum, etc) and promotion-related activity.

As a result, some have questioned loyalty programme ROI. ASDA and Safeway in the UK spent millions on loyalty programmes before abandoning them because of lack of provable return. In the United States, Publix and HEB Grocery have discontinued similar programmes. Ford USA withdrew its credit card reward programme.

A major issue affecting ROI calculation is the worry that loyalty programmes essentially reward customers for purchases that they would have made anyway. According to the international research project on loyalty programmes conducted by the Retail Advertising and Marketing Association, 87 per cent of customers said they would purchase from a company even if they were not in a programme.

Companies are legitimately concerned that customers become more loyal to the programme than to the brand. Customers will choose an offering solely for the rewards and then quickly defect for greater rewards elsewhere. Programme membership does not always generate satisfaction. If anything, programme members are more likely to criticize.

Other arguments include a lack of strategic differentiation. Any loyalty programme can be copied. Just ask American Airlines. Finally, some believe strongly that branding is all about an emotional connection. To them, establishing a 'mercenary' relationship with customers based on awards undercuts that connection.

KEEPING THE FAITH: MAKING LOYALTY PROGRAMMES WORK

A successful loyalty programme includes the following five steps.

Step 1: Determine programme parameters

Will the loyalty programme be open to all customers, or just a profitable segment? If it is open just to a segment, identify the characteristics and motivations of potential members.

Aim to make the programme pay for itself after 18–24 months. Tesco limits its marketing budget, including its loyalty programme, to 1 per cent of gross sales. It drops any activity that does not produce a sustainable sales uplift.

Calculating loyalty programme costs essentially involves subtracting the gross sales prior to a programme, administrative costs and the costs of incentives from the gross sales after the programme. In other words, profit/loss = (units sold × gross margin after loyalty programme) – (value of discounts, rewards, etc) – (units sold × gross margin before loyalty programme) – administrative costs.

This calculation can be applied to various segments (high, medium and low usage) within the loyalty programme. A major what-if involves costs versus appeal of the awards. In general, substantial benefits to the heaviest users are the least cost-effective, while substantial benefits to the medium users show the greatest return. For light users, the most cost-effective programme offers below-average benefits.

Step 2: Design programme

Based on membership and cost, outline programme elements, including rewards, recognition, benefits, partners and communications/promotion. Characteristics of a good loyalty programme include differentiation, attractiveness and, of course, affordability. Programmes can get quite complicated, with award points varying according to products purchased, purchase locations and member standing, but simplicity is vital. Benefits, rewards and requirements must be quickly under-standable, by both employees and customers. If employees do not under-stand how the programme works, neither will customers, and efforts to sign up members will languish.

Programmes must have realistic, identifiable and attainable award levels. That makes it more likely that customers will sign up and stay with the programme, and that employees will promote it more. Rewards redemption must be as simple and as rapid as possible. Customers do not want to jump through hoops for a benefit after giving a company business.

A loyalty contract with members is critical. This implicit contract states: 'Be a loyal member and, the more you do business with us, the more benefit you will accrue.' The loyalty contract must include strict privacy protection.

A good start for loyalty programme design is PAS (Publicly Available Specification) 46 published by the British Standards Institution in 2002. PAS 46 outlines a seven-step framework for improving data collection, analysis, set-up and feedback for loyalty programmes. The framework states that information and feedback must be collected from complaints and enquiries as well as surveys, focus groups and customer visits. After consolidating information from all sources, the organization must communicate results to employees. It must also develop initiatives to maximize loyalty and organizational performance. Finally, benchmarks must be established to quantify loyalty regularly.

Be sure to get the set-up right. Few things will damage a brand more than cancelling a programme that the best customers belong to.

Step 3: Collect data and analyse

A loyalty programme can be implemented as easily as distributing punch cards. Although such simple programmes can help increase retention, the real value of loyalty programmes is missed. The real value lies in the data collected from the initial enrolment process and subsequent purchases.

Not surprisingly, loyalty programmes quickly generate tremendous amounts of data. As a result, strong database and analytical capabilities are critical. Analyses not only can improve customer penetration and profitability but also can upgrade planning and merchandising, inventory management, pricing and other operational areas. According to research firm IDC, analytical software generates an average five-year ROI of 431 per cent.

Analyses can include lifestyle and demographic profiling, preferences, acquisition, number of active customers, average purchase and frequency of purchase, defection rates, redemption rates and, of course, costs. A key report is lost-customer reporting, which highlights members who have not made a purchase within a specified period. Advanced analyses can look at marketing ROI, customers on the edge of defection and potential for up-sell/cross-sell.

Analysis can produce substantial benefits. An example is the American Express Membership Rewards programme. There were 1.5 million UK American Express cardholders in 1996. However, American Express had signed up only 35 per cent of those card members for the reward programme, which awards points for purchases.

Further acquisition branding efforts were delivering diminishing returns. So American Express took a different tack. It used analytical software to profile existing customers and learn the characteristics of high-potential prospects. Analyses then identified American Express cardholders who were not reward programme members but still matched the characteristics of high-value members. The analyses then went deeper, identifying which high-value prospects would increase card usage if they became members.

Prospects who passed both filters were divided into 10 deciles. Those in the top three deciles represented the most profitable prospects because they were the most likely to convert and to increase use of the card. The next three deciles (4–6) would be moderately profitable. American Express would just break even or lose money on members of the bottom deciles. As a result, telemarketing campaigns focused solely on the top six deciles. The remainder were ignored.

Additionally, American Express researched the attitudes of potential prospects to determine the need for a different approach to acquisition branding. It found out that many prospects were not interested in paying a membership fee and thought too many points were required to qualify for awards.

As a result, the programme was redesigned. Changes included attracting more partners such as restaurants, theatres and other retail establishments to expand the benefits, especially for those who did not travel much. American Express also developed a new programme. Participants could sign up without paying a fee, but would be awarded points at a lower rate than 'full' members. Because of lower costs, members in the 'no-fee' programme were as profitable as the 'full' members. Penetration increased significantly.

In another case, analysis identified the high-value customers of a financial institution who would keep a credit card regardless of special offers. The company then substantially reduced the value of offers to those loyal customers while increasing the budget to extend offers to customers who appeared on the verge of defection. Analytics helped one telecommunications customer reduce churn by 3 per cent, retaining 9,000 customers responsible for US $4.5 million in revenue.

Step 4: Measure and track

The most important measurement, of course, is the impact on profitability. Costs that must be considered include set-up, advertising and promotion, enrolment, database, software and other IT expenses, editorial and production for loyalty communications, rewards and fulfilment. Also calculate pre- and post-programme customer profitability to determine the programme's effect. Look at other data as well, especially retention rates. Retention rates that continue to fall even with a loyalty programme indicate severe problems. If a card is being used, track how much of total spending is coming through the card. A successful programme involving a card will show 80–90 per cent of all sales resulting from card usage.

More sophisticated calculations will look at the profit cannibalized by rewards given to those who would have purchased anyway. One methodology is to compare sales growth and redemption rates. For example, a major cereal manufacturer established a test loyalty programme based on discount coupons that increased sales by 7.1 per cent. However, the coupon redemption rate jumped to 22 per cent when it had averaged 5 per cent. The manufacturer concluded that the loyalty coupons were cannibalizing too many existing sales, and ended the test programme.

After introduction, survey members about the value they are receiving. How likely are they to recommend the brand? Has it changed their attitudes or purchase behaviour?

Take early measurements with a grain of salt. The first few months of a programme typically show high enrolment and spending levels.

Step 5: Improve and enhance

What are you going to do once you are knowledgeable about the purchases, habits and preferences of programme members? Ensure that service, quality and other issues continue to meet customer requirements for accountability. The most rewarding loyalty programmes will not keep members if offerings do not provide value.

A loyalty programme must be continuously supported and promoted, both to members and to employees. Create specialized websites. Online systems should allow members to check points and redeem rewards 24 hours a day. Ensure point-of-sale (POS) promotion. According to the Point of Purchase Advertising Institute (POPAI), more than 70 per cent of purchasing decisions in mass merchandisers and supermarkets are made in the store. Maintain communications through relevant opt-in e-mails and other media. An ideal vehicle is magazines. American Express has its *Departures* magazine for Platinum Card holders and Bloomingdale's has launched the fashion and lifestyle magazine *B*. Many car dealerships send out monthly e-mails with information about 'hot cars', maintenance and travel. Based on its analyses, Tesco sends a magazine with segment-specific content and six highly targeted coupons to each member four times a year. Four coupons are for products the customer already buys, and two are for products that the customer has never bought, but is likely to buy.

Adjust the programme frequently to keep pace with changing requirements, offerings and customer demands for value. Use analyses to determine what worked and what did not. Test current and planned elements of the programme. Establish a historical track record to illuminate trends and performance. Track data by store / region, product and customer. Enhance the programme with targeted promotions to increase customer penetration.

Cross-market with complementary products and services. An ideal alliance, for example, is between a cinema and a nearby restaurant. Both benefit by encouraging visits and retention.

As one of the newest and most comprehensive loyalty programmes, Cendant Corp's TripRewards programme incorporates most of the features of successful loyalty programmes. Cendant is one of the world's largest hotel franchisors, the world's largest car rental operator, the world's largest real estate brokerage franchisor and one of the largest retail mortgage originators in the United States. Cendant's brands include the Amerihost Inn, Days Inn, Howard Johnson, Knights Inn and Ramada. TripRewards is growing at a rate of 125,000 members per month, and exceeded 3 million members in 2004.

TripRewards members can earn and redeem points at any of Cendant's 6,000 North American hotels. They also earn points on cars rented through Cendant's Avis or Budget brands; for filing tax returns with the company's Jackson Hewitt tax preparation service; and for attending presentations for subsidiary Holiday Network timeshares. Points also accrue through car service partners Aamco Transmission, Munro Mufflers and Pep Boys; and retailers Eddie Bauer, Kohl's, LL Bean and Bose. TripRewards members can opt to earn airline or rail miles with Continental Airlines, Delta Air Lines, Air Canada and Amtrak.

The programme features a broad array of awards, ranging from magazine subscriptions to holiday stays. Corporate research indicated that, the sooner members can begin redeeming rewards, even at a low level, the more likely they are to use the programme.

Initially, TripRewards faced three challenges. One was fairly migrating members of previous member chain programmes to TripRewards. Another involved consolidating its database, including cleaning and updating customer files. This effort included upgrading customer segmentation and targeting software. The final challenge was promotion. Cendant used an extensive multimedia campaign to introduce TripRewards. Franchisees received detailed training about the programme, and were required to promote it during check-in. All promotion stressed programme simplicity.

The launch is a model for loyalty programmes. Since the launch, retention of hotel loyalty programme members has improved, and the length of stays at Cendant properties has increased. Franchisee profitability is up. Research shows that last year's customers are staying 100 per cent more often this year.

FUTURE OF LOYALTY PROGRAMMES: TRENDS WITH THE MOST IMPACT

After enjoying tremendous growth in the 1980s and 1990s, loyalty programmes have plateaued during the past few years. However, several developments will give loyalty programmes a boost, in terms of both usage and corporate value.

Technology, including smart cards, radio-frequency identification devices (RFID) and other 'contactless' payment systems, is already reshaping loyalty programmes. First introduced in the mid-1980s, smart cards are a type of credit card with an embedded chip for storing data. Because of their data collection capabilities, range and ease of use, smart cards offer tremendous potential for loyalty programmes. They enable programmes to be tailored so that each customer receives varying discounts, awards or product promotions.

Smart cards have been widely adopted in Europe, partly because credit card verification is more difficult in Europe than in North America. Strong security capabilities also help reduce fraud. In Turkey, the Garanti Bank Bonus MasterCard smart card programme has more than 2 million members who can earn points at 18,000 stores. The Premium Club, a coalition programme in Poland, has partners that include Statoil, KFC and Pizza Hut. In Singapore, smart card points are awarded for purchases at the InterContinental Hotel or at a nearby shopping centre.

By contrast, US acceptance has been slow. Retailer Target ended a trial of its smart card loyalty programme, a major setback to smart card acceptance. However, usage is expected to grow substantially, especially since progress on such standards as EMV (Europay, MasterCard and Visa) is being made. Standardization will allow cardholders to use smart cards worldwide.

Other advances include RFID, wireless POS systems and biometrics. RFID devices enable wireless communication with POS devices within a metre or so. MasterCard has experimented with contactless RFID systems involving Chevron, CitiGroup, JP Morgan Chase and Loews Cineplex. Studies are under way to use RFID to identify high-profit customers in banks and casinos quickly so they do not, in the words of one steady customer, 'have to stand in line behind drunk conventioneers and screaming kids'. However, remember that technology must always remain secondary to loyalty programme design and relevance.

Another trend involves increased programme flexibility. For years, coalition programmes have given members choices in *where* they earn a programme's currency. Now they are giving members choices in *how* they earn them. For example, members of Hilton Hotel's HHonors programme can choose between 10 HHonors points and 1 airline mile per dollar spent, 10 HHonors points and 500 airline miles per stay or 10 HHonors points plus 5 bonus HHonors points per dollar spent. Members can switch choices at any time. Additionally, Cendant's TripRewards allows members to earn points, airline miles or rail points for hotel stays.

A final trend involves real-time rewards. Instead of waiting four to six weeks for awards, members can be rewarded and/or recognized with discounts or premiums at the point of sale.

CONCLUSION

The film *Minority Report* featured the ultimate loyalty programme. When Tom Cruise's character walked into a clothing shop, a robot scanned his retinas and asked 'How did the assorted tank tops work out for you last time?'

That is what today's loyalty programmes seek to do – identify customers based on past purchases, encourage them to buy more with relevant offers and reward them for past patronage.

Loyalty programmes can be executed in several ways, such as an independent effort or as part of a coalition with others. Getting members to sign up and awarding points is generally not difficult. The hard part comes from ensuring that loyalty programmes increase retention and profitability. In fact, several studies have indicated a weak correlation between programmes and profitability, especially since administrative, analysis and rewards costs can mount. Airlines, for example, are so worried about the unfunded liability associated with the billions of reward miles on their books that they are constantly rumoured to be looking at abandoning their loyalty programmes. Additionally, programmes are easily copied, erasing any long-term competitive advantage.

For loyalty programmes to succeed, extensive analysis is required on two fronts. The first is to ensure that customer equity, reflecting retention, penetration and customer profitability, exceeds the multiple known and hidden costs associated with a loyalty programme. Ideally, the analysis looks at whether the awards programme is subsidizing sales that would have been made otherwise. Analysis is also required for targeted offers, improved pricing and knowledge about new opportunities.

But the most important point to remember is that a loyalty programme is just one element of acquisition and retention. A loyalty programme does not ensure loyalty. Numerous surveys indicate that consumers value service and responsiveness more than any loyalty programme. Even the best loyalty programme will not mitigate the impact of a missed order or late shipment. If anything, loyalty programmes increase the fundamental requirement for operational excellence and service. As always, the best way to reward customers – and ensure continued loyalty – is always to provide them with economic, experiential and emotional value.

Takeaways

- What are loyalty programme goals? Encourage future purchases or reward existing relationships? What is the customer appeal? Is it open to the best customers or all customers? Does it generate sufficient usage? What sets it apart from competitive loyalty programmes?
- How strong are data collection and analytical skills? How are customer data being leveraged?
- How well is the programme coordinated with other branding activities? Is it being used as a promotional tool to drive cross-selling or as a substitute for price cuts? What are the plans for ongoing programme promotion and enhancement?
- What are the criteria for success? How are costs and benefits tracked and measured?
- What emerging technologies may affect administration or usage of your loyalty programme?

13

Orchestrating allies: no brand is an island

'There can be no communication if it is conceived as going from the "I" to the "thou". Communication works only from one member of "us" to another.'

Peter Drucker, legendary management consultant

In the customer economy, no company can brand by itself. Branding requires the help of allies, who range from brand ambassadors to strategic partners to supply chain vendors. It is these allies who help recruit new customers, ensure that products are delivered on time and ensure that service meets requirements. As a result, a critical part of branding requires recruiting and orchestrating these allies to deliver maximum customer value.

A conductor always works from sheet music to unite the elements of an orchestra in harmony. Companies seeking to ProfitBrand must use a similar guide. Instead of notes and chords, this guide consists of a combination of the voice of the customer, knowledge about segment and other profitability, and the measurements that ensure accountability. Such information is used both to inform allies about what is required to deliver customer value and to ensure that, like an orchestra, all the elements are working harmoniously towards a common goal.

Four allies propel the success of any brand – evangelists, supply chain partners, channels and strategic partners. Companies must orchestrate these allies so that they all mutually work towards increasing customer value. Evangelists are used to increase brand adoption and support retention. Suppliers must meet quality, delivery and other standards. They must also contribute toward innovation and cost reduction. Channel partners, consisting of retailers, resellers, distributors, integrators, agents and other intermediaries, must expand capabilities for doing business on customer terms. Strategic partners must provide access to markets, innovation or funds that expand branding efforts.

AMBASSADORS AT LARGE: LEVERAGING EVANGELISTS

Is it any wonder that start-up airline JetBlue has been such a success? A survey found that 59 per cent of JetBlue customers polled flew JetBlue for the first time because they were referred by a friend or relative. In the same survey, 98.7 per cent said they definitely would or probably would recommend JetBlue to others.

Many marketing activities focus on the individual. Look at the popularity of one-to-one marketing. But a substantial amount of research, based on the belief that we are social animals first and individuals second, indicates that success depends on how well marketing reaches a group, not individuals. This research finds that groups account for more than 80 per cent of the influence on individual purchases, while only 10 per cent is directly attributable to marketing activities. Anyone who has seen how chants or 'the wave' gets started at stadium events, or how individuals in crowds act differently from when they are alone, can understand why the herd instinct is so strong.

As a result, one important ally to orchestrate is the group. So-called 'tribal marketing' is based on the belief that, if the group adopts the brand, individual acceptance will follow. Ideally, the group – or tribe – mirrors profitable customer segments.

The most dominant form of group orchestration is, of course, word-of-mouth marketing (also called buzz marketing, street marketing, guerrilla marketing, renegade marketing, virtual marketing, ambush marketing, vanguard marketing, ambient marketing, covert marketing, under-the-radar marketing, below-the-line marketing, diffusion marketing or viral marketing). Word-of-mouth marketing seeks to influence the influentials in each group, also known as carriers, trendsetters and evangelists.

McKinsey & Company estimated that word of mouth influences about two-thirds of the US economy. Consultancy Cap Gemini Ernst & Young found that 70 per cent of new car buyers were influenced by word of mouth; only 18 per cent reported an effect from advertising. Based on a 2003 study of 3,000 visitors to WashingtonPost.com, RoperASW concluded that 10 per cent of Americans can potentially influence the habits of the other 90 per cent.

Word-of-mouth power derives from the recognition that others are backing up their recommendations with their reputations. The power is enhanced by the knowledge that such recommendations are made without self-interest.

Häagen-Dazs owes its popularity today to word of mouth. Samples of the premium ice cream let influential customers taste the richness in exclusive shops and hotel restaurants and at such upmarket events as Grand Slam tennis tournaments, polo tournaments, sailing regattas and Conservative Party events. The resulting word of mouth was powerful enough to fuel growth without advertising. The brand started in 1961, but the first ad did not appear until 1991.

Several tactics can help orchestrate groups. One common method is to seed the influentials with samples. To help promote the Ford Focus, Ford gave advance models to employees of celebrities like Madonna and Adam Sandler, hoping that sightings of the car outside hip restaurants and clubs would fuel sales. Giving the car to 120 of these influentials helped Ford sell 286,166 units the first year after introduction. Additionally, Procter & Gamble has signed up almost 300,000 US teenagers to receive samples, coupons and invitations to review offerings – and hopefully talk to their friends.

Another tactic is to simplify endorsement. Make it easy to pass along a recommendation. The best known usage of this tactic was the free e-mail service Hotmail. Every e-mail sent with the service included a message encouraging the recipient to sign up for the service. The result was the fastest new product adoption rate in history – from zero to 12 million members in just 18 months. Bose includes a 'courtesy card' in the carrying case for its noise-cancelling headphones so customers can easily relay product information to others. Apple puts stickers of its logos inside the manual for its G5 computer.

An 'extraordinary' experience can also fuel word of mouth. One example: beautiful women approached men in bars, whispered 'save me' in their ears and slipped a phone number in their pockets. About 60 per cent of the men called the number, and heard about a game from Electronic Arts. A cigarette manufacturer dispatched crews with iced coffee and beach chairs to make exiled smokers more comfortable outside office buildings.

Because of their growing popularity in grassroots communications, companies are using blogs, or web logs, for brand promotion. But blogs have to be used correctly to generate positive word of mouth. The most important rule is to be authentic. By making up phoney posts, numerous firms have been guilty of 'astroturfing' – creating the perception of a grassroots movement where none exists. Be sure to be relevant and provide value as a resource.

Because word of mouth is difficult to control and track, companies are now trying to add structure and measurement. Several firms recruit 'brand evangelists' first to actively spread the word about client products and then to report on their activities. Others, like computer manufacturer Gateway, attempt to establish a relationship with about 150–300 key 'influencers' in a category to speed dissemination of the 'next big thing'. However, 'buzz' does not last long. One study about hot new TV shows indicated that word of mouth fades after six weeks.

Because of its power and low cost, positive word of mouth is every brand's dream. Frederick Reichheld said in *Harvard Business Review* (1 December 2003), 'The percentage of customers who were enthusiastic enough to refer a friend or colleague – perhaps the strongest sign of customer loyalty – correlated directly with differences in growth rates among competitors... Evangelistic customer loyalty is clearly one of the most important drivers of growth. While it doesn't guarantee growth, in general profitable growth can't be achieved without it.'

But word of mouth cannot be commanded. Word of mouth results from the same forces that deliver customer economic, experiential and emotional value – service, quality and the ability to do business on customer terms. Brands that fail to deliver such value quickly discover that word of mouth can be a double-edged sword. Poor word of mouth can break a brand much more easily than positive word of mouth can make it.

DELIVERING THE GOODS: ENLISTING SUPPLY CHAIN PARTNERS

In many ways, supply chain failings put retailer Kmart on life support as a brand. To drive store traffic, Kmart extensively relied on marketing circulars that promoted popular items. However, such marketing was not coordinated with its supply chain capabilities. As a result, promoted items were frequently out of stock. Customers seeking the hot items left disappointed. After several such disappointments, they never returned.

For much of the mass economy, supply chain management (SCM) did not exist. The term itself wasn't even invented until the early 1980s. Now, SCM is the basis for competition and the primary vehicle for delivering customer value. Brands can survive without knowing their brand equity. Without an effective supply chain, however, factories shut down, deliveries are missed and customers go elsewhere. CEOs and CFOs know that SCM is the mother of profitable and sustainable brands.

SCM is shorthand for the interconnected coordination of material flow, information and finances (credit terms, payment schedules, etc) as they move from supplier to manufacturer to wholesaler to retailer to customer. SCM is based on two principles. First, optimization of the entire supply chain is more important than the optimization of units in the process. Also, processes like planning, order management and warehouse management are more important than functions like sales, purchasing and production.

Supply chains are often visualized as serial linkages, like assembly lines with linear links passing from raw material producers to manufacturers and eventually to customers. That simplification hides a complex reality. Supply chains are actually semi-choreographed networks of interconnected activities affecting orders, manufacture, replenishment and delivery. Activities have conflicting objectives (cost versus speed versus quality) and require differing expertise. Each activity must deal with uncertainty and resource constraints, and the effects of each activity ripple throughout the supply chain.

Since supply chain costs make up 50–75 per cent of the final costs of goods, and up to 25 per cent of operating costs, according to the consulting firm AT Kearney, supply chain inefficiencies increase costs without increasing customer value. Like the iceberg that sank the *Titanic*, unseen costs from supply chain inefficiencies can damage any corporate ship. Boeing took a US $1.6 billion charge because of supply chain bottlenecks. Problems with supply chain software cost Nike more than US $100 million in lost sales, depressed its share price by 20 per cent and resulted in numerous class-action lawsuits.

Savings from supply chain optimization can be immense. In 2002, the integrated supply chain group within IBM, which oversees almost US $40 billion of annual spending with 33,000 suppliers, reported US $5 billion in savings from productivity gains and streamlining. The group followed up such success in 2003 with more than US $7 billion in supply chain savings and its lowest inventory levels in 30 years.

Manufacturing consulting firm Pittiglio Rabin Todd & McGrath (PRT&M) found that best-practice SCM companies had a 45 per cent supply chain cost advantage over median competitors. They enjoyed a 50 per cent faster order-to-cash cycle time. They also had 50 per cent fewer days of inventory. Additionally, by ensuring availability when customers were ready to buy, incidences of being out of stock declined by 2 per cent.

Elements of best-practice SCM include the following:

- *Inventory reduction:* Inventory is expensive and covers up manufacturing or other inefficiencies. Minimizing inventory reduces costs, frees up capital and accelerates profitability. Automation has helped to reduce inventory substantially during the past decade, but more must be done. One strategy is to move away from 'push' manufacturing to customer-economy 'pull' manufacturing (sometimes called 'lean' or 'agile' manufacturing). Mass-economy manufacturing is based on running machines at full capacity to maximize asset utilization. Large inventories are used as back-up in case of unexpected supply problems or demand.

  By contrast, 'pull' manufacturing seeks to respond to actual demand. Nothing is produced until needed, resulting in substantial inventory reduction. Set-up times and lot sizes are reduced as much as possible, and steps without value are removed from processes. 'Pull' manufacturing requires close coordination with suppliers for 'just-in-time' deliveries and other capabilities.

- *Logistics improvements:* Poor deliveries are a prime cause of customer unhappiness. Yet according to an *Economist* survey of 70 global companies, only 22 per cent were consistently able to deliver on time. One reason is that logistics represents one of the most complex supply chain activities. Fulfilment involves orchestrating a complex interplay of transport, supply and inventory, compounded by such interruptions as weather and traffic jams. According to Forrester, a single global shipment takes an average of 27 parties to go from point A to point B. If anything happens along that path – a flat tyre, missing paperwork, loading delays – goods are late.

  Since transport accounts for 30 per cent of all logistics costs, logistics systems can save money and ensure on-time deliveries. By using routeing and scheduling software, shoe retailer Stride Rite cut the time it took to ship shoes from Asia to its Kentucky distribution centre by a third. The result was a 30 per cent reduction in transport costs and a 25 per cent increase in inventory turns.

Outsourcing is another form of orchestration. All major carriers offer comprehensive logistics services. Ford uses UPS to reduce vehicle transit time between plants and dealers by four days, saving US $1 billion in vehicle inventory and more than US $125 million in inventory-carrying costs.

- *Better forecasting:* Accurate demand forecasting is one of the biggest supply chain challenges. Poor forecasts lead to lost sales or excess inventories and affect workforce, inventory and production management.

    Demand planning systems can help. These systems combine sales history, promotional plans and other information with sophisticated algorithms to predict demand for each product, reducing the possibility of over- or underproduction. However, the most important contributor to improved forecasts is better information sharing among all supply chain elements.

Best-practice SCM requires collaboration, communication and consolidation with suppliers. Unfortunately, company–supplier relationships have traditionally been adversarial. Some of Detroit's problems stem from the fact that they routinely pressure suppliers for lower pricing. By contrast, Japanese car manufacturers work cooperatively with suppliers to lower costs. This cooperation is one reason why Japanese competitors have an estimated US $300–600 per car cost advantage over US competitors.

While pricing is important, companies negotiating over decimal points miss an important point. In the customer economy, direct costs form only a portion of the cost of offerings. A larger portion comes from the indirect cost of processes – inventory, shipping, machine set-up, packaging, invoicing and payment, etc. Reducing these costs requires that companies and suppliers collaboratively address key issues. How can inventories be lowered? Can offerings be drop-shipped to customers? Can pre-assembly speed production? Collaboration must extend to other areas as well, including design, forecasting and shipping.

Such collaboration pays off. After assembling a team of more than 100 suppliers, Boeing Rocketdyne, the propulsion and power unit of Boeing, developed a low-cost, highly reliable rocket engine that used just six parts instead of the hundreds of components used in earlier designs. Manufacturing time was slashed by 63 per cent.

Orchestration requires giving partners, suppliers and even customers access to forecasts, product design information, inventory levels, etc. Cisco sends key suppliers proposed specifications for products under

development. This not only helps those suppliers plan their own capabilities, but also alerts Cisco to potential problems or costs. By sharing information, partners can conduct joint forecasting, planning and strategies.
The more information companies can share, the more efficient the supply
chain and the less likelihood of being out of stock or other supply chain
disruptions. Collaboration also means aligning processes and technologies wherever possible.

IndustryWeek's Census of Manufacturers revealed that nearly a third of
executives said sharing demand data with partners has 'significant
impact' on supply chain performance. The survey indicated that manufacturers who cooperate with suppliers enjoy higher on-time delivery
rates and cash-to-cash cycle times that are 10 days less than the median.
When the small tractor division of John Deere cooperated with two
dozen suppliers, the manufacturing cycle was reduced from 32 days to 2
days. Costs were cut by 5–25 per cent.

Despite its importance, information sharing remains a hurdle. The
IndustryWeek survey also indicated that more than 40 per cent of executives said information sharing remains a 'significant challenge'. That is
because suppliers often have differing infrastructures and business
processes. Many still depend on faxes for information exchange. The
formats of even common business documents like purchase orders differ.
No wonder one study found it took an average of three months to ramp
up just one electronic process with a single trading partner.

Finally, orchestration requires consolidation, or a reduction in the
number of suppliers. Many companies seek numerous suppliers
believing that a multitude of suppliers provides negotiating leverage,
and safety during shortages. They order staplers, for example, from 200
vendors when only three might be needed. That is a mass-economy view.
Actually, a large number of suppliers and other partners increases coordination costs. There's less loyalty, which means that suppliers are less
willing to innovate or invest on a brand's behalf. By contrast, since
consolidation gives each remaining supplier more business, companies
can raise standards for innovation, quality and delivery. Suppliers are
willing to invest more in the relationship as well as in improved quality
or responsiveness.

One study indicated that firms who had relationships with about half
as many suppliers (1.3 versus 2.8) had substantially fewer part defects
(0.35 per cent versus 2.6 per cent). When Xerox reduced its suppliers from
5,000 to about 500, reject rates on parts decreased by a factor of 13.

Cisco remains a superb example of what supplier orchestration can
accomplish. When orders come in, Cisco often communicates requirements

Table 13.1   Key supply chain metrics

Service	Order entry accuracy
	Order fill rate
	Percentage resolution on first call
	Customer returns
	Actual versus promised times
	Repairs/returns
	Complaints
	Supply chain cycle time
Process	Forecast accuracy
	Perfect order measure*
	New product time-to-market
Financial	Cash flow
	Revenues
	ROI/ROE
	Cash-to-cash cycle
	Cash turnover ratio
Purchasing	Supplier performance
	Material component quality
	Unity purchasing costs
	Expediting costs
	Warranty costs
	Field service repair costs
Manufacturing	Product quality
	Work-in-progress inventories
	Yields
	Cost per unit produced
	Set-up/changeover costs
	Source-to-make cycle time
	Production cycle time/time-in-progress
	Overtime costs
	Manufacturing productivity
	Capacity utilization
	Rework/scrap
Logistics	Inventory turns
	Inventory days of supply
	On-time delivery
	Fill rates
	Inventory accuracy
	Pick accuracy
	Shipment accuracy
	On-time shipment
	Delivery times
	Cost of carrying inventory
	Transport costs
	Warehousing costs

*Measures errors per order line during every stage of fulfilment to component suppliers and contract manufacturers, who assemble and test the product. More than 50 per cent of the time, products are shipped directly to customers without ever being touched by a Cisco employee. The pay-offs: no warehouses, no inventory and no delays in getting products into customer hands.

ADDING VALUE: LEVERAGING CHANNELS

Much of what's written about CRM and marketing addresses those who have direct customer interactions, like the airline, financial and hotel industries. That leaves a gap. Most goods and services flow through channels, or intermediaries such as distributors and retailers. Orchestration is required to ensure that customers continue to receive value, from both the manufacturer and the channel.

Distrust often colours the relationships between manufacturers and the channel. It is called channel conflict, but frequently it has been a war. According to Forrester, 66 per cent of manufacturers said channel conflict is their biggest issue. Manufacturers worry about partners who carried competitive products, chafe at the inability to connect with the ultimate customer and enviously eye the channel's 20–40 per cent mark-up. Companies have also felt hamstrung by dependence on partners. One Christmas, for example, Mattel could not sell its hottest toys because Toys 'R' Us cut inventory.

Channel partners echo such distrust. Retailers and distributors fear the internet and 'disintermediation', or the ability for direct manufacturer sales. They feel that vendors know little about them except a fax number. One-sided changes in vendor programmes outrages partners. At the heart of many issues is a disagreement concerning who 'owns' the customer.

This internecine debate is not in the interests of customers. If there is one core ProfitBranding lesson, it is this: the customer belongs to no one. It is the brand that belongs to the customer. That means companies, channels and suppliers have to provide customer value, not just value customers.

Although channel conflict is age-old, the internet threatened to turn war into Armageddon. Retailers felt threatened. They thought that the internet offered manufacturers a path to long-desired direct sales, with no reseller mark-ups and product display fees. After some unfortunate experimentation with internet sales, many companies are realizing that the internet has actually increased the need for a retail channel. One reason is because of brand proliferation. Many offerings look alike, or contain differences that are either irrelevant or hard to understand, especially in mature industries.

Differentiation can be provided by channels, which have such strengths as local outlets and salespeople, more immediate service and better customer knowledge. Retailers, agents and others can educate the customer about value, change price sensitivity or provide a variety of service-based differentiators. For example, mobile phone service sales are directly related to how well the channel representatives explain features, services and charges. Other assets of a channel include the ability to provide support such as warehousing, installation, financing and delivery.

Additionally, selling direct has disadvantages. While the 40 per cent-plus margins look attractive, required investments in infrastructures and inventory can be high. New competencies, such as return handling or small-order shipments, are also needed.

Smart companies are not using the internet to eliminate channels, but to enhance them. They are leveraging the internet for reseller recruitment, sales and inventory reporting, planning, training, support, order tracking, and lead and quote generation. GE recognized that quote responsiveness was critical to smaller electrical contractors, who often lose or win jobs based on the speed of the quote. So GE established a browser-based quoting system, eliminating the need to contact sales personnel.

As a result, channels retain their importance. Even companies that define e-business depend on partners. Cisco uses channel partners for 75 per cent of its business. Dell, which built its business on direct sales, does 15 per cent of its business through partners.

Companies can address channel issues with various internet strategies. Companies can launch businesses that do not conflict with existing channels, like Procter & Gamble did when it established Reflect.com, which sells customized cosmetics online. Or they can put partners online, either by establishing a website or by providing a marketing portal for customers. Cisco lets customers configure products on the web. Customers can then choose whether to order the products direct or from a reseller, who gets credit in both cases. Many campaign management systems allow leads to be collected and sent to resellers via the web. These leads can flow automatically into partner systems for their sales efforts.

Channel measurement is a vital part of orchestration. Measurement is one reason why Wilsonart took market leadership away from Formica, which had dominated the US $1.5 billion laminate industry since 1913. Wilsonart succeeded because it continually measured – and rewarded – distributor performance. Typical measures for distributors included a 45 per cent market share, 26 per cent gross margin, eight inventory turns per week, and over 98 per cent order completion. Distributors were jointly involved in setting such goals, and outside researchers are hired to evaluate hard-to-measure criteria like market share. The performance improvement led to an increase in customer retention and loyalty.

GRAND ALLIANCES: LEVERAGING PARTNERSHIPS

The power of strategic partnerships to enhance brands is well recognized. It's estimated that 20 per cent of non-financial news releases each day concern partnerships. Partnerships can range from mutual web page links to distribution agreements, outsourcing and co-marketing agreements. Advantages include gaining complementary products, markets and distribution channels. Other benefits include providing greater economies of scale/scope, faster time-to-market, risk minimization and enhanced credibility in new or existing markets.

Strategic partnering consists of three approaches. The first is resource sharing. Companies work together to develop offerings or open new markets when individual activity may be too risky or expensive. Inmarsat is a consortium that operates a telecommunications satellite. Members are simultaneously investors, customers, vendors and competitors. Strategic partnerships can also be complementary. Companies use compatible resources, such as the marketing strength of one and the product development capabilities of another, for mutual benefit. Sears worked with IBM to create a website about home decorating. Finally, partnerships can expand distribution. Strategic partnerships are especially important for establishing international footholds.

While alliances are important now, they will be vital in the demand economy. That's because of embedded systems, or the processing and communications power that will be incorporated into everything from toys to refrigerators. Embedded systems, for example, will enable the washing machine, box of washing powder and dress to communicate with one another to ensure a dress gets safely cleaned. When embedded systems allow automatic replenishment based on strategic alliances, how many are going to reprogramme, say, refrigerators to order another brand of milk?

Affiliates represent another type of partnership. Affiliate programmes establish a complementary, pay-for-performance network of websites with links to the sponsoring merchant. Each affiliate then gets a commission / referral fee for every sale or other visitor action. Referral rates range from 3 to 40 per cent, while some pay fixed fees. Generally, the response rate of affiliates is about twice that of banner advertising. Affiliate programmes are not a free ride. They require substantial work to set up and maintain, and as many as 85 per cent of affiliates generate only minimal sales.

While the benefits of partnership can be great, so can the risks of failure. Studies by Accenture, KPMG and others indicate that partnerships fail 25–75 per cent of the time. In 2002, France Telecom's mobile phone unit, Orange, teamed up with Thailand's TelecomAsia. On paper, the union looked great. Orange had marketing and technical expertise, and TelecomAsia had local knowledge. Less than two years later, the two companies went their separate ways. The main reason was that both companies failed to unite around a common vision of the best way to deliver customer value. Orange wanted to expand business methodically with a low-price strategy to attract as many subscribers as possible. By contrast, TelecomAsia wanted an expensive infrastructure that could support multiple services to attract higher-spending customers. Managers became more focused on fierce internal battles than on customers, and profitability suffered. Ultimately, both companies decided the relationship was not worth it.

Failed partnerships are common. Look at Unisys and AT&T, KLM and Northwestern, BMW and Rover, Danish beer maker Carlsberg and Thai-owned Chang Beverages, ABN Amro and the Bank of Asia; the list goes on. Most failures result from not thinking beyond the final handshake. The biggest landmine: 'Who owns the customer?'

To succeed, partnerships must create new value, not merely exchange existing skills. They must have strategic goals beyond another sales channel. This requires technological links among participants, multilevel collaboration and information sharing and, most importantly, the trust and loyalty that result from shared executive-level commitment.

CONCLUSION

Once every company wanted to brand alone as the king of the castle. That is no longer possible – or smart. A ProfitBrand is inextricably tied up with a company's evangelists, suppliers, channels and strategic partners. Success depends on how well, for example, companies can harness word of mouth and enlist the vast power of the group. Suppliers must collaborate on requirements, production, inventories and logistics. Companies must enhance the channel's ability to deliver value to customers by simplifying support and increasing training. And partnerships must be more than marriages of convenience.

Orchestration is much more complex and difficult than, say, developing a new advertising campaign. Traditionally adversarial relationships must be transformed into ones based on cooperation, consolidation, communication and customer orientation. Flows of material, information and finance among a network of customers, suppliers, manufacturers and distributors must be coordinated based on common objectives and data. Everyone must agree on cost and service trade-offs, performance levels, business rules, quality and other standards. Technology must be enlisted to facilitate the flow of information and ensure that everyone is working from common data. Manufacturers and the channel must lose their historic distrust and learn that, when the customer wins, they both win. The difficult art of pricing must bind strategic partners, not drive them apart.

But it is how these challenges are met – not how many awards are won – that determines which brands win in the customer economy. Brands can no longer seek to compete on the basis of their advertising claims or PR wins. The field is too crowded, products are too similar and consumers are either too jaded or too inundated with myriad messages for that to work any more. They must compete on their ability to deliver customer value, which requires orchestrating all the allies involved in meeting customer requirements. Operational excellence and even service are impossible without effective orchestration.

Takeaways

- What are you doing to generate word of mouth? How are you encouraging customers to provide referrals? Does your lead-tracking system incorporate word-of-mouth referrals?
- How effective and coordinated is your supply chain? Are relationships with partners supportive or antagonistic? What linkages do you have with suppliers? Are processes and systems integrated with partners? Is customer, sales, forecast and production information shared?
- Are you consolidating suppliers? Do the criteria for consolidation include supply chain performance, communication and collaboration as well as pricing?
- Are you meeting the channels' requirements for service, support and compensation? Can partners rapidly obtain pricing and/or delivery information? How is the internet being integrated into your relationship?
- What strategic partnerships do you have? What are you doing to sustain them and increase their profitability?

14

Conclusion

'Try not. Do.'

Yoda

The earliest television commercials consisted of no more than a person standing in front of a microphone reading a script. Why? Because that was the way commercials had always been done on radio. No one understood that TV represented a new force with its own rules, imperatives and effects.

That early advertising is a metaphor for branding today. Companies are attempting to brand using iconic techniques that once worked well in the mass-economy world of control and predictability. That world, unfortunately, is at its last gasp, fatally wounded by expanded online and offline competition as well as retailer and customer empowerment. It is the customer economy now. Customers define brands now, and companies must respond to new business imperatives.

It is the customer economy now, and the world is about to move into the demand economy. Yet branding remains stuck in a bell-bottom time warp, preoccupied with issues that first evolved 30 or more years ago. Branding experts debate issues – 'awareness', 'positioning', 'brand equity', 'creativity' – that are both largely a matter of opinion and increasingly irrelevant to CEOs and CFOs. 'Awareness' does not indicate loyalty, profitability or any other aspect of a customer relationship. It does not motivate to purchase, and to purchase again. 'Awareness' is general, when targeted segmentation is required. 'Positioning' lingers from a time when mass-media hegemony and limited competition allowed companies the luxury of believing that mind share was more important than profitability. 'Brand equity' remains a chameleon measurement that exists only in the eye of the beholder. And 'creativity' may be a branding watchword, but what is required to deal with the imperatives of the customer economy is imagination.

Compare this mummification with other facets of business, which have imaginatively adapted to the evolution to the customer economy. In management, the concepts of teams, empowerment and flat organizational structures represent significant advances since the 1980s. The role of the supply chain, once a province of the purchasing department, now impacts almost every top executive decision. Finance has developed innovative concepts like EVA (economic value added) and ABC (activity-based costing). Even the lowly warehouse now involves advanced technologies and algorithms that dynamically balance service and costs.

When companies attempt to brand in the customer economy with dated and faded mass-economy tactics, results are painfully predictable. Companies seek to build brands, but instead build only expensive failures. Disloyalty increases. And competition degenerates into pricing wars. Just because something once worked well does not mean it will work again. Admiral Horatio Nelson's HMS *Victory* was a premier warship of its day, but it would not last long against any of today's ships.

Because many involved in branding keep looking into a rear-view mirror, up to 95 per cent of all products fail to become brands. That is understandably unacceptable to CEOs and CFOs, especially considering the trillions of dollars spent on branding. Instead of trying to relive the golden age of mass-economy branding, branding must adapt to the imperatives of the customer economy – profitability, accountability and sustainability.

Any branding plan, discussion or concept that does not address profitability has little value to CEOs and CFOs. Without profitability, branding expenditures waste resources. Without profitability, customer value cannot be delivered. Ultimately, without profitability, there is no brand.

Brands – and everyone involved in branding – must be accountable. Accountability requires quantifiable measurement. Because of historical difficulties in measuring the effects of advertising, PR and other activities, marketing has long escaped the stringent requirements for accountability demanded from the rest of the organization. But technology and other tools are making it easier to observe, track and calculate branding effectiveness, enabling greater accountability.

Branding must meet CEO and CFO demands for accountability, which requires frequent (if not continuous) and relevant measurement. Companies must constantly measure and track branding, and operational and service performance from the customer perspective. Accountability starts with profitability and customer equity.

Metrics also include financial (profitability, percentage of sales, ROI), responsiveness (calls-to-resolution, e-mail and telephone call-backs), results (conversion ratios, up-sales and cross-sales), time (frequency, lag between transactions), quality (defects, warranty claims) and service (defections, complaints). Measurements must reflect customer realities and requirements, not internal benchmarks. Satisfaction is a noble goal, but it is better to meet the quantifiable standards by which customers hold you accountable.

Finally, branding requires sustainability, or the ability for brands to last and recoup investments. CEOs and CFOs are recognizing that brands are strategic assets. They are as important to long-term success as intellectual property or equipment and buildings. Like other strategic assets, branding requires long-term investments. Although ROI is critical, it is important to remember that not every branding investment produces an immediate, short-term return. Additionally, branding investments must not be limited to advertising, PR or other marketing. Investments in service, supply chain excellence or database skills are also required. Brands are built not by the mass-media power to make promises, but by organizational capabilities to honour commitments.

Sustainability requires looking at brands in terms of relationships, not transactions. 'Relationship' may have a soft meaning, but it has a hard measure – retention. When almost every competitive advantage can be duplicated, companies must focus on the advantages no one else can enjoy – the continuing relationship with the customer, and the knowledge that results from that relationship. The mass-economy days when companies could differentiate themselves in terms of product functionality or even 'positioning' sales copy are long gone. Today, it is customer relationships that differentiate and sustain brands.

To meet requirements for profitability, accountability and sustainability, several steps are required. First, and most importantly, strategic focus must change. Because the mass economy rewarded economies of scale, CEOs and CFOs concentrated on achieving gains in sales and market share. However, such concentration sometimes led to neglect of the most important goal of all – profitability growth. What good does it do to have customers who write large cheques and enable large market share if they are ultimately unprofitable because of acquisition and service costs?

Table 14.1 Branding versus ProfitBranding

Category	Mass-economy branding	ProfitBranding
Primary strategic goal	Market or sales growth	Profitability growth
Paradigm	We sell	Customers buy
Symbolism	Hunter	Farmer
Profitability driver	Sales growth	Customer, account and product penetration
Branding focus	Acquisition	Retention
Brand management focus	Perception	Tactical and strategic branding systems
Branding responsibility	Marketing department	Organization/supply chain
Profitability source	Products	Customers
Measurement	Indefinite	Specific to profitability, behaviour
Sales focus	Amount of transaction	Customer, account and product penetration
Sales planning	Percentage sales growth	Integrated with customer plans and budgets
Customer loss	Unnoticed	Profitable customers recovered

Concentrating on market share leads to over-dependence on pricing and promotion. This attracts price-sensitive customers who are least likely to be loyal. Retention falls, acquisition and other costs rise, and profitability suffers. While sales and market share growth must be a part of the executive agenda, it is profitability that ultimately determines brand success and sustainability. It is not about how many customers you have, or how much you sell. It is only about the maximum number of the right customers – those with the greatest lifetime value.

Focusing on sales or market share leads to another strategic failing – viewing brands in terms of products. Branding discussions revolve around product capabilities, extensions or profitability. But the debate forgets the first lesson of business – profits come from customers, not products. As Peter Drucker says, 'The question "What is our business?" can, therefore, be answered only by looking at the business from the outside, from the point of view of the customer and market. All the customer is interested in are his own values, wants and reality. For this reason alone, any serious attempt to state "what our business is" must align with the customer's realities, situation, behaviour, expectations and values.' In other words, the debate must always focus on delivering economic, emotional and experiential value to customers, followed by a discussion on how to maximize the extraction of that value through effective pricing or other tactics.

Profitability and customer focus come together in the prime metric for the customer economy – customer equity. Customer equity, or the lifetime profitability of the customer, ensures brand sustainability, makes retention branding more powerful than acquisition branding, unifies the organization around delivering customer value and helps allocate resources more effectively. Customer equity calculations allow brands to target and serve segmented customers more effectively. Customer planning then directs capabilities and services toward the 20 per cent of customers who generate 80 per cent of the profits. Such planning also seeks to address the estimated 15 per cent of customers who are unprofitable. Profitable, marginally profitable and unprofitable customers must not be treated alike.

Customer equity must not be confused with 'brand equity'. While the concept of brand equity does have some value, it is a weak marketing measure for three reasons. First, no standardized, universally acceptable calculation exists. The world accepts 'metre', 'total sales' and 'Six Sigma' because those standards are replicable, but it will be a long time before brand equity is anything but an eye-of-the-beholder way to evaluate marketing strength. Next, brand equity cannot determine accountability. Suppose brand equity is estimated at US $100 million. What are the relative contributions of advertising, PR, distribution and channel efforts towards that total? Finally, brand equity is a measure that provides no customer value. No consumer ever chooses products based on relative brand equity.

The next step is shifting branding emphasis from acquisition to retention. Although the majority of branding funds are devoted to acquisition, retention is the most powerful weapon to build brands. The longer customers stay, the more profitable they become. They lower the cost of sales and become an unpaid sales force. Each customer represents one less prospect for competitors. Retained customers also fuel innovation and growth, improve employee morale and even reduce the cost of capital. If this is true, why would any company want to anger any profitable customer with poor service, inaccurate fulfilment or any other all-too-common failing.

Acquisition branding remains vital. But retention branding must no longer be an afterthought, receiving only a small percentage of branding money. When new customers are motivated by price or other promotion, they are more likely to be disloyal. By contrast, existing customers are more profitable, cost less to serve and can become brand ambassadors. While acquisition branding may bring customers in the door, it is retention branding that keeps them there, increases their profitability and ensures sustainability.

Everyday operational excellence, stretching from initial prospect contact to final recovery effort, is paramount. Before a brand can establish a relationship, it must first represent a company the customer wants to have a relationship with. That means each interaction must be characterized by quality, reliability and responsiveness. It is no longer enough to execute. You must execute well. Otherwise, disaffected customers will not only leave but bad-mouth. As Jeff Bezos, founder of Amazon.com, pointed out, 'Branding is what people say about you when you leave the room.'

Everyday operational excellence requires strategic and tactical systems. Strategic systems like balanced scorecards define and quantify optimal customer relationships, provide a consistent methodology for execution and track progress toward goals. Tactical systems for CRM, lead management and campaign management institutionalize customer knowledge. This empowers organizations with common information and processes to meet prospect requirements and deliver customer value. Without both types of systems, companies cannot squeeze costs to compete more efficiently, nor can they leverage customer knowledge and relationships to compete more effectively.

Even more important than systems, however, are people and processes. If each person in an organization and supply chain is committed to delivering customer value, then brands will thrive. Each employee must be supported by customer-centric processes and tools, which can range from advanced communications technologies and standards to new organizational positions.

The sustainability of a brand derives from the ability to leverage customer knowledge to do business on customer terms. That knowledge enables communications relevancy, segmentation and the ability to deliver – and extract – customer economic, experiential and emotional value. Every company must track and analyse customer information. This information includes when customers join, how often and how much they buy, what offers they respond to, and when and why they defect. Most important, it includes knowing how customers hold brands

accountable. The information must be used to meet customer requirements for reliability, quality and responsiveness consistently.

Companies must also know customer profitability. This information is
vital not only for maximizing corporate profitability, but also for
targeting prospects likely to be profitable. Advanced analysis can enable
effective customer planning, or outlining the resources required to attract
prospects and ways to increase customer, product and account penetration. Knowledge about customer profitability is also used for
customer recovery.

It is a customer-economy paradox: the more that brands have been
recognized as strategic corporate assets, the less effective traditional
branding efforts have become. To maximize the value of brands as
strategic assets in this new era, CEOs and CFOs must drive their organization – and especially their marketing departments – toward
ProfitBranding. ProfitBranding incorporates the imperatives of the
customer economy. It addresses the issues at the top of every executive
agenda – profitability, accountability and sustainability. And it lays the
groundwork for success in the next era of branding, the demand
economy.

Branding has no silver bullets or magic potions. It takes hard work to
meet the requirements of demanding customers in an increasingly
competitive world. But it is a lot harder to succeed using mass-economy
tactics that have little more going for them than the passion of true
believers paying homage to ancient gods. Trying mass-economy
branding tactics must end. Now it is time to do. To succeed in the
customer economy and beyond, companies must ProfitBrand, or create a
'long-term profitable bond between an offering and its customers, based
on trust, loyalty and accountability'.

Afterword

'I know what branding is all about and how important it is. But I am frustrated because my CEO and CFO do not understand branding. What book can I recommend that will explain branding to them?'

That question frequently gets asked. The answer is that CEOs and CFOs usually are not the ones who need to read branding. A better question is 'What books should I read to understand how to run a successful business?'

If you accept the premise that branding rests on delivering economic, emotional or experiential value to customers to establish profitable bonds, branding can no longer be limited to advertising, PR, direct mail or other traditional marketing. If you believe that brand success ultimately derives from how well it consistently meets service, quality and other customer requirements, then tactics based simply on promotion will not be able to sustain brands during the customer economy or emerging demand economy.

Branding is about the business of business. Most of all, it is about the business of creating and keeping profitable customers. As a result, rather than business executives learning more about branding, it is time for branding executives to learn more about business.

The first place to start is the supply chain. Every branding executive must have at least a high-level knowledge of procurement, manufacturing, warehousing and transport, and supply chain KPIs (key performance indicators). Unless supply chain capabilities enable brands to get into customer hands when required, brands will die.

A second area to study is technology. Technology is key for improving not only internal and supply chain activities, but also customer relationships. *CIO* magazine reports that only about 25 per cent of businesses have close, coordinated relationships between their CMOs and CIOs, although about 40 per cent are working to strengthen ties. That is a step in the right direction, but the goal needs to be 100 per cent.

Finally, branding executives must increase their knowledge about statistical and financial analysis. Branding today is characterized by too much waste and ineffectiveness. Knowing the numbers that count leads to improved pricing and customer profitability as well as to more efficient and effective marketing.

The most important lesson: listen to your customers. The best, most powerful book about branding or even business cannot teach you more than your customers. Your customers will tell you what marketing works, how to improve relationships and what the most relevant benchmarks are. In other words, they will tell you how to ProfitBrand.

If you have questions or comments, please contact me: nick@fusionbrand.com.

References

Aaker, David (1991) *Managing Brand Equity: Capitalizing on the value of a brand name*, Free Press, New York

Hallberg, Garth (1995) *All Customers Are Not Created Equal: The differential marketing strategy for brand loyalty and profits*, John Wiley, New York

Kaplan, Robert S and Norton, David P (1996) *The Balanced Scorecard: Translating strategy into action*, Harvard Business School Press, Boston, MA

Keller, Kevin (2003) *Strategic Brand Management: Building, measuring and managing brand equity*, Prentice Hall, Upper Saddle River, NJ

Lenskold, James (2003) *Marketing ROI: The path to campaign, customer and corporate profitability*, McGraw-Hill, New York

Locke, Christopher *et al* (2001) *Cluetrain Manifesto: The end of business as usual*, Perseus Books, New York

McLuhan, Marshall and Powers, Bruce R (1992) *The Global Village: Transformations in world life and media in the 21st century*, Oxford University Press, New York

Miniter, Richard (2002) *The Myth of Market Share: Why market share is the fool's gold of business*, Crown Business, New York

Nagle, Thomas and Holden, Reed (1994) *Strategy and Tactics of Pricing: A guide to profitable decision making*, Prentice Hall, Upper Saddle River, NJ

Novo, Jim (2001) *Drilling Down: Turning customer data into profits with a spreadsheet*, Booklocker.com, Bangor, ME

Reichheld, Frederick (2001) *Loyalty Rules!*, Harvard Business School Press, Boston, MA

Reichheld, Frederick F and Teal, Thomas (1996) *The Loyalty Effect: The hidden force behind growth, profits and lasting value*, Harvard Business School Press, Boston, MA

Ries, Al and Trout, Jack (1986) *Positioning: The battle for your mind*, Warner Books, New York

Selden, Larry and Colvin, Geoffrey (2003) *Angel Customers and Demon Customers*, Portfolio, New York

Schultz, Don and Walters, Jeffrey (1997) *Measuring Brand Communication ROI*, National Association of Advertisers, New York

Further reading

Aaker, David (1996) *Building Strong Brands*, Free Press, New York

Anderson, David M (1997) *Agile Product Development for Mass Customization, Niche Markets, JIT, Build-to-Order, and Flexible Manufacturing*, McGraw-Hill, New York

Anderson, James C and Narus, James A (2003) *Business Market Management: Understanding, creating, and delivering value*, 2nd edn, Prentice Hall, Upper Saddle River, NJ

Argenti, Paul (1998) *Corporate Communication*, McGraw-Hill, New York

Barlow, Janelle *et al* (2000) *Emotional Value: Creating strong bonds with your customers*, Berrett-Koehler, San Francisco

Berry, Jon and Keller, Ed (2003) *The Influentials: One American in ten tells the other nine how to vote, where to eat, and what to buy*, Free Press, New York

Blattberg, Robert C, Getz, Gary and Thomas, Jacquelyn S (2001) *Customer Equity*, Harvard Business School Press, Boston, MA

Bradley, SP and Nolan, RL (1998) *Sense and Respond: Capturing value in the network era*, Harvard Business School Press, Boston, MA

Brown, Stanley (2000) *Customer Relationship Management: Linking people, process, and technology*, John Wiley, New York

Butscher, Stephan (1998) *Customer Loyalty Programmes and Customer Clubs*, Gower, London

Cairncross, Frances (2002) *The Company of the Future*, Harvard Business School Press, Boston, MA

Cannie, Joan Koob *et al* (1992) *Keeping Customers for Life*, AMACOM, New York

Champy, James (2002) *X-Engineering the Corporation: Reinventing your business in the digital age*, Warner Books, New York

Chopra, Sunil and Meindl, Peter (2000) *Supply Chain Management: Strategy, planning and operations*, Prentice Hall, Upper Saddle River, NJ

Clancy, Kevin J and Krieg, Peter C (2000) *Counterintuitive Marketing: Achieve great results using uncommon sense*, Free Press, New York

Collins, James and Porras, Jerry (1994) *Built to Last: Successful habits of visionary companies*, HarperCollins, New York

Cortada, James W, Hargraves, Thomas S and Wakin, Edward (1999) *Into the Networked Age: How IBM and other firms are getting there now*, Oxford University Press, New York

Cristol, Steven and Sealey, Peter (2000) *Simplicity Marketing: End brand complexity, clutter and confusion*, Free Press, New York

Cross, Robert (1997) *Revenue Management: Hard-core tactics for market domination*, Broadway Books, New York

Curry, Jay (2000) *Customer Marketing Method: How to implement and profit from customer relationship management*, Free Press, New York

Cusack, Michael (1998) *Online Customer Care: Strategies for call center excellence*, Quality Press, Milwaukee, WI

Doan, Robert and Simon, Hermann (1997) *Power Pricing: How managing price transforms the bottom line*, Free Press, New York

Docters, Robert G *et al* (2003) *Winning the Profit Game: Smarter pricing, smarter branding*, McGraw-Hill, New York

Drucker, PF (1974) *Management: Tasks, responsibilities, practices*, Harper & Row, New York

Engelson, Morris (1995) *Pricing Strategy: An interdisciplinary approach*, Joint Management Strategy, Portland, OR

Foster, Richard and Kaplan, Sarah (2001) *Creative Destruction: Why companies that are built to last under-perform the market – and how to successfully transform them*, Doubleday, New York

Fuld, Leonard M (1994) *New Competitor Intelligence: The complete resource for finding, analyzing, and using information about your competitors*, John Wiley, New York

Gladwell, Malcolm (2000) *The Tipping Point: How little things can make a big difference*, Little, Brown, New York

Godin, Seth (1999) *Permission Marketing: Turning strangers into friends, and friends into customers*, Simon & Schuster, New York

Godin, Seth and Gladwell, Malcolm (2001) *Unleashing the Ideavirus*, Hyperion, New York

Goldratt, Eliyahu M and Cox, Jeff (1992) *The Goal: A process of ongoing improvement*, North River Press Publishing, Great Barrington, MA

Goodman, Gary (2000) *Monitoring, Measuring and Managing Customer Service*, Jossey-Bass, San Francisco

Gordon, Ian (1998) *Relationship Marketing; New strategies, techniques and technologies to win the customers you want and keep them forever*, John Wiley Canada, Etobicoke, Ontario

Haeckel, Stephan and Slywotzky, Adrian (1999) *Adaptive Enterprise: Creating and leading sense-and-respond organizations*, Harvard Business School Press, Boston, MA

Hagel, John and Armstrong, Arthur (1997) *Net Gain: Expanding markets through virtual communities*, Harvard Business School Press, Boston, MA

Haig, Matt (2003) *Brand Failures: The truth about the 100 biggest branding mistakes of all time*, Kogan Page, London

Hammel, Gary and Prahalad, CK (1994) *Competing for the Future*, Harvard Business School Press, Boston, MA

Hammer, M and Champy, J (1993) *Reengineering the Corporation: A manifesto for business revolution*, HarperCollins, New York

Hesselbein, Frances (ed) (1997) *Organization of the Future*, Jossey-Bass, San Francisco

Hill, Sam and Rifkin, Glenn (1999) *Radical Marketing*, Harperbusiness, New York

Horovitz, Jacques (2000) *Seven Secrets of Service Strategy*, Financial Times/Prentice Hall, New York

Humby, Clive and Hung, Terry (2003) *Scoring Points: How Tesco is winning customer loyalty*, Kogan Page, London

Kanter, Rosabeth Moss (1994) *Collaborative Advantage: The art of alliances*, Harvard Business Review, Boston, MA

Kaplan, Robert and Cooper, Robert (1997) *Cost and Effect: Using integrated cost systems to drive profitability and performance*, Harvard Business School Press, Boston, MA

Knapp, Duane (1999) *Brand Mindset: Five essential strategies for building brand advantage throughout your company*, McGraw-Hill, New York

Kuglin, Fred and Rosenbaum, Barbara (2000) *The Supply Chain Network Internet Speed: Preparing your company for the e-commerce revolution*, AMACOM, New York

Moon, Michael and Millison, Doug (2000) *Firebrands: Building brand loyalty in the internet age*, McGraw-Hill, New York

Newell, Frederick (2000) *Loyalty.com: Customer relationship management in the new era of internet marketing*, McGraw-Hill, New York

Ogilvy, David (1985) *Ogilvy on Advertising*, Random House, New York

Pine, Joseph (1999) *Mass Customization*, Harvard Business School Press, Boston, MA

Poirier, Charles and Bauer, Michael (2000) *E-Supply Chain: Using the internet to revolutionize your business*, Berrett-Koehler, San Francisco

Porter, Michael (1998) *Competitive Advantage: Creating and sustaining superior performance*, Free Press, New York

Ranadive, Vivek (1999) *The Power of Now*, McGraw-Hill, New York

Rosen, Emanuel (2000) *Anatomy of Buzz: How to create word-of-mouth marketing*, Doubleday, New York

Rust, Roland T, Zeithaml, Valerie and Lemon, Katherine N (2000) *Driving Customer Equity*, Free Press, New York

Schmitt, Bernd H (1999) *Experiential Marketing: How to get customers to sense, feel, think, act, relate to your company and brands*, Free Press, New York

Scholtes, Peter *et al* (1996) *The Team Handbook*, 2nd edn, Joiner/Oriel, Madison, WI

Seely, John Brown and Duguid, Paul (2002) *Social Life of Information*, Harvard Business School Press, Boston, MA

Senge, Peter (1990) *Fifth Discipline: The art and practice of the learning organization*, Doubleday, New York

Shapiro, Andrew (2000) *Control Revolution: How the internet is putting individuals in charge and changing the world we know*, Public Affairs, New York

Slywotzky, Adrian *et al* (1998) *Profit Zone: How strategic business design will lead you to tomorrow's profits*, Times Books, New York

Sterne, Jim (2000) *Customer Service on the Internet: Building relationships, increasing loyalty, and staying competitive*, John Wiley, New York

Swift, Ronald (2000) *Accelerating Customer Relationships: Using CRM and relationship technologies*, Prentice Hall, Upper Saddle River, NJ

Tapscott, Don (ed) (1999) *Creating Value in the Networking Economy*, Harvard Business School Press, Boston, MA

Tiernan, Bernadette (2001) *The Hybrid Company: Reach all your customers through multi-channels, anytime, anywhere*, Dearborn Trade Publishing, Chicago

Upshaw, Lynn (1995) *Building Brand Identity: A strategy for success in a hostile marketplace*, John Wiley, New York

Windham, Laurie (1999) *Dead Ahead: The dilemma and the new rules of business*, Allworth Press, New York

Zabin, Jeff, Brebach, Gresh and Kotler, Philip (2004) *Precision Marketing: The new rules for attracting, retaining and leveraging profitable customers*, John Wiley, New York

Zemke, Ron and Bell, Chip (2000) *Knock Your Socks Off Service Recovery*, AMACOM, New York

Zemke, Ron and Woods, John (1999) *Best Practices in Customer Service*, AMACOM, New York

Zook, Chris and Allen, James (2001) *Profit from the Core: Growth Strategy in an Era of Turbulence*, Harvard Business School Press, Boston, MA

Index

Lightning Source UK Ltd.
Milton Keynes UK
176639UK00001BA/59/A